Tyrrell considers in turn Lonergan's cognitional analysis, epistemology, metaphysics, and formal proof for God's existence. Throughout the work the author stresses the personal self-appropriation of the Canadian philosopher-theologian's positions on knowing, objectivity, and being as the key to a correct understanding and critical validation of Lonergan's philosophy of God.

Bernard Tyrrell, S.J., is Assistant Professor of Philosophy and Religious Studies at Gonzaga University in Spokane, Washington. He has studied under Bernard Lonergan and Karl Rahner, and was the initiator of '' Ongoing Collaboration: The International Lonergan Congress '' held in Florida in 1970.

BERNARD LONERGAN'S PHILOSOPHY OF GOD

Bernard Lonergan's Philosophy of God

BERNARD TYRRELL S.J.

University of Notre Dame Press

American edition 1974
UNIVERSITY OF NOTRE DAME PRESS
Notre Dame, Indiana 46556

First published 1974 by
Gill and Macmillan Limited
2 Belvedere Place
Dublin 1 Ireland
and in London through association with the
Macmillan Group of Publishing Companies

© 1974 by Bernard J. Tyrrell

Jacket design by Hilliard Hayden

Library of Congress Cataloging in Publication Data
    Tyrrell, Bernard J. 1933-
    Bernard Lonergan's philosophy of God.
    Based on the author's thesis, Fordham University, 1972.
    1. God—History of doctrines—20th century, 2. Lonergan,
    Bernard J. F. I. Title
    BT102.T9 1974 211 73-22205
    ISBN 0-268-00540-0

Printed and bound in Great Britain

In memory of my mother
Mary Koreski Tyrrell
and with special thanks to
Joseph D. Collins

Contents

Foreword

STUDENTS of man's mental operations fall into three classes. There are behaviourists, phenomenologists, and traditionalists. The behaviourists feel that human psychology is to be studied in the same manner as animal psychology and, since they have no access to the immediate data of animal psychology, they rule out attention to the immediate data of human psychology. Phenomenologists, the more closely they follow Edmund Husserl, begin by bracketing external reality to concentrate all the more fully and freely on the content of our immanent, intentional operations. Traditionalists, finally, employ a faculty psychology : they advert to the immediate data of consciousness; but they go beyond the data to posit non-conscious faculties or potencies whence the conscious operations proceed.

These three classes provide no more than an initial orientation. They do not preclude subdivisions, overlaps, transitions. One may speak of 'intellect' or 'will' in accordance with common English usage and without any commitment to a faculty psychology. At the opposite pole, one may be a thorough-going Aristotelian and use the words to denote potencies because one wants a unified science with a metaphysics as the principle of unification and with the unification made effective by conceiving physical and psychological terms and relations as further determinations of metaphysical terms and relations.

My own writings are an instance of transition. I had been educated in the Aristotelian-Thomist tradition, and I had published two monographs on the thought of Aquinas.[1] My book, *Insight*, expressed a cognitional theory which, so far from depending on a metaphysics, presented a metaphysics derived from cognitional theory. Hence, though I used the English words, intellect and will, my cognitional theory was an intentionality analysis and not properly a faculty psychology.

It remains that intentionality analysis has ulterior implications. They were not adverted to in *Insight*. They came to the fore in subsequent incidental papers and more fully in my *Method in Theology*. Where faculty psychology leans to a priority of intellect over will, intentionality analysis has to conceive questions and answers for deliberation as sublating questions and answers both for reflection and for intelligence. There follows a fuller and happier apprehension of the human person and, in particular, of the human person's approach to God.

In this later view chapter XIX of *Insight* appears incongruous. It approaches the question of God in the old manner of the Aristotelian-Thomist tradition and not in the new manner made possible by intentionality analysis. The point was amply and vigorously made in the Lonergan Congress of Easter Week, 1970.[2] In the present volume Fr Tyrrell, who had so much to do with the Lonergan congress, gives full and professional treatment to the issues.

Bernard Lonergan

Introduction

THE philosophy of God of Bernard Lonergan can be conveniently envisaged first from a contextual viewpoint and then in terms of the stages of its internal development. Such an exposition of Lonergan's viewpoint requires an extensive consideration of two aspects of the problem not normally found in a study of natural theology. The first aspect is that of concrete context, an aspect to be explained and discussed throughout Part I. The second aspect is that of speculative context. Chapters 3 and 4 will indicate in detail this second aspect; Part I will make evident the intermeshing of the contexts. Since, however, the speculative context is internal not only to the thematic development of Lonergan's philosophy of God but also to the entire presentation of this book, it will be helpful to specify it a little further here. This further specification, in turn, will help to locate Lonergan's transcendental refections in a simple existential manner.[1]

In response to questions raised by Professor Andrew J. Reck at a special symposium held in 1967 Lonergan remarked: 'The procedure followed in *Insight* was to treat three linked questions. What am I doing when I am knowing? Why is doing that knowing? What do I know when I do it?'[2] The first question is a matter of cognitional analysis. It involves an invitation to the reader of *Insight* 'to discover his own cognitional operations in the data of his own experiences.'[3] Lonergan attempts to provide data out of which an answer to the first question may arise in the first ten chapters of *Insight*. The second question constitutes the epistemological moment of *Insight* and in principle regards chapters XI–XIII, i.e., the chapters on the self-affirmation of the knower, the notion of being and the notion of objectivity. The third question is the metaphysical moment and its answer is heuristically reached when (1) the isomorphism of knowing and being is affirmed, (2) the metaphysical elements in their distinctness and interrelatedness are understood and verified as truly ontological, not merely cognitional, elements and finally (3) openness to God or general transcendence is acknowledged.[4]

The second of the above questions, Why is doing that knowing? involves a dynamic threefold movement which should also be briefly considered here. Lonergan speaks of the epistemological moment in the dynamic metaphor of 'breakthrough, encirclement and confinement'.[5] He employs these dynamic military expressions not only to indicate the central importance of the epistemological moment in *Insight* but also—and principally—to stress the essentially dynamic quality of epistemology as he conceives it. For Lonergan, epistemology is not a deductive process but rather a matter of performance, of conversion, of personal knowing, in which one's attempts at thematisation of the cognitive process are rigorously tested in the vital terms of one's experience of the process itself. Breakthrough, then, for Lonergan, applies to the successful performance of self-affirmation of the knower. 'Encirclement' occurs when one understands that being is whatever one intelligently grasps and reasonably affirms. Lonergan acknowledges that encirclement, i.e. the recognition of being as the objective to be reached through intelligent grasp and reasonable affirmation, is implicit in the breakthrough but the notion of being is explicitly dealt with in chapter XII. Finally, 'confinement' has its grounds in the chapters on self-affirmation as knower, being, and objectivity, and it is achieved through a dialectical opposition of the twofold notions of the real, of knowing, and of objectivity.[6] Thus, 'Once the subject grasps that, unless he identifies the real with being, his statements are bound to be counter-positions that eventually are due for reversal, confinement has set in.'[7] It is, therefore, in the key epistemological chapters of *Insight* that the grounds for confinement are in principle given.

Indeed one may say that these chapters, in their context of cognitional theory,[8] provide a key to the appreciation of the cultural and speculative position of Lonergan. And a further aspect of the present book is that it brackets reflections on these chapters between considerations of the historically-conditioned graced transcendent intention that is man and of the unconditioned transcendent Mystery that is God.

In concluding this introduction I would like to thank my

mentor, Fr Vincent Potter, S.J. of Fordham University, and my readers Fr Gerald McCool, S.J. and Fr Patrick Heelan, S.J. for the invaluable criticisms, corrections and evaluations which made my original doctoral dissertation entitled *Bernard Lonergan's Philosophy of God* a possibility and consequently in principle this book. Again, I would like to express my deep gratitude to Fr William Ryan, S.J. of Gonzaga University who spent a summer reading my dissertation, cutting out excessive verbiage and introducing certain precisions which were a starting-point in transforming my dissertation into book form. I should like to thank Miss Patricia O'Connell for completing the index for the present work. To Dr Philip McShane, however, I owe a debt of tremendous gratitude for actually effecting the trans-formation of my thesis into a readable book. Dr McShane also added some creative and critical emendations of his own, and brought my book up to date with Fr Lonergan's most recent writings. For these many efforts of Dr McShane I can only express my very deepest thanks and heartfelt appreciation.

It is, however, to Fr Bernard J. F. Lonergan, S.J. to whom I owe the debt of deepest gratitude for the existence of this present work. Fr Lonergan taught me in numberless ways—through his writings, lectures and personal conversations—that the way to really philosophise is not to engage in a long series of Wolffian-type deductions from so-called first principles but rather to enter into one's own conscious self and to investigate empirically, or through what he refers to as the process of 'self-appropriation', what is really going on when one is knowing; why that process, empirically discoverable in one's conscious intentional operations, is not an exercise in mere subjectivity but the only way to achieve authentic objectivity; and what is really meant by the reality we claim to reach through the process of knowing, or what Lonergan now refers to as 'cognitive self-transcendence'. Above all, however, I am grateful to Fr Lonergan for pointing out to me, and many others, that not only are moral and religious conversion not matters of sheer indifference to the exercise of philosophic and theological thinking but that they are in fact necessary existential conditions of possibility for doing philo-sophy and theology in an objective, unbiased and authentic fashion.

Aquinas spoke of Aristotle as The Philosopher and Dante

described him as 'the master of those who know'. I would like to humbly suggest, though history alone must be the judge of the accuracy of my statement, that Bernard J. F. Lonergan is The Christian Thinker of the twentieth century.

THE NEW CONTEXT OF LONERGAN'S PHILOSOPHY OF GOD

I

The Historical Dimension

THINKERS do not operate in a vacuum. Hence, as contemporary hermeneutics indicates, to understand the content of a given thinker's work it is of crucial importance to grasp the context in which the thinker articulates his worldview.

It is the aim of Part I of this work to investigate four principal features which characterise the new context of Lonergan's philosophy of God. These features of the 'new' context of Lonergan's philosophy of God distinguish it in varying degrees from more classical approaches—this is the basis of the use of the adjective 'new'—as well as from diverse contemporary efforts. They do not, however, exhaust the possible features of the new context and hence should not be viewed in any rigid or exclusivist fashion.

First, then, Lonergan operates in a post-Kantian philosophic context which stresses the importance of the subject. There is accordingly at work in Lonergan's thought a shift from a certain classical cosmocentrism to an anthropocentricism whose matrix is historical development. Secondly, Lonergan is a 'modern' thinker who acknowledges the implications of the cultural shift from classicism to historical mindedness for contemporary philosophising. Lonergan thus makes it a point to attempt to philosophise in the context of historical mindedness, frequently indicating the ramifications which this cultural shift has for a contemporary discussion of the God problem. Thirdly, Lonergan functions both implicitly and explicitly as a 'Christian' philosopher. Anyone who wishes to do an adequate hermeneutical study of Lonergan's philosophy of God must take account of this dimension of his philosophy. Finally, Lonergan is 'existential' in his philosophising. This means in the present context that he acknowledges the need of both *de jure* and *de facto* existential conditions of possibility for any effective and fruitful approach to the problem of God as developed in *Insight* and elsewhere.

This fourth characteristic of Lonergan's thinking will occupy us in the next chapter.

Let us turn now to a consideration of the 'anthropocentric turn', which in Lonergan's case involves a centring of attention on the self consciously operating. The expression 'self-appropriation' might perhaps be said to epitomise Lonergan's 'anthropocentric turn'.

The subject of the present work is Lonergan's philosophy of God. Nevertheless, the critical validation of Lonergan's proof for the existence of God in *Insight* depends on the successful outcome of the self-appropriation to which Lonergan invites his readers at the beginning of *Insight*. His anthropocentric turn accordingly constitutes the foundation of his approach to the problem of God. It involves an invitation to a highly complex and subtle attempt at self-attention. It is a call to experience oneself experiencing, understanding and judging; to understand one's experience of oneself experiencing, understanding and judging; and, finally, to judge critically the correctness of one's understanding of oneself experiencing, understanding and judging. The call to self-appropriation also involves an invitation to appropriate oneself on the level of moral consciousness and decision. The analysis, however, of the process of self-appropriation will constitute a major part of this work, and so we have only sketchily introduced it here. A few further remarks are in order.

First, just as Lonergan holds with Rahner that the dogmatic theology of past ages must now become a theological, trans-cendental, anthropology,[1] so analogously it would appear that Lonergan would stress that any critically viable 'natural theology' must be in a fundamental sense anthropological in its roots. Thus, whereas the 'proofs' of Aquinas were cosmocentric in their emphasis, the proof for the existence of God which Lonergan elaborates finds its proximate basis in the existential subject's thematisation of his own cognitive experience.

Secondly, Lonergan's anthropocentric turn is in no sense meant to imply that Lonergan is a subjectivist. Rather the point is simply being made that it is in man and his operations that Lonergan finds the critical basis for setting up what will ultim-ately prove to be, in his opinion, a 'critically' validated proof for the existence of God. Thus, just as Lonergan, in an unpublished

lecture, 'The Future of Thomism',[2] stresses that there will be an
ever greater shift from soul to subject, so in his 'natural theology'
he moves away from an approach to the God-problem based on
metaphysical argumentation in terms of cosmic design to a
critical approach which has its foundations in a properly verified
thematisation of the operating subject.

Thirdly, Lonergan is most insistent that cognitional analysis
and epistemology must foundationally precede metaphysics if
the metaphysics is to be 'critically' viable.[3] This same require-
ment would also apply to any philosophy of God which would
claim to be critically viable.

Finally, it might be objected that in *Insight* Lonergan admits
that there are as many proofs for the existence of God as there
are modes of contingent existence,[4] and that accordingly the
classical proofs are valid. In the present writer's view, while
Lonergan does acknowledge a certain validity in the classical
approaches to God, still he would insist that the cosmocentrically,
or metaphysically, oriented proofs do not possess their own
inviolable cogency and *ultimate critical foundation* apart from
cognitional analysis and the critical validation of the experience
of oneself experiencing, understanding and judging.

We come now to the second feature of the new context
indicated at the beginning of this chapter.

The cultural shift from what Lonergan describes as the classicist world-view to historical-mindedness is what has made it
possible, and indeed necessary, to raise the problem of context
prior to the actual exposition and critical evaluation of Lonergan's
philosophy of God. Here we will discuss the cultural shift first as
it relates to Lonergan's overall philosophical approach and then to
certain aspects of the God problem. First we must indicate
Lonergan's conception of the relationship between the social and
the cultural.

For Lonergan the cultural presupposes the social. The social
is basically a way of living, a way in which men live together in
some orderly fashion. The social is thus discernible in family and
society, in Church and state. Men, however, not only live and
act but they wish to understand their living and performing:
'They wish to discover and to express the appropriateness, the
meaning, the significance, the value, the use of their way of life
as a whole and in its parts . . . such discovery and expression

constitute the cultural and, quite evidently, culture stands to social order as soul to body, for any element of social order will be rejected the moment it is widely judged inappropriate, meaningless, irrelevant, useless, just not worth while.'[5]

Culture is the meaning of a way of living. This meaning, however, may be discerned and expressed in diverse fashions. There is first an immediate level of meaning which would appear to constitute the spontaneous substance of any culture. This is the level on which meaning and value are felt, intuited, acted out in rites and symbols, language and art. This is the level of the intersubjective, of tone and gesture, smile and frown. It is the level of meaning present in the work of art prior to its critical interpretation or in the dream prior to its analysis. It is the level of meanings and values spontaneously operative in everyday life.

In any advanced culture, however, there is a second level of meaning or culture superstructure. This is the level of differentiated consciousness. 'It is not content to act out what it feels and intuits. Rather it seeks to mirror spontaneous living by analysing it, making all its elements explicit, subjecting them to scrutiny, evaluation, criticism.'[6] This is the level of the critic and the historian, the scientist and the technician, the psychologist and the economist, the philosopher and the theologian. Classical and modern culture both share in the two levels of meaning just described. Each involves both spontaneous and objectifying components. Besides these basic similarities, however, there are manifold differences.

Classical culture was born of the Greek effort to control meaning. It gave form and life to the civilisation of Greece and Rome. It was renewed in the European Renaissance. It was the chrysalis from whence issued modern languages and literatures, modern sciences and mathematics, modern philosophy and history, in a word: modern culture. It still held its own as recently as sixty years ago but today it is largely dead and forgotten. On the other hand, modern culture or the era of historical-mindedness had its real beginning, according to Lonergan's analysis, towards the end of the seventeenth century. Lonergan thus notes that Herbert Butterfield places the origins of modern science in the year 1680 and that Paul Hazard places the beginning of the Enlightenment at the same time. Lonergan acknowledges that new ideas and discoveries, which were subsequently integrated into modern science, occurred long before 1680 but he concurs with Professor Butterfield in the latter's stress on the significance of the latter part of the seventeenth century for modern culture.[7]

The differences between classical and modern culture in Lonergan's conception are many and varied. Thus, for example, classical culture did not conceive of itself as one culture among many. Classical culture conceived of itself as normative and universal. Barbarians ceased to be barbarians to the extent that they participated in the ideals and norms, the verities and laws, the manners and tastes of 'culture'. Modern culture, on the other hand, is historicist and empirical. It knows that culture is something found in every people, for in every people there is some apprehension of meaning and value in their way of life. Modern culture thus knows itself as one culture among many. It knows that cultures are man-made and can develop and change—indeed, that to an extent they not only can but should change. Modern culture is therefore a culture which knows about diverse cultures and relates them to each other genetically and historically since it knows that they are human creations and that man is a developmental being.

Perhaps nowhere, however, is there a greater contrast between classicist and modern culture than in the area of science. The difference is not quantitative but qualitative. It is not just a matter of knowing more but rather of a fundamental shift in the notion of science itself.[8]

The shift from classicism to historical-mindedness is of great importance for understanding the difference between classical Thomism and certain contemporary philosophical developments. In Lonergan's analysis, classical Thomism stressed logic rather than method, the metaphysics of soul rather than the self-appropriation of the subject, an apprehension of man in the static terms of unchanging human nature rather than in the dynamic context of historical development and generally the deductive rather than the empirical, the static rather than the dynamic, the abstract rather than the concrete, and the universal rather than the historical.

Again, it may be said that there is a certain foundational difference in approach between classicist and modern science and that this difference is equally reflected in the sphere of philosophy. Thus, the ideal of classical science was to achieve true and certain knowledge of causal necessity by moving deduct-ively from necessary self-evident first principles to equally necessary conclusions. Foundations in modern science, however, do not consist in first principles but in the method which gener-ates the conclusions, laws, and principles which the scientist makes use of.[9] Likewise, in classical Thomism the tendency was to begin with abstract propositions called first principles, and from these to deduce certain criteria, norms, laws, etc., in an effort to move from the abstract and universal towards the con-crete.[10] In the case of certain modern philosophical develop-ments—notably his own—Lonergan emphasises the importance of the shift from an approach which discovers its foundations in first principles to an approach which is transcendental and locates its foundations in the cognitive structural features of the conscious operating subject. The real invariant then in this particular transcendental approach to philosophy is not found in any set of abstract propositions or first principles but in the dynamic interrelated cognitive operations of the subject.

In his paper, 'Belief Today', Lonergan indicates the crucial import of the cultural shift—especially in its scientific aspect— for the philosophy of God in pointing out that 'the classicist did not advert to the real novelty of modern science, and so he could not conclude to the real novelty in modern philosophic problems and, particularly, in the problems concerning God.'[11]

Basically, in Lonergan's analysis, owing to the separations which took place in the development of Western thought first between theology and philosophy in Descartes and then between philosophy and science in Newton and Laplace, a scientific notion of causality was developed which has nothing to do with a philo-sophic notion of causality. It is true that modern science still speaks of causes, but it does not mean efficient, formal, material and final: it means rather correlations. Modern science then takes as its data man and the world. In accord with its own methodological canon that to be scientific a hypothesis must be verifiable, modern science systematically prescinds from the prob-lem of God. The hypotheses of modern science arise from the data of sense or of consciousness and can only be verified in terms of the same data. But, as Lonergan puts it :

God is not a datum of human experience for, in this life, we do not know God face to face. Again, between this world and God there is no relationship that can be verified, for verification can occur only between data, only with regard to objects that lie within this world and so can present us with data.[12]

Modern science accordingly forces the philosopher to ask how he can speak about God or claim to mean or know anything about God when God is not an immediate datum of either sense or consciousness, and hence is not verifiable in the scientific use of the term. The philosopher is impelled to ask what kind of knowledge his knowledge of God might possibly be.

Again, there is a sense in which it is meaningful to speak of God as absent from modern science. The natural scientist, for example, who is strictly concerned with the particular object of his science and not with the nature, foundations, and ultimate implications of his science has no need of the hypothesis of God. Yet, as history has shown, as the distinctions between theology and philosophy and between philosophy and science became separations there was a tendency first for philosophy to arrogate to itself the role theology formerly played and then for science to do the same thing in regard to philosophy. In these cases the philosopher became a *théologien malgré lui* and the scientist became a philosopher *malgré lui*. Newman, as Lonergan observes, alluded to this sort of phenomenon when he remarked that if a certain area of knowledge came to be overlooked, ignored, or omitted by a cultural community then among other effects the rounded whole of knowledge would be mutilated and 'the remaining parts would endeavour to round off the whole once more despite the omission of a part and, as a result, they would suffer distortion from their effort to perform a function for which they were not designed.'[13]

Lonergan indicates in a 1959 book review that the attempt at integrating the differentiations of science, philosophy and theology through a study of method is a *'scienza nuova'*, or Christian philosophy at its deepest level.[14] Here also he indicates that 'in substance' the question of Christian philosophy—to which we turn presently—'asks how a Catholic can attempt total reflection on man's situation.' This reference of Lonergan to 'total reflection on man's situation' brings to the fore once again the importance of context in any philosophical reflection since the context is a most important dimension of man's concrete situation. In regard to the problem of the absence of God in modern culture, accordingly, it is important to understand not only in what fashion God may be said to be absent from the cultural superstructure of science, but also 'from this everyday, familiar domain of feeling, insight, judgment, decision,' as well.[15]

Lonergan observes that the context in which modern science and the humanities have evolved has been in large measure one of indifference if not outright hostility to God and religion. One need only think of the chief writers of the Enlightenment as well as of a Freud or a Marx to realise how much agnosticism or atheism are woven into the basic fabric of modern culture. Nor is this Godless mentality restricted to the élite only. It is transposed from the erudite language of theory and technology through metaphors, narratives, catch phrases and images into something which practical intelligence can comprehend. The net result is that the biases of common sense tend to reinforce the biases of intellectuals and God is rendered yet more absent from the minds and hearts of modern man.

Lonergan, furthermore, notes that 'modern culture involves a re-interpretation of man and his world, a transformation of the ordering of society and of the control over nature, and a new sense of power and responsibility' and 'all three have a bearing on the absence of God in modern culture'.[16] This is the case because all three of these aspects of modern culture have man as their immediate focus and are in large measure the concern of individuals and groups which regard God as anti-man and as a classicist idol which must be overthrown.

There is then a crisis situation which has arisen as a result of the shift from classicism to historical-mindedness and it is perhaps especially manifest among Christians and other theists. The secularist is to a large extent the creator of modern culture both in its basic thrusts and in the contextual ambience within which these thrusts occurred and is consequently to a greater or lesser extent at home in modern culture. The Christian, on the other hand, or, more accurately, the Catholic Church, has to a great extent remained aloof from the developments of modern culture until rather recently. 'From that enormous development the church has held off : it could praise the ends; it could not accept the means; and so it could not authentically participate in the process that eliminated the standardised man of classicist thought and ushered in the historical consciousness of today.'[17] The Catholic Christian today then is caught in a crisis which the secularist does not experience in the same fashion because the Christian must not only assimilate whatever is good in the cultural shift but also discern what is extraneous and unnecessary in this shift.

Moreover, proper discernment of what is wheat and what is chaff in modern culture as viewed from a Christian perspective is an enormous task because, as Lonergan stresses, most of our knowledge is a matter of belief rather than of immanently generated knowledge. Thus, men of common sense accept on the testimony of others countless items of their everyday knowledge and the same is true of scientists. The engineer, for example, relies on the correctness of his slide rule and the scientist on thousands of experiments performed by his predecessors. Belief consequently is a major component of culture and it becomes an ever greater factor as the need for collaboration increases. The individual can verify very little for himself. All of this means, of course, that the occurrence of a great cultural shift is going to cause problems for everyone but especially for those whose radical *Weltanschauung* is in one fashion or another challenged by diverse aspects of this shift. As Lonergan expresses it :

In times of little social or cultural change, beliefs are stable and little open to question, but in times of great social and cultural change, beliefs too are changing and, because they are only beliefs, because they are not personally acquired knowledge, such change leaves believers at a loss. They are disorientated. They do not know which way to turn. They feel that all they have taken for granted is menaced. They may be tempted to unbelief as a liberation, or, again, they may dread it as destructive of truly human living.[18]

In view of the present crisis which is radically not so much a crisis of faith as of culture[19] it would seem that it must be the aim and principal task of a Christian philosopher to bring clarity out of confusion first by understanding the meaning of the cultural shift in so far as it affects philosophy and theology and then by attempting to articulate a philosophy of God which will take cognisance of all that is rich and positive in the thrusts of modern culture and hence will prove viable in the sophisticated ambience of this culture. Moreover, this would seem to be precisely what Lonergan is attempting as he endeavours to work within the exigences of the new cultural context and to meet the new questions which arise within this context.

There remains to be considered, in this chapter, Lonergan's position as a Christian philosopher.

Since 1928 when Emile Bréhier gave his lecture in Brussels on the question of the existence of a 'Christian' philosophy, there has been a long series of disputes regarding the possibility and nature of such an intellectual endeavour as 'Christian' philosophy. Bréhier denied its possibility, but in 1931 Gilson, in a paper read before the *Société française de philosophie*, affirmed, and today continues to affirm, the existence of a multiplicity of truly Christian philosophies.[20]

Our discussion here will not be exhaustive. We employ two approaches to determine what is Christian about Lonergan's philosophy. The first analyses the context in which he has philosophised and is philosophising. The second approach considers what he has explicitly stated about the possibility or actual occurrence of a Christian philosophy.

THE CHRISTIAN CONTEXT OF LONERGAN'S PHILOSOPHICAL ENDEAVOUR

There is the earlier context in which Lonergan philosophised, namely that of his historical studies of the nature of operative grace and of the *verbum* in the thought of Aquinas.[21] This context of Lonergan's philosophising is our immediate concern. As far as Lonergan's more recent philosophising is concerned, since it occurs almost exclusively within theological works and hence in an explicit Christian context, there is no need here to elaborate any further on the *de facto* Christian context of Lonergan's later philosophising.

In his study of operative grace in Aquinas, Lonergan's primary concern was to do a proper hermeneutic of Aquinas' thought on operative grace. Lonergan noted from the outset that there were differences between Thomas' earlier expositions of operative grace, and that it was accordingly necessary first to engage in a study of the historical background of theological speculation on grace. He thus proceeded in his first article to consider the divergent views of Augustine, Anselm, Peter Lombard, Philip the

Chancellor, Albert the Great and Bonaventure before entering into a detailed analysis of the general movement of the thought of Aquinas.

In the articles which followed, Lonergan indicated how Thomas was able to work out his theorem of actual grace once he had clearly grasped the distinction between habitual and actual grace, and once he was able to work out an analogy of nature which corresponded to the problematic of actual grace.

As Lonergan's analysis of Aquinas' development indicates, Aquinas also made great use of the secular Arabic, Platonist and Aristotelian philosophies at his disposal, while at the same time profoundly transmuting them according to the exigencies of the Christian mysteries which he was endeavouring to articulate systematically in order to gain some fruitful, though admittedly limited and analogous, knowledge of them. Thus, Lonergan found it necessary to follow Aquinas as he worked out his notions of 'the nature of operation, promotion, application, the certitude of providence, universal instrumentality . . . the analogy of operation . . .' as well as 'the idea of freedom, . . . [and] the various ways in which . . . he conceived God to move the will, the meaning of his central theorem of divine transcendence and, to some extent, its relation to subsequent theories.'[22]

Lonergan culminates his study of operative grace with a penetrating analysis of Aquinas' notion of human freedom and divine transcendence. The result of Lonergan's study was not only a dismissal of the Bañez-Molina controversy as beside the point, but a radical affirmation of the existential possibility of the effective operation of human freedom in the face of—actually, in and through and because of—divine transcendence. This human freedom-divine transcendence problematic is explicitly Christian both *de facto* in its historical origin and *de jure* in that this problem, implicit though it may have been at earlier stages in the development of Christian reflection, lies at the very core of Christian revelation itself. The Lonergan of *Grace and Freedom* may therefore be termed Christian *qua* philosopher because the context in which he worked was in large measure Christian and because the central problematic with which he dealt originated in reflections on Christian revelation, evoking profound metaphysical considerations. Indeed, Lonergan incorporates his interpretation of Aquinas' theorem of divine transcendence into his own philosophical analysis of general transcendental knowledge in *Insight*. This last point serves not only to indicate the fundamental continuity which exists in the thought of Lonergan between the period of *Grace and Freedom* and that of *Insight* but, more importantly for our present concern, the Christian matrix out of which certain key philosophical reflections of Lonergan on the God-problem arose.

In his studies of the *verbum* in Aquinas' thought, Lonergan was concerned with the proper human analogue for understanding the divine processions in a necessarily imperfect yet none the less fruitful fashion. To this end he engaged himself first in a lengthy psychological analysis of the nature of understanding as it expresses itself in the inner words of definition and judgment. Next, he entered into a discussion of certain issues in which cognitional analysis and metaphysics are inextricably joined together. Finally, in the fifth article—'*Imago Dei*'—Lonergan applied the results of his analyses in the first four articles to an analogous explanation of divine knowledge and, more specifically, of the processions of the Word and of the Holy Spirit.[23]

With regard to the problem of the specific context of the articles on the *verbum*, we might note certain of Lonergan's comments about Augustine in his comparatively recent Introduction to the book version of the articles. In the first paragraph of the Introduction, Lonergan comments that in working out the concept of the *verbum* Aquinas was attempting to fit an Augustinian creation into a framework which was Aristotelian.[24] Further on, Lonergan stresses that the basic context in which Augustine developed his thought on the *verbum* was Trinitarian and that its fundamental impetus was anti-Arian.[25] Here there is clear evidence of the specifically Christian context of Lonergan's *verbum* studies. He affirms a clear dependence of Aquinas on Augustine, and of both on Christian revelation for their respective reflections on the *verbum*. And Lonergan himself, of course, is dependent on the entire tradition.

Again, in his Introduction to the *verbum* analysis, Lonergan proceeds to describe Augustine in an existential fashion which throws yet more light on the Christian ambience of the studies of the *verbum* and also serves to provide a bridge to a more general discussion of Lonergan's explicit comments on such problems as the nature of Christian philosophy in terms of the grace-nature distinction. In Lonergan's view Augustine was 'a convert from nature to spirit; a person that, by God's grace made himself what he was; a subject that may be studied but, most of all, must be encountered in the outpouring of his self-revelation and self-communication.'[26] Augustine, then, in Lonergan's interpretation, through his conversion became a subject radically aware of himself and an incipient master of interiority. Thus, for example, Augustine became capable of such grace-illuminated introspection that he was able to speak subtly of the interior *verbum* as a 'non-linguistic utterance of truth,'[27] as 'not primitive but derived,'[28] as 'total . . .'[29] in its dependence, as 'not blind or automatic, but conscious and cognitive.'[30]

In Augustine's description of various qualities of the inner word there is a seminal attempt at what Lonergan describes as 'self-appropriation'. Thus, it might properly be said that just as Newman was led to a certain 'self-appropriation' in terms of his reflections on the meaning of his assent to the truths of faith, so analogously Augustine was introduced through his conversion and his reflections on the Trinitarian mystery to a depth of interiority and self-scrutiny he might not otherwise have achieved.

In terms of the present context and as a link to what is shortly to be discussed, the following comment of Lonergan is worth citing in full:

If one supposes Augustine to be right (in speaking of the *verbum*) and, at the same time, entertains an admiration for Newman, one is going to ask whether the Augustinian couplet *memoria* and *verbum* is parallel to Newman's couplet of illative sense and unconditioned assent. But if one desires to get beyond words and suppositions to meanings and facts, then one has to explore one's own mind and find out for oneself what there is to be meant; and until one does so, one is in the unhappy position of the blind man hearing about colours and the deaf man reading about counterpoint.[31]

Here Lonergan expresses his admiration for the intellectual prowess and achievement of Augustine and Newman, but at the same time indicates the need for the individual to explore his own mind if he is to come to a personal understanding of what

B

it is for a man to understand and to know. Moreover, although he acknowledges a certain *de facto* dependence on Christian revelation for the type of subtle self-appropriation which occurred in Augustine and Newman, Lonergan in the above quotation does not invite us to reflect, as Augustine did, on the Trinity or, as Newman did, on the meaning of one's assents to the truths of faith. Rather, he urges the reader to investigate his own mind and to find for himself '. . . what there is to be meant'.

The exploration of one's own mind evidently is not an exclusively Christian undertaking. As Lonergan observes at the beginning of his article, 'The Natural Desire to See God',[32] the questions *is it?* and *what is it?* are natural to every man. To ask these questions does not require an acquired habit, such as playing the violin does, nor does it require any gift of divine grace.[33] Aristotle, for example, pointed out some three centuries before the Christ-event that wonder is natural to all men.[34] And, as Lonergan himself indicates, Aristotle's grasp of the nature of insight was too uncannily brilliant to have occurred without the exercise of very subtle psychological introspection.[35] If such activities, then, as wondering, inquiring, understanding, reflecting and judging are natural to all men, one is strictly in the realm of the profane, or non-supernatural, in attempting to describe or explain these inter-related cognitive activities.

At this point a question arises which goes beyond the issues of the Christian context and problematics that Lonergan dealt with in his studies of operative grace and the *verbum* to a more radical foundational question. Thus, although the 'self-appropriation' which took place in Augustine, Aquinas and Newman occurred in a sacral or, more specifically, explicitly Christian context, the pagan Aristotle was also quite capable of performing a highly subtle form of introspection. It is, therefore, imperative to ask if for Lonergan there is any validity in speaking of a 'Christian epistemology or a 'Christian' metaphysics in any other than an accidental, extrinsicist, or, at best, historical sense.

LONERGAN'S EXPLICIT VIEW OF CHRISTIAN PHILOSOPHY
In point of fact, Lonergan does explicitly use the term 'Christian philosophy',[36] and he has both spoken and written about what he refers to as the origins of Christian realism.[37] Lonergan

indubitably maintains that there is an epistemology and a metaphysics implicit in Christian revelation.[38] Yet, although he is most firm in holding this position, he would certainly contend that in so doing he in no way contradicts the view that a pagan—we are speaking now abstractly and not necessarily existentially—could by engaging in critical introspection arrive at an epistemological and metaphysical position which would coincide with the epistemology and metaphysics Lonergan affirms to be implicit in Christian revelation. Moreover, the basis for this contention would seem to be most fundamentally rooted in the fact that Lonergan rigorously argues for the distinction between grace and nature and entertains no sympathy even in his most recent works for the position of those who would *in principle* deny this distinction.

Accordingly, if we push the analysis a bit further, Lonergan would never concede that epistemology or metaphysics are any more 'supernatural' sciences than are physics or chemistry. They are, in other words, 'natural' sciences in the sense that the term 'natural' may be employed in contradistinction to the term 'supernatural'. Of course, in designating both physics and metaphysics as 'natural sciences' we imply no reductionist sense. Thus, for example, just as for Lonergan chemistry differs from physics on the one hand and from biology on the other, so even more radically epistemology and metaphysics would differ from any of the empirical sciences.

But what then does Lonergan mean when he speaks of 'Christian realism' or of an epistemology and metaphysics which are implicit in revelation? As is obvious from what we have just said, he does not mean that this realism or epistemology and metaphysics are 'Christian' in an absolutely exclusivist sense. This fact, however, does not negate the possibility that there is something in revelation and man's response in faith to the revealed word which implicitly involves a certain type of realism, and hence an epistemology and metaphysics.

Yet, before proceeding to discuss in more detail the nature of the realism which Lonergan affirms to be implicit in the revelation-response context, it will prove methodologically helpful for us to ask what its *a priori* conditions of possibility are, or in other words, what makes it possible on the most radical foundational level for a Christian realism to exist.

In a most general fashion, the *a priori* condition of possibility for Christian realism as Lonergan conceives it is the existence in God's mind of an intelligible world order in which nature and grace exist as distinct yet intelligibly interrelated principles of being within this world order. Lonergan writes in reference to this point :

I would affirm that world-order is prior to finite natures, that God sees in his essence, first of all, the series of all possible world orders each of which is complete down to its least historical detail, that only consequently inasmuch as he knows world-orders does God know their component parts such as his free gifts, finite natures, their properties, exigences, and so on.[39]

Of course, in setting forward what is referred to as the *a priori* condition of possibility for Christian realism, one assumes the fact of revelation, and one makes use as well of a principle which Lonergan will only affirm once he has proved the existence of God. One must proceed in this manner, however, in order to provide the background for making basically intelligible what Lonergan means by Christian realism and why he can argue that there is a metaphysics intrinsic to revelation which is at the same time a *natural* and not a *supernatural* science.

Reverting once again to the discussion of the *a priori* condition of possibility for the existence of Christian realism, the most important point to grasp is that grace and nature, though distinct principles of being, are not related to each other in some vague extrinsicist fashion, but rather are enfolded in the unity of a world-order which is known by God prior to the distinct component parts of the world order. We should keep in mind this most general *a priori* condition of possibility for the existence of a Christian realism as our discussion moves to a more specific and concrete analysis of the interrelatedness of grace and nature as manifested on the level of subject and the subject's operations. This brief analysis in turn will lead into a specific discussion of the elements of Lonergan's notion of Christian realism and the historical development which he studies in order to articulate this notion's meaning.

In an article entitled 'Openness and Religious Experience', Lonergan speaks of openness as (1) fact, (2) achievement and (3) gift.[40] For Lonergan openness as fact is the pure desire to know.

It is what Aristotle was referring to when he spoke of wonder that is the origin of all science. It is what Aquinas referred to when he spoke of man's natural desire to know God through his essence. Secondly, there is openness as achievement. Openness as achievement is basically the self in its self-appropriation and self-realisation. Finally, there is openness as gift. Man by nature wants to know everything about everything. Yet, to know everything about everything one would have to know the essence of God. Man can, of course, by nature constantly enlarge his horizon perspectives. The differentiations and ever higher integrations which have occurred and are constantly occurring within human consciousness bear eloquent testimony to this fact. Yet, we must make a distinction here. There are possibilities of horizon-enlargements built into the very structure of human consciousness. But, there is also an ultimate enlargement which lies beyond the limits of any horizon-enlargement available to the native resources of natural intelligence. This enlargement is the face-to-face vision of God, knowledge of God not through any finite species but through the essence of God himself. This ultimate horizon-enlargement can only come as a gift from above, descending from the Father of light.

Moreover, as Lonergan puts it, 'in the language at once of Scripture and of current philosophy, man is fallen. There is then a need of openness as a gift, as an effect of grace, where grace is taken as *gratia sanans*.'[41] But the ultimate grace is God's personal face-to-face gift of himself to man of which, in Lonergan's analysis, the *lumen gloriae* is the created contingent term verifying as consequent condition the truth of the reality of God's ultimate Self-gift.[42]

Lonergan stresses that these three aspects of openness are to be intimately interrelated. Thus, in the concrete universe which is the world-order of our experience, 'openness as fact is for openness as gift.'[43] Likewise, 'openness as achievement rises from the fact and conditions and, at the same time, is conditioned by the gift.'[44] These three forms of openness are linked together in the concrete historical development of the human spirit. It is this intimate linkage which explains the primacy of religious experience in the world of man and the non-extrinsic quality of the relationship between nature and grace.

Openness as fact, therefore, is an *a priori* condition of the

possibility for openness as achievement. If there were not the
fact of the existence of the natural desire to know, there would
be nothing in which achievement or self-appropriation could
occur. In similar fashion, openness as fact is an *a priori* condition
of the possibility for openness as gift. For, if the pure desire to
know were not unrestricted or, in other words, correlative to the
totality of being in its complete universality and concreteness,
there would be nothing for the Gift to communicate itself to in
a face-to-face intercommunion of knowing and loving.

With the above analysis of the *a priori* condition of possibility
for the existence of a Christian realism clearly in mind, it is now
possible to focus attention directly on the problem of Christian
realism, or in other words, of the epistemology and metaphysics
which Lonergan claims to be implicit in Christian revelation. The
procedure here will be first to begin with a definition of three
forms of *realism* as Lonergan envisages them and then to indicate
more concretely in just what fashion he relates these three forms
of realism to the revelation-response context and to the historical
evolution of Christian consciousness.

THE THREE FORMS OF REALISM

Lonergan, in *De Deo Trino*, speaks of three forms of realism :
non-critical, dogmatic and critical.[45] Obviously, all men do
actually know various realities. Yet, the three types of realists
assign different criteria for why they think they know things to
be real. Lonergan thus proceeds with a simple example to indicate
the differences in criteria which the various *realists* employ to
justify their form of *realism*.

The naïve, or non-critical, realist says that he knows that a
given mountain is real because he can see it with his eyes, touch
it with his hands and feel it under his feet. The *reality* of the
mountain is so obvious and clear for the naïve realist in terms of
immediate sensation and perception that he attributes any further
attempt to assign more subtle criteria for the knowledge of the
really real to a certain 'stupidity or perversity'[46] of mind. In
contrast, the critical realist, while he acknowledges that he can
see the same mountain with his eyes, tread upon it with his
feet and touch it with his hands, insists that he can only *know*
that it is real by affirming it to be so through correct judgment. In Lonergan's view, the crucial function of judgment in

achieving knowledge of the *real* or *what truly exists* goes unrecognised and unacknowledged by the non-critical realist.

Then there is the dogmatic realist. Lonergan defines the dogmatic realist as the type of realist who either through a rare and quite extraordinary natural acuity of mind, or through the influence exercised upon him in an implicit fashion by the revealed word of God, agrees with the critical realist without, however, understanding why he is in agreement. Moreover, owing to the nescience inherent in dogmatic realism, it easily becomes mixed with naïve realism. Yet, it is also foundational to critical realism. Critical realism remains to be discussed in chapters 3 and 4, but it will prove helpful to analyse somewhat more closely here what is meant in terms of our present context by realism, dogmatic, and the implicit character of dogmatic realism.

Both the Old and the New Testament place a primary emphasis on the revealed *word* of God. Again and again the expression occurs : 'For thus says the Lord'.[47] Moreover, the word of the Lord is to be held fast by the disciples of the Word : 'But even if we or an angel from heaven should preach to you a gospel contrary to that which you received, let him be accursed.'[48] This stress on unswerving adherence to the word of God is grounded in the word itself and explains that celebrated formula so often repeated by Church councils throughout the centuries: 'If anyone shall say . . . let him be anathema.' Basically, then, there is a realism contained in the word of God both because this word must be sincerely believed and not contradicted, and because it is true and corresponds to reality as it actually is. For realism in the most general sense means that a truth acknowledged in the mind corresponds to an existent state of affairs. Such is precisely what the Christian believes to be the case when he accepts God's word.

This realism is dogmatic not only in the sense that it pertains to the very essence of dogma, but also because it is posited without philosophical reflection. It is the philosopher's explicit task to assign adequate and sufficient reasons for any affirmation he may make. Dogmatic realism, however, does not consist in philosophical reasoning but is totally operative in so far as the revealed and preached word of God is sincerely accepted.

It is characteristic of dogmatic realism, however, that dogmatic realists do not recognise it as such. Thus, although Isaiah,

Paul, and Athanasius were all dogmatic realists, they did not explicitly advert to their realism. All that Lonergan is affirming is that they had minds, sincerely acknowledged and accepted the word of God, and acted according to the reality revealed to them and known in faith through the word.

Owing to the dynamics of the dogmatic realism inherent in the word of God as sincerely believed, a dialectic naturally arises which tends to expel elements of naïve realism with which it can become entwined, and implicitly to lay the grounds for the development of critical realism. So, many of the pre-Nicene Christian writers who believed the word of God and even died for it were dogmatic realists, i.e., they did not think that what was known by the senses was *uniquely* and *exclusively* the real but rather they above all clung to the reality revealed to them through the word of God. Yet there were inconsistencies which only dialectic could resolve.

THE ORIGINS OF CHRISTIAN REALISM

Lonergan finds the origins of Christian realism in the development which leads from the God of Scripture to the God of the Fathers and councils. In both the Old and New Testaments God is characterised as One who acted, spoke, promised, threatened. The Fathers, however, from the second to the fourth century were concerned with the Trinitarian problematic and from the fifth to the seventh with Christological issues. There was then a gradual shift from the scriptural descriptions of God as related to us to an explanatory viewpoint, which through the employment of non-scriptural terms attempted to speak of God as he is in himself. The 'middle term', so to speak, between Scripture and the early councils was development, and more specifically a development which was at its core dialectical.

At the beginning of the Christian era, there were Judaeo-Christians who were not able to transcend effectively their Old Testament background and who tended to think of the Son as an angel.[49] They attempted to conceive of the God of New Testament revelation in terms of the symbolism of the Old Testament. Then again there were the gnostics who engaged in a pseudo-symbolic type of speculation. It was speculation because they dealt with ultimates but it was pseudo-symbolic because they personified abstract notions, intermingling sensitive images with their abstractions.[50] Further, there were the Marcionites who viewed the God of the Old Testament as evil,[51] and the adoptionists who held that Christ was only a man.[52] All of the above, although important in terms of background, were not within the main stream of Christian development. More significant by far were Irenaeus, Tertullian, Clement of Alexandria, Origen, Arius and Athanasius—to name but a few of the most important figures involved in the dialectic which led to the Nicene definition.

Irenaeus was orthodox but tinged with naïve realism. Against the Marcionites he affirmed that the God of the Old Testament was the Father of Jesus Christ.[53] But in attempting to prove that there was only one God, Irenaeus concentrated on the fact that God contained all things, and so, Lonergan argues, it is difficult in view of context and terms employed not to see a rather materialistic conception operative in this proof.[54]

Tertullian exemplifies the same difficulty as Irenaeus but even more clearly. For Tertullian there was no question that the Son was truly God and distinct from the Father. Yet, it was equally necessary that the Son be a body since for Tertullian a spirit to be real had to have a body. This position in turn led Tertullian to affirm that the Son was temporal and a portion of the divine substance of which the Father was the whole and also that the Son was subordinate to the Father as the one obeying is subordinate to the one commanding. These latter affirmations, of course, involved at least an implicit contradiction of his basic affirmation that the Son was truly God.[55]

Clement of Alexandria was likewise involved in what Lonergan retrospectively designates as non-critical realism. Clement clearly argues that the angels and God himself have bodies although their matter is far too subtle for us to be able to see them. Clement thus confused the notion of body with the notion of reality, as Tertullian had done.[56]

In attempting to come to grips with gnostic exegesis, however, Clement was forced to transcend a mere naïve realism. In the eighth book of his *Stromata* Clement recommended a methodological approach to exegesis. Thus, he stressed that if the exegete makes use of a name he should define it and define it in terms that are better known than the particular name in question.[57] He argued in this manner in order to overcome the symbolic limitations of gnostic exegesis. If the only interpretation of Scripture were symbolic, then it would be impossible to say what the symbols in Scripture were symbols of. It was accordingly necessary to appeal to some other criterion than the symbolic, and so the need for a correct notion of reality implicitly arose.[58]

In Origen likewise there is a certain transcendence of naïve realism but the transcendence is in the direction of a Middle Platonism.[59] Origen excluded all materiality from his conception of the Father and the Son and so struck a blow against the position which tended to view the generation of the Son by the Father in material, imaginable terms.[60] But, Origen taught that the Father knew himself far more perfectly than did the Son[61] and that the Father was *the* God—*ho Theos*—whereas the Son was God or *Theos* by participation.[62] Origen's approach was Platonist and involved radical difficulties whose heretical implications he probably did not grasp.[63]

Irenaeus, Tertullian, Clement of Alexandria and Origen all struggled to articulate their understanding of the word of God in terms fit for their own peculiar cultural milieu and background. Yet, although they remained fundamentally orthodox in their sincere acceptance of the divinity of the Son, their reflections were often inadequate, involving some statements which were at least implicitly contradictory to their profession of faith in the Son's divinity. This contradiction between profession of faith and certain reflections on the meaning of the truths of faith within unique philosophico-cultural contexts moved the dialectic forward towards its implicit resolution in the Nicene definition.

With the advent of Arius, however, the pre-Nicene dialectic received tremendous impetus toward immediate resolution. For Arius, unlike the Christian teachers and Fathers whom we have just been considering, saw clearly that if he was to cling firmly to his particular view of the nature of God he would be logically required to deny the divinity of the Son.

More specifically, Arius held that the most radical and defining attribute of God was that he was unbegotten and unoriginate. Accordingly, since the Scripture speaks of the Son as begotten, Arius felt compelled by logical consistency to deny the divinity of the Son and to speak of him instead as a perfect creature.

Arius, moreover, shifted the whole locus of discussion onto a new more technical plane of discourse. And, this shift to a more explanatory type of propositional expression was in part responsible for the Council's introduction of a non-scriptural term into its definition.[64]

At Nicea itself the Fathers affirmed in opposition to Arius and those likeminded that there was one God, whom they immediately named the Father Almighty, and that the Son was 'God of God, begotten not made, of one substance with the Father' and 'consubstantial with the Father'.[65] They did not, however, expressly teach that the Father and the Son possessed one and the same substance. Lonergan observes none the less that the affirmation of one substance was logically implied in the Nicene decree.

More specifically, the Fathers at Nicea taught monotheism. But they also taught that both the Father and the Son were true God. This implied of necessity that they possessed numerically one and the same divinity. Athanasius in his writings indicated that the Fathers at first wrote that the Son was the true image of the Father and most similar to the Father in all things without any variation,[66] but that, when they saw how the Arians were twisting these statements to their own advantage, they were forced to re-express in clearer terminology what they had decreed. Accordingly, the Fathers stated that the Son was not only similar to the Father, but the same thing by similitude.[67] Thus, in Lonergan's analysis, it was the intention of the Nicene decree to go beyond similitude to the notion of radical identity. And, as a matter of historical fact, what was logically implicit at Nicea was explicitly deduced and expressed at least by the time of the Council of Serdica in 343, where it was taught that the Father and the Son possessed one and the same *hypostasis*.[68]

In the light of the preceding analysis it should be at least skeletally clear what immanent dialectical forces were at work prior to Nicea and why the Nicene definition of the Son's consubstantiality with the Father was, as it were, a *de facto* historical inevitably. In Lonergan's opinion, the most radical explanation of the genesis of the Nicene definition lies in the exigences of intelligence, reasonableness and responsibility which characterise the human spirit and in the intrinsically luminous or supereminently intelligible quality of the revealed word of God.

To be precise, the life-giving word of God is addressed to the

mind and heart of man, and through the special help of the
Spirit of the Father and the Son man is enabled to respond to
the word in faith.[69] Here it must be stressed, if the proper relationship between nature and grace is to be maintained that,
although the light of faith and the gift of hope-filled charity are
required if a man is sincerely to adhere to the word in faith and
to do the truth in love, the light of faith presupposes as the condition of possibility of its own effectiveness the full, free symbiotic
cooperation of man's native intelligence and reasonableness.

In terms of these symbiotic operations, man through his grace-
illumined spirit makes an unconditional assent to the revealed
word of God and vigorously reacts against any affirmation which
contradicts the word he has sincerely accepted in faith. Here
there is a clear manifestation of the distinction and intimate
relationship between grace and nature as concretely embodied in
the symbiotic unity of faith-illumined intelligence that assents to
the living word of God.

In terms of the above the precise meaning of dogmatic realism
is also concretely exposed. Thus, the word of God, though radically mysterious, as is its Source, is intelligible. In fact, it is supereminently intelligible, and yet directly addressed to the human
heart and mind. The word of God as accepted through the light
of faith exercises its force on the human spirit, impelling it
through the light of its supereminent intelligibility towards an
ever greater fidelity to the exigences of intelligence and reasonableness. Now this is precisely what is meant by the dogmatic
realism inherent in the word of God. Because man is intelligent
he is by nature open to a revelation in terms of *logos*. Inversely,
because the word is intelligible, and proceeding from the very
Ground of human intelligence itself, the revealed *logos* as
accepted freely through grace-illumined acts of faith leads the
believer toward an ever greater fidelity to the exigences of his
own rationality.

Of course, there is a difference, on the one hand, between
existential fidelity to the revealed word and the exigences it
imposes on human rationality and, on the other hand, a thematised understanding of the type of exigence for the human spirit
implicit in the word of God. Thus, every Christian who is faithful
to the word and the exigences it imposes on the human spirit is
a dogmatic realist. But to be a critical realist and explicitly to

relate this realism to the Christian context, one must not only be faithful in one's commitment to the word and its exigences for human intelligence. One must also understand and properly verify one's understanding of the nature of human intelligence, the function of the light of faith in human intelligence, a certain imperfect and analogous conception of the revealed word of the Word and the interrelationship of the three. Finally, one may be in principle either a dogmatic or critical realist even though one has not *explicitly* heard the word of God preached. In Lonergan's estimation, however, this latter instance is very rare indeed.[70]

In concluding this section on Lonergan's notion of Christian philosophy, it will prove helpful briefly to situate the preceding analysis within a more precise philosophic context. Accordingly, at Nicea, as viewed from Lonergan's perspective, the Council through its affirmation of the consubstantiality of the Son with the Father—as explained in the famous Athanasian rule—laid the foundations for critical realism.[71] This is so, first of all, because through the Athanasian rule the imagination was transcended, i.e., the Athanasian rule is no more imaginable than is the second law of thermodynamics, since the rule simply asserts that whatever is predicated of the Father is likewise to be predicated of the Son, except the name Father. Secondly, the Council laid the grounds for a critical realism in the sense that truth, and hence being, were at least implicitly affirmed to be ultimately attainable not through sense data alone or mere conception, but through judgments or, in other words, through true propositions.

Now, just as Lonergan in his cognitional theory conceives of knowledge as a process which involves experience as well as understanding and judgment, so in his analysis of the Nicene problematic he indicates how essential sensible images were as aids for the development of the Athanasian rule. For example, without an image such as the sun as origin of light, Athanasius would never have been able to get an insight into the intelligibility or *ratio* of consubstantiality.[72] For there is no insight without phantasm and its heuristic suggestive function. Hence the visible world, the world of sense and imagination, is an essential condition of possibility for the occurrence of insights through which intelligibilities are grasped which may then be expressed in abstract propositions, such as, for example, the Athanasian rule. Yet a mistake occurs when the world of sense experience is made the sole criterion of what is real. And this mistake, Lonergan avers, was made to a greater or lesser degree by a number of the early Christian thinkers.

In Lonergan's view, ideas are required if the question is ever to arise as to whether or not a given state of affairs is true or false. But if ideas or mere syntheses of concepts are made the sole criteria for what is real, there is scope again for error. Such was the error of Middle Plantonists like Origen and, to an extent, Clement of Alexandria. These men saw clearly that the senses and their data could never be adequate criteria for judging the really real but they failed to see that truth is reached in an absolute, unconditioned sense only through correct judgments and propositions. This notion of truth and judgment is what Lonergan believes to be the implicit achievement of Nicea, which is most especially manifest in the genius of Athanasius.

In conclusion, Lonergan is convinced that there is a specific type of realism—the realism which affirms that truth is known through correct judgments—at the core of the Christian message itself and that when the human mind, open by nature to the possibility of a free revelation on the part of God, sincerely accepts this revelation it is impelled by its own innate dynamism, metamorphosed and empowered by the force and light of the revealed word, to rise above every form of empiricism and idealism toward a critical realism.

We may end by quoting a more recent comment of Lonergan's, which places the issue of Christian philosophy in a context which harmonises with our discussion of this chapter and opens up the topic of the next :

Now from a rationalist or deductivist viewpoint it may seem of great importance to determine just what is presupposed and just what is implied by any of the meanings attributed to the word philosophy. But I believe such importance to be greatly reduced, if not to vanish, when the rationalist or deductivist viewpoint is rejected, when procedures are, not from premises to conclusions, but from data through understanding to judgments and decisions, when significant decisions are highly personal and indeed existential matters of conversion, and when conversions are not logical consequences of previous positions but rather notable rejections of previous positions.

So with regard to Christian philosophy my views are rather humdrum. There is no philosophy that sets up an exigence for God's gift of his love, or that constitutes a sufficient preparation for that gift. There is a philosophy that is open to the acceptance of Christian doctrine, that stands in harmony with it, and that, if rejected, leads to a rejection of Christian doctrine.[73]

2

The Existential Dimension

IN *Insight* Lonergan explicitly states that unless the context indicates otherwise what he means by the terms 'exist', 'existence', and 'existential' is what is known through questions to which a 'yes' answer is given.[1] Thus, 'existence' or the 'existential' is not what is known through answers given to 'what' or 'why' questions such as 'What is an eclipse?' or 'Why is this an eclipse?' but rather through 'yes' answers to such questions as 'Is what I am experiencing an eclipse?' or 'Do eclipses occur very often?' Presupposed in all this, of course, is that the 'yes' answers are correct answers. Otherwise one is not, in fact, knowing 'existence' or the 'existential'.

In *Insight*, however, the context does occasionally admit of other uses of the word 'existential'. Thus, in his Introduction to *Insight* Lonergan employs the term 'existential' in a somewhat negative sense in writing of ' "existential" concerns that invade and mix and blend with the operations of intellect to render it ambivalent and its pronouncements ambiguous.'[2]

But in the Epilogue of *Insight* Lonergan employs the term 'existentialist' in a positive manner writing of the consideration, by philosophy and the human sciences, of man in his concrete performance.[3] The work *Insight* does not involve an invitation to do some reading or thinking about man as he might exist in some state of pure nature or in a state other than the one in which the reader finds himself, but rather to engage in a 'coming-to-grips' with the self one happens to be. Lonergan's basic philosophy, concerned as it is with the subject's performance, must in fact be considered existentialist, and if the term 'self-appropriation' adequately expresses the goal of *Insight*, the term 'conversion' serves to indicate most forcefully the radical 'existential' character of the process of self-appropriation. In Lonergan's more recent lectures, and especially in *Method in Theology*, conversion is central. Nevertheless, his rather constant explicit use of the term 'conversion' in his more recent writings must not lead one to suppose that this emphasis is something *radically* new in him. On the contrary, *Insight* may, in fact, be most properly designated as an invitation to intellectual and, indirectly, to moral conversion. And it terminates by inviting the reader to face the problem of evil in the world and to seek personally to identify its solution in the area of religion. Lonergan's explicitly 'existential' concern with the problem of conversion emerges as early as his *De Constitutione Christi* which was published in 1956. In the section entitled—significantly for the present discussion—'De Existentia', Lonergan describes in a somewhat global fashion the three conversions man is summoned to undergo if he is to 'exist' authentically as a man,[4] and raises the issue interestingly in terms of Kierkegaard's self-posed question regarding the authenticity of his existence as a Christian and of the existentialists' question as to what it means to be genuinely a man. He situates man's need for conversion within the general context of man's existence as a being who must pass from potential dominion over himself to actual dominion through a long and arduous process of freely willed self-development. In this context, he contrasts man with entities which exist in a lower order of the hierarchy of being in terms of the disparate fashion in which laws operate in these lower entities and in man.

Lonergan first indicates that on the strata of the chemical elements chemical laws operate and *dominate* but in such a manner that all the laws of physics likewise hold. On the plant level, the laws of biology function and *dominate* but in such a way that all the laws of physics and chemistry are allowed their proper scope of operation. Likewise, on the level of the animal, the laws of sensitive psychology are operative and *dominate* in such a fashion that no physical or chemical or biological law is violated. There is manifest, then, on the chemical, vegetable and animal levels a certain *Aufhebung* in which the laws of the lower genus are at once retained and yet sublated in such a way that they become perfectly subordinate to the *domination* of the higher synthesis. Man, however, offers an exception to this rule. In man the highest specifying element— his intelligence and freedom—does not exercise automatic control over his *inferior pars*. Rather, to 'exist', to become a truly authentic human being, man must freely move himself out of the state of potentiality to the state of radical dominion and full human actuality.[5]

Lonergan goes on to attribute certain qualities to conversion which are equally applicable to intellectual, moral and religious conversion. Thus, conversion is at once intimate, radical, conscious and deliberate.[6] In his more recent writings and lectures Lonergan has emphasised the social aspects of conversion. So, for example, in 'Theology in its New Context' he describes conversion as 'an ongoing process, at once personal, communal and historical.'[7] Most assuredly, for Lonergan conversion is always 'intensely personal, utterly intimate.'[8] Yet it is 'not so private as to be solitary. It can happen to many and they can form a community to sustain one another in their self-transformation. . . . Finally, what can become communal, can become historical. It can pass from generation to generation.'[9]

Again, Lonergan underlines the need for the unconverted individual to realise personally, and at least to confess to himself, a certain need for conversion if he is ever to be converted. Thus he regularly notes that if, for example, it took such an acute genius as St Augustine years to realise that he had identified his notion of the 'really real' with body,[10] how much greater confusion must exist in those of lesser talent who have never clearly and distinctly faced the problem, let alone resolved it, and how very important it is for these individuals in some way at least to grasp a certain need for conversion. One might extend the remark to the spheres of the ethical and the religious. Indeed, we may pass on immediately to relate Lonergan's usage of the term 'conversion' more specifically to the basic problematic of this work : the God problem in Lonergan's philosophy.

First then, three basic conversions—intellectual, moral, religious—may be viewed as existential conditions of possibility for any fruitful understanding and validation of a critically grounded philosophy of God, such as that of Lonergan. Thus, intellectual conversion may be accurately described as a *de jure* existential condition of possibility, and moral and religious conversions as *de facto* conditions of possibility for anyone to understand properly and critically validate for himself the truth of Lonergan's approach to the problem of God. An exposition of the three conversions is, therefore, of great hermeneutic importance. However, we add at once that intellectual conversion, pertaining as it does to the internal development of the philosophy of God, will be dealt with more properly in Part II. Lonergan, however, for the sake of comparison and differentiation frequently treats of the three conversions together. Accordingly, we will treat briefly here of intellectual conversion in order to indicate its distinction from, and relationship to, moral and religious conversion.

The procedure in the following three major divisions of this chapter will be to analyse each of the conversions and then to examine their interrelationship. Before entering into this detailed analysis, however, we will offer a possible explanation for Lonergan's use of the term conversion in a philosophical context and attempt to indicate exactly what it means to designate the conversions as either *de jure* or *de facto* existential conditions of possibility for accurately grasping Lonergan's philosophy of God.

INTELLECTUAL, MORAL AND RELIGIOUS CONVERSION

What perhaps initially strikes the reader of Lonergan is the strangeness of using the term 'conversion' in a philosophical context. Lonergan, however, especially in his more recent lectures and essays, constantly does so. In fact, he goes so far as to describe intellectual conversion as the core moment in philosophy. There is no simply hermeneutical answer to the question of usage, but Lonergan's writings do suggest a possible line of response.

Lonergan's early philosophical studies involved a prolonged study of Newman's *Grammar of Assent.* This work involves a certain concrete epistemology of moral-religious assent and lays great stress on the personal responsibility involved in real assent. Likewise, in *Insight,* Lonergan stresses the element of personal commitment and responsibility involved in judging. He cites the de la Rochefoucauld witticism to the effect that everyone complains about his memory but no one about his judgment.[11] He notes that the pusillanimous refuse to judge even when the evidence is in, whereas the brash make haste to pronounce judgment long before such evidence. These examples, as is clear, do not bear directly on the phenomenon of conversion but they do indicate the importance of personal involvement and responsibility in Lonergan's conception of knowing. And these latter qualities are, of course, right at the heart of the conversion phenomenon.

In a reply to Professor Andrew J. Reck, who had spoken somewhat critically of Lonergan's 'allegiance to neo-Thomism',[12] in terms of its effect on his cognitional theory, Lonergan indicated that his 'interest in Aquinas came late',[13] whereas in the early thirties he began 'to delight in Plato, especially the early dialogues, and then went on to the early writings of Augustine.'[14] In this context it is interesting that in the Introduction to *Insight* Lonergan refers to both Plato and Augustine, and explicitly to the latter in terms of the effects of Neoplatonism and religious conversion on his philosophical thinking.[15] Lonergan indicates that both Plato and Augustine transcended their imaginations to discover that the real and body were not identical. For Lonergan this achievement of Plato and Augustine indicates a crucial breakthrough. Indeed, Plato offers a historical precedent, and even an explicit source of inspiration for Lonergan's employment of the expression, 'conversion', in describing the ascent from the cave as a conversion, or a turning round, of the soul from darkness to light.[16]

Lonergan is not a Platonist but he does acknowledge that in man there are two modes of knowing—one a form of animal knowing and the other specifically human—and that a specifically philosophical conversion is needed in order to move from the status of '*homo sensibilibus immersus* to *homo maxime est mens hominis.*'[17] He accordingly praises Plato for discovering the element in man's knowing which transcends sense knowledge, or imagination, though he is at fundamental variance with the Greek philosopher on certain other basic issues.

It is noteworthy that not only does the use of the term 'conversion' in a philosophic context occur in both Plato and Lonergan, but also that certain descriptive expressions of Plato regarding this conversion find an almost literal echo in Lonergan. For example, in Plato's words, as the liberated prisoner emerges from the cave and approaches the light 'his eyes will be dazzled, and he will not be able to see anything at all of what are now called realities.'[18] In a strikingly similar manner Lonergan, in *The Subject*, writes of intellectual conversion as a matter 'of moving out of a world of sense and of arriving, dazed and disoriented for a while, into a universe of being.'[19]

We should not overlook the influence of Augustine on Lonergan in this context. Lonergan states that it was in the throes of a religious conversion that Augustine slowly mastered the idea derived from the Neoplatonist tradition and nourished in a Christian ambience that 'the name, real, might have a different connotation from the name, body.'[20] He thus intimately associates Augustine's religious conversion with his growth in philosophical thinking.

Lonergan, then, in the tradition of Plato, Augustine and Newman—to name but three—envisaged philosophical thinking in a very dynamic existential fashion. Knowing is a personal achievement which involves commitment and responsibility. And if this is true of any instance of knowing, it is preeminently the case in regard to knowing knowing. Indeed, for Lonergan the shift in philosophical viewpoint which critical realism demands is as existential, difficult, and radically transformative of human consciousness as are moral and religious conversion. In fact, in a most recent essay Lonergan says that of the three conversions the intellectual is the most rare.[21]

Intellectual conversion is spoken of as a *de jure* existential condition of possibility for arriving at a personally validated understanding of Lonergan's philosophy of God, because Lonergan's proof for the existence of God is intrinsically dependent for its validity on the adequacy of his basic cognitional analysis and epistemological positions.

Moral and religious conversion, on the other hand, are defined as *de facto* existential conditions of possibility for personally validating the truth of Lonergan's philosophical approach to God. Negatively this means that moral and religious conversion, unlike intellectual conversion, do not constitute intrinsic moments in the immanent unfolding of Lonergan's proof for the existence of God. Positively it means that the individual who undertakes the task of critically evaluating a philosophy of God does not operate in a vacuum but rather as a responsible historical agent in whom basic moral and religious options are *de facto* or actually existentially operative—either in a negative or positive fashion—and that these options ineluctably exercise an influence, for good or ill, on the individual's entire project of thinking about God.

We may profitably put this in the context of Lonergan's

discussion, in chapter XVII of *Insight*, of the appropriation of truth. 'The essential appropriation of truth is cognitional',[22] but 'our reasonableness demands consistency between what we know and what we do; and so there is a volitional appropriation of truth that consists in our willingness to live up to it.'[23] Lonergan stresses, however, that good will is an existential condition of possibility for reaching the truth in the first place.[24] Bad will makes truth unwelcome and a process of enquiry may be either halted at the start or hindered at every stage of its prosecution. Newman makes this same point when he writes : 'I have already alluded to the influence of moral motives in hindering assent to conclusions which are logically unimpeachable. According to the couplet :

> A man convinced against his will
> Is of the same opinion still;

assent then is not the same as inference.'[25]

Newman observes further that just

as assent sometimes dies out without tangible reasons, sufficient to account for its failure, so sometimes, in spite of strong and convincing arguments, it is never given. We sometimes find men loud in their admiration of truths which they never profess. As, by the law of our mental constitution, obedience is quite distinct from faith, and men may believe without practising, so is assent also independent of our acts of inference. Again, prejudice hinders assent to the most incontrovertible proofs.[26]

The business of attaining truth requires the harmonious co-operation of all man's powers—the subconscious, perception, imagination, memory, etc.—'but for the collaboration of all our powers towards the grasping of truth, bad will substitutes their conspiracy to bring forth doubts about truth and evidence for error.'[27] Lonergan's stark conclusion is that 'without good will he (man) cannot proceed to the attainment of truth.'[28] Such a statement concretely conveys what is meant by saying that moral conversion is a *de facto* existential condition of possibility for validating for one's self the truth of a correct philosophy of God.

Finally, there is religious conversion, described as the same type of existential condition. Nor is such a condition or its discussion to be excluded because of its theological dimension. First, religion as a phenomenon is open to philosophical consideration as even a brief perusal of the history of philosophy shows. Moreover, it is the very nature of philosophy not to set aside any dimension of reality from its purview. Secondly, such an exclusion would constitute a withdrawal from the new context as discussed in the previous chapter. But let us postpone further consideration of religious conversion till we have dealt in more detail with intellectual and moral conversion.

Intellectual conversion

First, intellectual conversion is intimate, radical, conscious, and deliberate because it involves a personal grappling with the self. In this personal grappling, the spontaneous tendency to conceive of the real in terms of 'body' must be overcome through a type of self-transcendence in which the individual moves out of the world of the immediacy of the sensible, into the world of the intelligible and being where the real is what is known through the mediation of the inner words of understanding and judgment.

Moreover, in terms of the God problem, intellectual conversion is most radically an 'existential' condition of possibility for the validation of Lonergan's basic approach to the divine because it consists fundamentally not in an analysis of the logical consistency of propositions but in a dynamic act of self-realisation on the intellectual level. Further, intellectual conversion is a *de jure, intrinsic* condition of possibility for understanding and affirming the validity of Lonergan's approach to the God problem because Lonergan's whole proof for the existence of God hinges on the validity of his affirmations of the identity of the real with being and of the complete intelligibility of the real. And, to arrive at these affirmations the individual must first have succeeded in affirming himself as a knower in the sense indicated in chapter XI of *Insight* and also in affirming the validity of the notions of being and of objectivity as set forth by Lonergan in chapters XII and XIII. The central importance of these affirmations emerges most clearly when one reflects that it is towards the act of self-affirmation that all the prior chapters of *Insight* flow, and that it is this concrete performance that grounds the development of the remaining chapters of *Insight*, and especially the chapter on general transcendent knowledge.

To be yet more specific, for Lonergan the crucial breakthrough is achieved once an individual, through a dialectic of performance and concept, verifies for himself that the particular sequence of dynamically interrelated cognitional acts he experiences himself to be performing are, in fact, what constitutes knowing. This is so because the notions of being and objectivity, such as Lonergan thematises them in chapters XII and XIII, are really explications of what was radically implicit in the preceding chapters and above all in the act of self-affirmation itself. The affirmation of the existence of a universe of proportionate being isomorphic to the knower is the product of the same type of sequence of interrelated operations as is the self-affirmation of the knower. In the former instance, however, the datum to be affirmed is the proportionate universe rather than the self. The affirmation of the existence of God, however, occurs in terms of the same sequence of interrelated cognitional acts but is unique, different from the two prior affirmations in that God is not an immediate datum of either sense or consciousness. Still without the prior affirmations critically achieved in intellectual conversion, the proof expressed in chapter XIX of *Insight* could not even be formulated, much less affirmed.

Intellectual conversion is a difficult affair. As early as his 1958 article entitled '*Insight* : Preface to a Discussion', in arguing that the world of each man's 'Sorge'—i.e., his individual interests and concerns—must be constantly and unremittingly submitted to the corrections in horizon made by true judgment, Lonergan writes :

I am inclined to believe, however, that this consistent and sedulous correction does not occur without a specifically philosophic conversion from the *homo sensibilibus immersus* to *homo maxime est mens hominis (Sum. theol.*, 1-2, q.29, a. 4 c). This existential aspect of our knowing is the fundamental factor in the differentiation of the philosophies in *Insight*.[29]

In this respect Lonergan has not changed his position, as evidenced by his recent lecture, *The Subject* :

There is a final point to be made. The transition from the neglected and truncated subject to self-appropriation is not a simple matter. It is not just a matter of finding out and assenting to a number of true propositions. More basically, it is a matter of conversion, of a personal philosophic experience, of moving out of a world of sense and of arriving, dazed and disoriented for a while, into a universe of being.[30]

None the less, Lonergan acknowledged that one should not imagine that men necessarily live in an either-or type of situation in which they are either converted or not : rather, they tend to oscillate between sensism and intellectualism. He compares the diverse grades of 'ex-sistentia' in which men may live to the tremendous wave variations which exist in the oceans and to the constant ebb and flow of tides.[31] Our earlier analysis of the Nicean problematic and its dialectic might serve as a sort of model of the manifold existential fluctuations endemic to the human condition.

Moral conversion

Moral conversion, like intellectual conversion, is at once intimate, radical, conscious, and deliberate because it involves a freely espoused transvaluation of values on the highest level of human consciousness. In *The Subject* Lonergan chooses to reserve the term 'existential' for the human subject as operating on the fourth level of consciousness, i.e., 'as a doer, as one that deliberates, evaluates, chooses, acts.'[32] Lonergan's more restricted use of the term 'existential' in *The Subject* indicates the primacy he accords to the fourth level of human consciousness.

What, then, is moral conversion? In *De Constitutione Christi* Lonergan describes moral conversion, although not explicitly making use of the term, as involving a certain 'night of the sensitive soul',[33] through which a purgation is effected which enables the individual to dedicate himself totally, efficaciously, and perseveringly to those values which intelligence grasps to be truly good. Thus, for example, the individual is led to understand that the universe involves a certain order, of which he is a subordinate part, and that he must dedicate himself to goals which transcend his own self-interest.[34]

Moral conversion, therefore, in a most general sense, involves a real self-transcendence or a moving beyond the objects of desire and fear, all merely personal satisfactions and tastes and preferences, into a world of objective value.[35] Here one commits oneself to a certain course of action or way of living because it is existentially grasped as the intelligent and responsible thing to do.

Whereas the self-transcendence of intellectual conversion is intentional, a 'coming to know, not what appears, not what is imagined, not what is thought, not what seems to me to be so, but what is so',[36] moral conversion involves not only a getting beyond the subject by knowing what in fact is so, but an inner transformation of the subject through doing what one knows to be truly good. It is, in Lonergan's terms, real self-transcendence.

Before we engage in a more detailed analysis of moral conversion let us return to the question of its nature as a *de facto* existential condition of possibility of the critical affirmation of God. We will include in our considerations, as far as is convenient, religious conversion, since the same basic explanation of their peculiar status as conditions applies to both and helps to make intelligible their interrelatedness within human consciousness.

The point, then, in describing moral and religious conversion as only *de facto*, existential conditions of possibility is simply this : to indicate as clearly as possible that the decisions which constitute the essence of moral and religious conversion are *not* factors intrinsic to the procedure in *Insight* which constitutes Lonergan's proof for the existence of God. The proof for the existence of God is a matter of experience, understanding, and judgment. It does not involve the fourth level of consciousness as one of its constitutive moments.

In both *The Subject* and 'The Natural Knowledge of God' Lonergan makes it quite clear that what is first in man's intention is the good[37] and not, in its deepest roots, any finite good or goods, but the good that is God, or *the good God*. There is at the core of man's being a transcendental drive or orientation, which, though fundamentally one, may be spoken of first as the notion of being and finally as the notion of value as it dynamically unfolds in promoting man through a series of *Aufhebungen* from insight and its diverse thematisations through reflective understanding and judgment to the level of decision and of rational commitment to values both ethical and religious, and hence ultimately to God.

The *good God*, therefore, is the ultimate objective of human intentionality and the radical goal of all human striving. For this reason, once the dynamic functional interrelatedness of man's intellective operations, as well as the intentional primacy of the existential—the fourth level of consciousness—is acknowledged, it becomes strikingly manifest how crucial both moral and religious conversion are as *de facto* existential conditions of possibility for a concretely fruitful approach to the problem of God in the context of Lonergan's systematic.

Although the term 'conversion' does not even appear in the rather exhaustive index to *Insight*, man's need for moral as well as intellectual and religious conversion is at least indirectly indicated in a variety of ways. Consequently, as a means of understanding in a more comprehensive fashion the nature and scope of moral conversion, and ultimately its relevance to the achievement of a proper understanding and critical validation of Lonergan's philosophy of God, it will prove helpful to discuss first Lonergan's treatment in *Insight* of the role of bias in human affairs and its proper antidote, as well as certain key concepts in the eighteenth chapter of *Insight* where Lonergan extends the process of self-appropriation into the area of moral consciousness. This analysis will in turn provide an apt context in which to relate self-appropriation of the fourth level of consciousness to moral conversion in terms of the relevance of both to a proper understanding of Lonergan's approach to the divine.

In chapter VII of *Insight*, Lonergan analyses the manner in which individual, group and general bias, each in its own fashion, contribute to a deterioration of the human condition; the 'creation' of an objective surd in society; the emergence of major cycles of decline and consequently, the need for a reversal of the cycles of decay in terms of a progress whose principle is liberty.

More specifically, there is first individual bias. This type of bias seeks not what is in accord with true self-love, i.e., wisdom and virtue, without which one can be a true friend neither to oneself nor to others, but is ruled instead by desires and fears. This egoism is not of necessity *unintelligent*, for it is clearly and in a brilliantly destructive fashion operative in 'the cool schemer, the shrewd calculator, the hardheaded self-seeker'.[38] Yet, it overrides intelligence and sins against the light when it discovers that fidelity to the exigences of detached intelligence would mean self-abnegation and the transcendence of a life-pattern in which personal desires and fears are made absolutely normative for action.

Group bias, like individual bias, involves an interference with fidelity to the normative exigences of intelligence. Individual bias, however, goes against normal intersubjective feelings—e.g., the spontaneous attachment of mother and child, man and wife, individuals within a clan or tribe. Group bias, on the contrary, finds itself supported by these very intersubjective bonds. Group bias does not have to defy the judgments of others since all within the group think for the group and judge the rest of the world accordingly. Moreover, just as individual bias impedes development in the individual and leads to his deterioration as an authentic human being, so group bias introduces a surd on a much broader level into the generative principle of a developing social order and is blind to those insights 'that reveal its well-being to be excessive or its usefulness at an end.'[39] Finally, since there are many groups, each with its own biases, group struggles against group and class against class, and hence there arises ever greater violence and the dominance of the surd.

Last, but in no sense least in view of its frightening implications for world-order, is general bias. General bias briefly, is at its core the failure of most men to make rationality the centre of their lives, their thinking, their judging. The consequence is an indifference to problems that require long-range solutions. There results the cumulative deterioration of the social situation and the mounting irrelevance of the pure, disinterested, and detached desire to know. These evils manifest themselves in the retreat of culture into an ivory tower, the reduction of religion to a solely inward affair of the heart, and the emasculation of philosophy to the point where it becomes a matter of mere technical competence.

Yet, the longer cycle of decline can be reversed, for man is free. Here, of course, the ever present need for moral conversion is implicitly affirmed. In chapter VII of *Insight*, however, Lonergan does not analyse in any detail the precise nature of freedom, since his methodological procedure involves reserving the discussion of such notions as truth, error, right and wrong, to later chapters. He does indicate, however, that since in man evolution becomes reflective and man becomes 'the executor of the emergent probability of human affairs'[40] he is free to erect a human science capable not only of knowing history but also of directing it. This heightened state of enlightened cultural consciousness to the exigences of which common sense itself might finally choose to submit for the sake of survival, Lonergan names 'cosmopolis'.[41]

Implicit in Lonergen's discussion of the role of bias, its effects and their possible reversal is an invitation to moral conversion. For, if freedom is the principle of progress,[42] it is only through the effective authentic use of freedom, i.e., through the existential transvaluation of values which is moral conversion that man can offset the effects of decline and make cosmopolis an operative ideal.

In chapter XVIII of *Insight* Lonergan extends the process of self-appropriation into the area of freedom and moral decision or, as he designates it, of rational self-consciousness.

First, there is the development inherent in the chapter itself. It begins with a general analysis of the notion of the good. On the level of experience, good is the object of particular desire. On the level of understanding, it becomes the good of order where concrete possibilities for ordering the manifold of human desire are discerned. On the level of judgment it becomes value, i.e., a good of order precisely in so far as it is a possible object of rational choice. The value is a true value, however, only to the extent that the choice is truly rational and does not result from a flight from self-consciousness or from rationalisation or from moral renunciation.[43]

Next, there follows an analysis of the notion of human freedom in its 'essential' characteristics, i.e., as a *process* involving sensitive experience, practical insight, practical reflection, and decision. Out of this analysis of 'essential' freedom there emerge considerations of the relationship between 'essential' and 'effective' freedom, the external and internal conditions required for the exercise of effective freedom, the possible liberating functions of satire and humour, and finally the fact of moral impotence.

There is in chapter XVIII a certain movement from the 'essential' nature of freedom to a consideration of its 'effective' actualisation. The logic of this development is understandable enough when one reflects that, although it is only from the existential exercise of freedom that the verified thematisation of its 'essential' nature can arise, logically and ontologically it is 'essential' freedom—i.e., the dynamic structure of man's rational self-consciousness—which grounds the possibility of 'effective' freedom—i.e., the actual operational range of any given individual's rational self-consciousness or, in other words, the relative frequence with which given acts of choice actually occur.

Further, although the most immediate aim in the eighteenth chapter is to aid the reader to self-appropriate himself on the fourth level of consciousness, there is no indifference as to whether or not an individual actually proceeds to live according to his properly verified thematisation of the nature of rational self-consciousness. Thus, Lonergan's discussion of the great limitations which external and internal factors may impose on the exercise of effective freedom is quite existential as is his discussion of the function of satire in helping bring men to their 'moral senses'. Likewise, his analysis of man's *de facto* moral impotence is a very concrete invitation to the reader to ask himself if there might not perhaps exist some higher solution to the problem of man's incapacity for sustained development.

Insight, then, is an invitation to self-appropriation both on the level of rational consciousness—the level of experience, understanding, and judgment—and of rational self-consciousness. This latter moment in the process of self-appropriation involves a correct understanding and verification in terms of the data of the fourth level of consciousness, the level of decision and moral consciousness. We should clarify this distinction between self-appropriation on the level of rational self-consciousness and moral conversion.

Intellectual conversion is identical with self-appropriation on the level of experience, understanding and judgment. Moral conversion, however, is not identical with the extension of self-appropriation into the sphere of moral or rational self-consciousness. This point becomes clearer when one reflects that in order to sin an individual must experience the dynamics of rational self-consciousness, i.e., experience that his doing ought to be in conformity with his knowing and yet refuse to freely make his doing conform with his knowing. Accordingly, a certain knowledge of moral consciousness is compatible in some sense with the absence of moral conversion.

It remains true, however, that there is an intimate connection between the achievement of self-appropriation on the fourth level of consciousness and moral conversion. The fullness of self-appropriation on the level of moral consciousness involves such a subtle awareness of the nature of virtuous living that it would be existentially or *de facto* impossible for an individual who made no attempt to live according to the exigences of rational self-consciousness to ever correctly thematise the traits of these exigences.

A certain paradox, then, would seem to be operative in the dynamic process of achieving self-appropriation on the level of moral or rational self-consciousness. On the one hand, moral conversion is not a *de jure* condition of possibility for achieving some minimal degree of understanding of the nature of rational self-consciousness. On the other hand, bad will or the absence of moral conversion blinds an individual and makes him incapable of understanding what he does not experience, namely, the deepest nature of moral commitment and full actualisation on the level of rational self-consciousness. Just as the message of Scripture is that the unspiritual individual is incapable of grasping the spiritual truth which alone makes man free, so the immoral man is existentially unable to grasp the true nature of morality.

Again, the attempt to achieve self-appropriation on the level of moral consciousness should enable a person to become more deeply moral. Thus, if an individual attempts to grasp the nature of rational self-consciousness, then to the extent that he is able to correctly thematise the nature of his moral consciousness he will experience a greater call to live according to the moral exigences which he has articulated. For it is difficult for an individual to act against the light. Consequently, the more luminous a man's understanding of his own inner moral exigences is, the more irresistible will he find the impetus of these exigences to be.

Moral conversion, then, is in some sense both a *de facto* condition for and yet, paradoxically enough, a result of the dynamics of self-appropriation extended to the level of rational self-consciousness. Moral conversion, however, and self-appropriation on the fourth level of human consciousness remain quite distinct realities.

Up to this point in the analysis of moral conversion its vital relationship to the overall problematic of Lonergan's approach to the divine has perhaps been more implicit than explicit. Yet, the relevance of the conversion analysis to the God problem is in certain aspects quite simple to articulate.

In his talk, 'The Natural Knowledge of God' Lonergan discusses the problem of Vatican I's declaration that the existence of God can be known with certainty by the light of unaided reason. He indicates that the Council was concerned with a *quaestio juris* and not a *quaestio facti*.[44] In other words, the Council fundamentally intended to affirm the natural possibility, the intrinsic natural capacity of the human intellect unaided by grace to arrive at certain knowledge of the existence of God. The Council did not, however, intend to affirm that man's natural potentiality for reaching certain knowledge of God's existence without the aid of grace had ever been or would ever be *de facto* actualised.

In regard to the actualisation of this natural potentiality in man, Lonergan is at pains to emphasise that there are many *de facto* existential requirements or conditions of possibility for an individual to grasp a valid argument for God's existence.

Such conditions are always very numerous. In the present instance men must exist . . . They must have attained a sufficient differentiation of consciousness to think philosophically. They must have succeeded in avoiding all the pitfalls in which so many great philosophers have become entrapped. They must resist their personal evil tendencies and not be seduced by the bad example of others. Such are just a few very general conditions of someone actually grasping a valid argument for God's existence.[45]

Lonergan thus clearly affirms the need for a certain moral conversion in an individual if he is to be in fact capable of grasping a valid proof for the existence of God.

In his lecture, *The Subject*, Lonergan stresses the primacy of the existential subject, the individual who 'freely and responsibly makes himself what he is',[46] and indicates how each level of conscious activity affects all the other levels:

The experiential, the intelligible, the true, the real, the good are one, so that the understanding enlightens experience, truth is the correctness of understanding, and the pursuit of the good, of value,

of what is worthwhile in no way conflicts with, in every way promotes and completes, the pursuit of the intelligible, the true, the
real.[47]

The obverse, of course, of the latter part of Lonergan's statement would be that the pursuit of what was evil, a false value
and one not authentically worthwhile, would conflict with,
undermine, and most seriously hamper 'the pursuit of the intelligible, the true, the real'.

It follows from the immediately preceding analysis, as well as
from what was noted earlier, that there is a very close interdepen-
dence in Lonergan's view between intellectual and moral conversion. Certainly knowledge is not to be identified with virtue.
On the other hand, the diversity of operations and conscious
states in a man must not be stressed to the point where their
unification in the one conscious subject, who is the source of these
operations, is belittled or ignored.

In *Insight* Lonergan demonstrates how intimate and all-
important the relationship between the intellectual and moral
states of consciousness in a man is when he discusses how danger-
ous the process of rationalisation can be. Unlike the attempt to
escape self-consciousness or the conscious adoption of 'moral
renunciation', where the individual simply gives up any hope of
amending his ways, rationalisation is an attempt to revise one's
knowing so as to bring it into harmony with one's doing, regardless of the consequences this involves. This is a bold and danger-
ous game because 'it is a playing fast and loose with the pure
desire to know in its immediate domain of cognitional activity'.[48]
There is, therefore, a close link between intellectual and moral
conversion because a radical failure in the realm of ethical
activity can involve an attempt to corrupt intelligence at its very
source and thus make it *practically impossible* for an individual
to identify the intelligible with the real and hence can make any
effort to demonstrate the existence of God almost literally
unthinkable.

Thus, if it is true that the self-affirmation of the knower is
alone the intrinsic, existential condition of possibility for any
correct understanding and validation of Lonergan's approach to
the problem of God, it is equally true that in Lonergan's interpretation, unless the existential subject clearly recognises the facts

C

in regard to bias and moral impotence, it is unlikely that he will ever be able to achieve an authentic self-affirmation of himself as a knower, let alone a critically intelligent grasp of a valid argument for the existence of God.

Finally, the consideration of the nature of self-appropriation on the level of rational self-consciousness and the relationship of this mode of self-appropriation to moral conversion is also most important because it is only on this level that the question of whether or not the world is good arises.

As observed earlier, man experiences in himself a spontaneous intending of the good, of value. This intending is radical and *a priori*. In Lonergan's analysis, just as the pure desire to know is the driving force of the spirit which first manifests itself in wonder and then moves the enquirer through insight and concep-tualisation to reflective understanding and judgment, so the notion of value is a prolongation of a single transcendental intending into the realm of value and the good. It is this opera-tive presence of the notion of value which leads man to ask if the world is good and so inevitably to ask if there exists a good God.

This question about God is one to which it will be necessary to return when the question of Lonergan's notion and affirmation of God arises. We have briefly alluded to it here merely to indicate the importance of the present discussion of self-appro-priation on the level of rational self-consciousness for an ultimate, explicit analysis of Lonergan's treatment of the God problem.

Hopefully, then, the continuity between *De Constitutione Christi, Insight* and Lonergan's more recent works as regards the role of moral conversion in philosophising about God is by now fairly clear. Certainly the stress on moral conversion is much more explicitly in evidence in his more recent works, but it was also, though in a more germinal fashion, very definitely present in many ways in *Insight*.

Lonergan terminates his chapter on the possibility of an ethics by asking whether a solution to the problem of man's moral impotence 'has emerged or is yet to emerge'.[49] Lonergan, then, in accord with his methodology in *Insight*, proceeds to raise the question of God before attempting 'an investigation of the ulterior finality of man'[50] in terms of the possibility of the existence of an actual solution to the problem of man's moral impotence. However, in keeping with the method of the present study and with the new context, it is the question of religious conversion which arises next.

Religious conversion

Religious conversion in Lonergan's estimation is in its ultimate implications the complete unmerited fulfilment of man's orientation towards self-transcendence and the most radically transforming element in human consciousness. It includes within itself in an at least implicit fashion intellectual and moral conversion and is their ultimate *de facto* existential condition of possibility. As Lonergan expresses it in *De Constitutione Christi*: 'This supernatural conversion, which includes the natural within itself, although principally directed towards the end of eternal life, nevertheless carries with it those elements which also enable a man to exist (existere) in this life.'[51] Lonergan is averring that this supernatural conversion not only invites and entices, but almost compels a man to 'exist'.[52] He makes this same point in more technically precise language in *Insight*:

> general transcendent knowledge is concerned with the ultimate condition of the possibility of the positions [the positions in Lonergan's terminology embody the basic epistemological stance of critical realism], and special transcendent knowledge [cf. the chapter in *Insight* which heuristically treats of a possible supernatural solution to the problem of evil] is concerned with the *de facto* condition of the possibility of man's fidelity to the positions.[53]

To more adequately appreciate Lonergan's position one must consider a number of interrelated categories which he employs. It should be noted, however, that while we here treat in turn such notions as 'horizon', and 'world', they express, rather, different aspects of a dynamic whole. Ultimately, of course, there is a certain order of priorities operative among the various 'parts' involved in the dynamic phenomenon we are at present scrutinising. The aim of the present analysis will be a unified articulation of these priorities.

Horizon

Lonergan's notion of 'horizon' may be initially described by engaging in a brief phenomenological analysis of questioning and of man's exercise of effective freedom. In regard, then, to the

phenomenon of questioning in general a distinction may be drawn
between the 'known', the 'known-unknown', and the 'unknown-
unknown'. The 'known' indicates the range of questions in any
given area which I can effectively answer. The 'known-unknown'
refers to the range of questions in any given area which I can
ask and find worth while but which I actually cannot answer.
Finally, the 'unknown-unknown' indicates the range of questions
I do not raise and which I would not find worth while or significant even if I did raise them.[54] Analogously, on the level of
moral activity, Lonergan, in analysing the extent of man's effective freedom, represents a man's basic field of freedom as a
circular area. Within this circular area he locates a central core
where man is effectively free. Encompassing this luminous core
is a penumbral area in which an individual's unhappy conscience
is at work, suggesting to him that he can do better if he tries, and
an outer shadow to which the individual scarcely if ever turns
his attention.[55] Horizon, then, in terms of the phenomena of
questioning and of man's exercise of effective freedom, may be
understood in the former case as the limit or boundary between
the known-unknown and the unknown-unknown and in the
latter as the boundary between the penumbral area and the area
of the outer shadow.

In a more generic sense, however, a horizon for Lonergan
is that which 'is specified by two poles, one objective and the
other subjective, with each pole conditioning the other'.[56] Thus,
for example, in the horizon of the physicist the objective pole is
the specific domain of physics as attained by the scientific methods
acceptable to physicists, and the subjective pole is the physicist
practising these methods. In the horizon, however, of the 'wise
man' or philosopher in the Aristotelian sense, 'the objective pole
is an unrestricted domain, and the subjective pole is the philosopher practising transcendental method, namely, the method that
determines the ultimate and so basic whole.'[57]

World

Lonergan also employs the term 'world' in the context of
horizon and its objective pole. For him a 'world is not a certain
object but rather a complex of objects and not so much of objects
known in act as of objects which are able to be known'.[58] In the
dynamic context of operations it might be said that just as a

single object is what is known through a determinate combination of operations, i.e., through experience, understanding and
judgment, so a world is what is to be reached through a complex
set or combination of differentiated operations.

In his 1962 Latin lectures, *De Methodo Theologiae*, Lonergan
defines 'horizon' as the actual capacity of the subject for eliciting
a given set of operations.[59] In these same lectures Lonergan describes 'world' as what is known through a given complex
combination of differentiated operations.[60] 'World', then, in these
lectures, seems to be identifiable with what Lonergan, in his
later book review 'Metaphysics as Horizon', describes as the
objective pole specifying a horizon and 'horizon' with what he
in this same review speaks of as the subjective pole specifying a
horizon.[61]

Further, in his *De Methodo Theologiae* Lonergan distinguishes
three sets of dialectically interrelated worlds. We may, however,
limit our consideration to the division of worlds which Lonergan
employs in 'Existenz and Aggiornamento',[62] as well as in *The
Subject* and in *Method in Theology*.

Lonergan then speaks of the world of immediacy, the world
mediated by meaning, the world constituted by meaning, and the
world of interiority. The world of immediacy is the world of the
infant, the world 'of what is felt, touched, grasped, sucked, seen,
heard—it is the world to which the adult returns when with an
empty head he lies in the sun. . . . It is the world of pleasure and
pain, hunger and thirst, food and drink, surrender, sex, and
sleep.'[63]

The world of immediacy is quite distinct from the world
mediated by meaning. Entrance into this latter world requires
the leap of insight which introduces man into the world of meaning. In this leap man experiences himself as not only capable of
tasting, touching, etc., but also of 'meaning', and this involves a
fundamental horizon expansion and hence the discovery of a
qualitatively distinct and more 'meaningful' world.

Again, the world mediated by meaning is further differentiated
when the individual discovers that the 'meant', the 'bright idea',
the hypothesis, is not of necessity identical with what is, with
what happens to be the case. When a man makes this latter
discovery, he achieves a type of cognitive self-transcendence in
which he reaches objectivity. At this point 'one is beyond the

subject and one has reached a realm that is non-spatial, atemporal, impersonal. Whatever is true at any time or place, can be contradicted only by falsity.'[64]

Again, there is the world not only mediated by meaning but also constituted by meaning. The state, the law, the economy, education, etc., all of these are the product of free subjects and the embodiment of human creativity.

Finally, there is the world of interiority. This is the world of the subject experienced as subject. It is the heightened awareness of this world which for Lonergan grounds the entire philosophic enterprise. It is about entrance into this world that he is speaking when he states:

It is not just a matter of finding out and assenting to a number of true propositions. More basically, it is a matter of conversion, of a personal philosophic experience, of moving out of a world of sense, and of arriving, dazed and disoriented for a while, into a universe of being.[65]

The horizon-statement relationship

A horizon is prior to all statements made within a given world of meaning. We can perhaps best point out the exact significance of this assertion through an example drawn from a discussion of Lonergan's position regarding the nature of philosophy. For Lonergan, in the area of philosophy it is precisely the priority of horizon to the meaning of statements which explains why realism and a philosophy in general cannot be proved deductively. For 'horizon is prior to the meaning of statements'.[66] This means that 'every statement made by a realist denotes an object in a realist's world, . . . [and] every statement made by an idealist denotes an object in an idealist's world.'[67] Thus, 'the two sets of objects are disparate; and neither of the two sets of statements can prove the horizon within which each set has its meaning, simply because the statements can have their meaning only by presupposing their proper horizon.'[68] Lonergan makes this same point in relating foundations as a functional speciality to the speciality, doctrines:

Foundations present, not doctrines, but the horizon within which the meaning of doctrines can be apprehended. Just as in religious living 'a man who is unspiritual refuses what belongs to the Spirit of God; it is folly to him; he cannot grasp it' (1 *Cor.* 2 : 14), so in theological reflection on religious living there have to be distinguished the horizons within which religious doctrines can or cannot be apprehended; and this distinction is foundational.[69]

For Lonergan, therefore, sets of statements (within a philosophical world) or doctrines (within a theological context) presuppose a horizon within which they can be understood. But this leads us back to the more radical problem of the origin of horizon itself.

Horizon: relative and basic

Horizons are either relative or basic (Lonergan also refers to the latter as absolute). A doctor, for example, has a relative horizon which a lawyer does not share, and vice versa. Each, however, may be open to the existence of the other's horizon and indeed to the fact of the existence of an almost endless variety of relative horizons, e.g., psychological, social, cultural, educational, or historical. Basic or absolute horizon, however, is another matter. It embraces the realm of fundamental intellectual, moral and religious involvement. Here one is on the foundational level of truth or falsity, value or disvalue, God or not God. Basic horizon encompasses man's fundamental orientation on the epistemological-metaphysical, axiological, and theological levels. Whereas differences of relative horizon need not of necessity imply the rejection or exclusion of those relative horizons in which a given individual does not happen to participate or show interest, fundamental commitments on the level of basic horizon, on the contrary, necessarily imply a radical option, and at least the implicit exclusion of opposed stands.

Conversion and basic horizon

Conversion is the key to the constitution of a basic horizon but the relationship of conversion to the basic horizons of philosophy, morality, and religion may be explicated in either a negative or a positive fashion. First, let us remark on the relation of intellectual and moral conversion to the horizon-world interrelationship. This will serve as a bridge to the discussion of Lonergan's hermeneutics and religious conversion, for, as *de jure* 'natural phenomena', these conversions possess a certain autonomy which makes it possible for them to serve as analogous jump-off points for understanding in an imperfect but fruitful manner the 'supernatural phenomenon' of religious conversion.

On the level of philosophy, the horizon of critical realism which results from what Lonergan terms intellectual conversion stands in opposition to all forms of radical materialism, positivism, empiricism, and reductionism. Yet, these latter philosophical *Weltanschauungen* do involve a stance within the basic philosophic horizon. This stance, however, from the Lonergan perspective, is not the result of an intellectual conversion in an authentic sense but instead is explicable precisely because authentic intellectual conversion has failed to occur : the significance of the shift from the world of immediacy to the world mediated by meaning has been missed.

The idealist, on the other hand, does in a sense acknowledge a world mediated by meaning. Like St Augustine he grasps that the real is not to be identified with body, but fails to appropriate the real distinction between understanding and judgment. It would seem that the idealist undergoes the first moment of intellectual conversion which is to comprehend that the real is not to be identified with body but does not realise in himself the second moment of intellectual conversion, which is the understanding that the real is not to be identified with either body or with ideas or concepts, but rather with what is known through correct judgments.

Materialism and idealism, therefore, which both represent philosophical positions of a most radical and fundamental nature, stand within a basic horizon, but this horizon is to be defined in terms of a certain absence of authentic intellectual conversion rather than through a positive relationship to conversion. The basic horizon of critical realism, however, is precisely defined in terms of the occurrence of an intellectual conversion through which the horizon is properly constituted.

On the moral level, a hedonistic way of life or any life-style which makes sensitive desire and fear normative for human action stands in an antithetical relationship to a way of life which makes value the criterion for human ethical activity. The hedonist stands in a relationship to a basic horizon since he embodies in himself a basic life orientation, but his stance is properly defined in terms of an absence of real self-transcendence or moral conversion. Like the materialist philosopher, the hedonist and all others whose lives are ruled by desires and fears remain locked within the confines of the sensory or aesthetic sphere.

The ideologist, on the other hand, who opts for a specific good of order, e.g., *laissez-faire* individualism or totalitarianism, but without properly locating it within a hierarchy of values respecting both the individual and common good, does indeed transcend the aesthetic horizon of sensitive desire and fear and so in this sense is operating on a higher level of human intentionality. Yet, he fails to undergo a radical moral conversion in which the hierarchy of objective values as creatively grasped by the authentic subject becomes normative for action. The ideologist is within a basic horizon not unlike that of the idealist, but specified negatively in terms of the absence of an authentic conversion on the ethical level. The basic horizon of the authentic subject, in contradistinction to the horizons of the hedonist and the ideologist, is defined precisely in terms of a moral conversion through which the horizon is properly fixed in the realm of value.

Finally, it is the presence or absence of authentic conversion which most properly defines the basic horizon of religion, just as analogously it is the presence or absence of authentic conversion which defines the basic horizons of philosophy and morality. However, the meaning and function of religious conversion in relation to the basic horizon-world interrelationship will best be developed within the context of an analysis of certain aspects of Lonergan's hermeneutics, to which we turn.

Lonergan wrote *Insight* in the period prior to Vatican II and, as is obvious from his current writings, if he were now to write a work similar to *Insight* he would no doubt do it differently— perhaps quite differently. At 'Ongoing Collaboration: The International Lonergan Congress', for example, Lonergan acknowledged that chapter XIX of *Insight*, which forms the nucleus of his philosophy of God, might suitably be located within a theological context. 'I'd be quite ready to say: let's drop chapter XIX out of *Insight* and put it inside of theology. I say that pretty well in my article in the *Proceedings of the American Catholic Theological Society* in 1968.'[70] Lonergan did not deny the validity of the chapter's basic argument for the existence of God. He did acknowledge, however, a stress on the importance of context which shows the impact which the post-Vatican II era has had on his own thinking.

In his recent talks and essays, Lonergan stresses that it is most important for thinkers and writers to attempt to understand the historical-cultural contexts in which they operate and to acknowledge as far as possible the basic horizons and worlds within which their statements acquire specific meaning. In an unpublished lecture on hermeneutics, Lonergan attacks what he refers to as 'the Principle of the Empty Head'.[71] Although he discusses it in the context of the interpreter of a text, it has relevance to the author of a text as well, and is illuminating for the present discussion. In this lecture Lonergan enunciates the 'Principle of the Empty Head' as follows:

'The Principle of the Empty Head' contends that, if one is to be objective, if one is not to drag in one's own notions, if one is not to settle in an *a priori* fashion what the text must mean no matter what it says, if one is not to 'read into' the text what is not there, then one must drop all preconceptions of every kind, see just what is in the text and nothing more, let the author speak for himself, let the author interpret himself.[72]

In Lonergan's analysis the 'Principle of the Empty Head' is the expression of a naïve intuitionism which asserts that in order to grasp a text all one need do is take a good look. On the contrary, Lonergan insists that an interpretation will succeed precisely to the extent that one is rich in personal experience, broad understanding and profundity of judgment. In other words, the richer a person is in knowledge and understanding the more likely it is that he will be able to interpret correctly.

The 'Principle of the Empty Head' also has a certain relevance in regard to authors as well as interpreters. So, just as Lonergan would say that a scriptural interpreter such as Rudolf Bultmann who acknowledges explicitly the philosophical presuppositions underlying his hermeneutical approach is better off than his less sophisticated critics who operate with unacknowledged philosophical presuppositions, so Lonergan would stress that a philosopher who is explicitly cognisant of the historical-cultural context in which he does his philosophising will be more likely to philosophise in a concrete, relevant and proper fashion. As Lonergan succinctly puts it: 'The condition of one who understands is always better than that of one who does not understand.'[73] This aphorism of Lonergan viewed in terms of its radical intellectualist implications stands in diametric opposition to what he names the Principle of the Empty Head.

If it is most important for both author and interpreter to be as knowledgeable as possible in regard to contexts, *a prioris*, and cultural variables that are inevitably operative in the composition and interpretation of texts, this is above all the case in regard to literature, philosophy and theology. These are areas of basic horizon and hence of conversion.

In commenting on 'the development of the interpreter', Lonergan remarks:

The major texts, the classics in religion, letters, philosophy, theology, not only are beyond the original horizon of their interpreters but also demand an intellectual, moral, religious conversion of the interpreter over and above the broadening of his horizon.

In this case the reader's original knowledge of the thing is just inadequate. He will come to know the thing only in so far as he pushes the self-correcting process of learning to a revolution of his own outlook. He can succeed in acquiring that habitual understanding of the author that spontaneously finds his wave-length and locks on it only after he has effected a radical change in himself.[74]

The point here is of critical moment for understanding the role of religious conversion in his analysis of hermeneutics. Lonergan is referring explicitly to the interpreter of outstanding works of religion, literature, and philosophy but, as in the case of the 'Principle of the Empty Head', his point also has a certain indirect relevance to potential authors. For example, in reply to a question regarding foundational theology posed to him by Fr Gerard Owens C.SS.R., at the 'Congress on the Theology of Renewal', Lonergan made the following response as summarised by Lawrence K. Shook:

[Lonergan pointed out that] acceptance of the truths of faith pertains to religion, but not all who accept (that is, are converted to) the truths of faith possess that 'reflection upon conversion' which is the foundation for the theology. This, he [Lonergan] went on to say, leads to the further question of whether one who does not accept the truths of faith can be a theologian. There is no room for such a theologian in theology in this technical sense of finding its foundations in accurate reflection upon conversion.[75]

For Lonergan it is impossible for a writer who has not himself undergone religious conversion to reflect authentically and accurately upon religious conversion. In like manner, it is impossible for an interpreter to evaluate correctly a text on religious conversion if he himself has not undergone religious conversion.

To exemplify in a concrete fashion the dynamic role of conversion and especially of religious conversion in the interpretation of a classic we might consider Dante's *Comedy*. One of the most renowned Dante experts, Dorothy L. Sayers, remarks that Dante

wrote his *Comedy* . . . for the 'common reader', and, taking as its basis two popular types of story which everybody knew and loved—the story of a vision of Hell, Purgatory, and Paradise, and the story of the Lover who has to adventure through the Underworld to find his lost Lady—he combined them into a great allegory of the soul's search for God. He made it as swift and exciting and topical as he could; he lavished upon it all his learning and wit, all his tenderness, humour and enthusiasms, and all his poetry. And he built it all closely about his own personal experience; for the redemption he tells of is first and foremost his own. Anybody who doubts this has only to read the *Vita Nuova*, the *Convivio*, and the *Commedia* in the order in which they were written and see how, with the return of Beatrice, Dante has come back to his earlier self. It is the return to love and humility, and, with humility, to joy.[76]

In Dorothy Sayers' view, Dante's greatest work was in a sense an extended allegorical thematisation in the most exquisite poetic terms of the poet's own interior transformation on the moral, intellectual, and religious levels of consciousness.

The multi-dimensional *Comedy* involves the interplay of a number of relative and basic horizons, and the consequent 'worlds' fixed or delimited by these horizons. Dante, for example, in a letter to his patron Con Grande della Scale, indicated that besides its literal meaning (the account of the poet's journey from hell through purgatory to heaven), the *Comedy* involves multiple allegorical meanings. Theologically, for example, the dark wood in which Dante finds himself at the beginning of the poem is a symbol of radical spiritual alienation from God. Politically, the wood stands for political anarchy of Dante's Italy; and, morally, it symbolises the immoral or fundamentally evil way of life.

The *Comedy* further involves an interweaving of the relative horizons of social system, literary convention and medieval science, as well as of the basic horizon of philosophy (*à la* Thomas Aquinas), morality, and religion.

It is the religious horizon which grounds the *Comedy*, providing the central unifying factor for the other horizons within it. As Dorothy Sayers observes, the *Comedy* is 'a great Christian allegory, deriving its power from the terror and splendour of the Christian relevation.'[77] To ignore the work's theological structure is to be doomed to disappointment and never to see 'the architectural grandeur of the poem as a whole.'[78]

Clearly religious conversion is a *de facto* existential condition of the possibility of arriving at an adequate and authentic interpretation of the *Comedy*. Likewise, the interpreter needs moral conversion and at least seminal intellectual conversion—both at least implicitly contained in religious conversion—since the *Comedy* is at once the allegorical embodiment of the dynamics of moral conversion and the articulation of the highly spiritual philosophical vision of Thomas Aquinas. Moreover the conversions required must be adequately incarnated to effectively mediate the interpretation. Here we may recall Lonergan's comment:

Conversion, as lived, affects all of a man's conscious and intentional operations. It directs his gaze, pervades his imagination, releases the symbols that penetrate to the depths of his psyche. It enriches his understanding, guides his judgments, reinforces his decisions.[79]

The nature and uniqueness of religious conversion

Religious conversion is both similar and dissimilar to intellectual and moral conversion. It is, like them, existential, personal and intimate. But, the dissimilarities between religious conversion, on the one hand, and intellectual and moral conversion, on the other, outnumber the similarities.

The basic dissimilarity between religious conversion and the others is explicable in terms of the grace-nature distinction. Man is by nature a dynamic, positive exigence, actively striving for cognitional and real self-transcendence. In regard to the total self-transcendence which is religious conversion, however, man is by nature an obediential potency through religious conversion, but he is not by nature an exigential striving for this ultimate form of self-transcendence.

Charles Curran, in his article 'Christian Conversion in the Writings of Bernard Lonergan',[80] argues that Lonergan should cease to emphasise the distinction between moral and religious conversion, and rather speak of two conversions: the intellectual and the 'existential conversion with its moral-religious-Christian aspects.'[81] Curran argues that since religious conversion does not occur without moral conversion, and since moral conversion in the present concrete existential order cannot occur without religious conversion, they should not be distinguished as Lonergan presently distinguishes them. However, this distinction as Lonergan currently employs it is basic to his overall approach.

For Lonergan, the grace-nature distinction continues to retain its validity and its importance.[82] For him it is as natural for man to seek real or moral self-transcendence as it is to ask questions and to strive for cognitive self-transcendence. Nor does the fact that man in the present order cannot achieve a sustained radical moral self-transcendence without grace militate against the retention of the distinction between moral and religious conversion. Grace does not remove man's natural exigence for moral self-transcendence but sublates and perfects it while in no way rendering it inoperative. Thus, analogously, just as Lonergan stresses that although grace is *de facto* required for man to achieve a sustained radical moral conversion, the moral fulfilment man achieves with the help of grace is *as such* the fulfilment of a natural exigence and not of an obediential potency.

Moral conversion, then, is a real self-transcendence through which an individual rises above domination by desires and fears, pleasures and pains, and enters into that phase of consistency between his knowing and his doing where allegiance to true values is the operative force in his moral life. Religious conversion, however, is that total self-transcendence in which the freely bestowed love of God becomes the first principle of all one's knowing and doing.

Religious conversion involves a certain inversion of the ordinary intentionality dynamics of human consciousness. In Lonergan's analysis, the ordinary process is to move from experience through understanding and judgment to decision, action and love. In this context the old adage that nothing can be loved which is not already known makes sense. As Lonergan puts it, 'being in love occurs on the fourth level of waking consciousness and, ordinarily, this fourth level presupposes and complements the previous levels of experiencing, understanding and judging.[83] None the less, 'what ordinarily is so, admits exceptions, and such an exception would be what Paul described to the Romans as God's flooding our hearts with his love.'[84] In this latter case 'love would not flow from knowledge but, on the contrary, knowledge would flow from love.'[85] This fact points up the radical difference between religious self-transcendence and moral conversion. The active potentiality for real self-transcendence or moral conversion is *de jure* within man's natural capacity and flows out of the natural exigence which a man experiences of making his doing and loving consistent with his knowing. Total self-transcendence or religious conversion, on the contrary, is supernatural and the free, unowed, gift of God. As Lonergan expresses it :

The fulfilment that is being in love with God is not the product of our knowledge and choice. It is God's gift. So far from resulting from our knowledge and choice, it dismantles and abolishes the horizon in which our knowing and choosing went on, and it sets up a new horizon in which the love of God will transvalue our values and the eyes of that love will transform our knowing.[86]

Religious conversion has a radical effect on the whole man. It effects a transvaluation of values and a transformation of all of man's conscious and intentional operations. The state of being in love with God becomes a first principle of all man's thinking and doing, and in this sense is the originating source of the context of contexts and the grounding dynamic principle of man's ultimate horizon. Religious conversion is the key *de facto* existential condition of possibility for any authentic thinking about God either in a philosophical or theological context.

Religious conversion in Christian and non-Christian contexts
    Religious conversion adds a dimension of complexity not operative on the levels of intellectual and moral conversion because it is supernatural and because it operates in non-Christian as well as in Christian contexts. This latter fact has emerged more clearly since Vatican II where the truth that God's grace is accessible to all men, and indeed effectively operative in all men of good will, received a new and more important emphasis.

Lonergan, in his reflections on the nature and scope of religious conversion, has in recent essays attempted to work out the manner in which religious conversion in its occurrence is manifested in both Christian and non-Christian contexts. To understand more adequately the sense in which religious conversion may be said to be a *de facto* existential condition of possibility in Lonergan's analysis for any profitable approach to natural theology, it will be helpful to analyse its meaning in both Christian and non-Christian contexts.

For Lonergan, as a Christian theologian, religious conversion in either a Christian or a non-Christian context has to be understood as intrinsically involving faith, hope and love on a supernatural level. More specifically, he conceives of the dynamic state of being in love with God as the core reality of Christian conversion and of all authentic religious conversion. This love is a gift. It is God's love flooding our hearts and it is unrestricted. It is the radical fulfilment of our obediential capacity for total self-transcendence. As fulfilment it brings a deep-set joy, a radical peace, and the power as a child of God to be a principle of benevolence and beneficence, of collaboration and love in regard to one's neighbour. This love is also the source of a knowledge which apprehends value and disvalue, good and evil. This knowledge Lonergan describes as the faith which is the eye of love, or as the knowledge which the heart alone possesses. Here by 'heart' Lonergan means man as transformed on the fourth level of consciousness—decision—by the gift of God's love.

Lonergan also speaks of the knowledge born of love as a certain 'universalist faith'.[87] This 'universalist faith', or transvaluation of values, that results from God's gift of his love 'does not presuppose any specific set of historical conditions. It can be bestowed on the members of any culture at any stage in its development. The values that are transvalued may vary, but the process of transvaluation has its constant ground in God's gift of his love.'[88]

Though Lonergan will not limit participation in God's gift of his love and in the 'universalist faith' and hope which flow from this gift to any particular cultural level or set of historical circumstances, it obviously only exists within concrete cultural and historical situations. Lonergan derives his definition of religious conversion basically from the data of explicit Christian relevation as interpreted within the horizon of Catholicism. Lonergan thus acknowledges the scriptural stress on the primacy of charity and God's universal salvific will, as well as on certain other revealed truths. He then concludes to a certain hypothetico-systematic statement about religious conversion which he suggests may be applicable in both non-Christian and explicitly Christian contexts. The dynamic state of being in love with God, he suggests, is the distinctive characteristic of religious conversion wherever it occurs. Accordingly, in reflecting on the study made by Friedrich Heiler of qualities common to the world's great religions, Lonergan notes that these qualities may be said to be implicit in the state of being in love with God. He sums up Heiler's list of seven areas common to the world's great religions, i.e., Christianity, Judaism, Islam, Zoroastrian Mazdaism, Hinduism, Buddhism, and Taoism, as follows:

First, the existence of a transcendent reality; secondly, the immanence of that reality in human hearts; thirdly, the characterisation of that reality as supreme beauty, truth, righteousness, goodness; fourthly, the characterisation of that reality as love, mercy, compassion; fifthly, our way to that reality is repentance, self-denial, prayer; sixthly, our way is love of one's neighbour, even of one's enemies; seventhly, the way is love of God, so that bliss is conceived as knowledge of God, union with him, or dissolution into him.[89]

Lonergan proceeds to indicate in what manner these seven characteristics might be seen to be implicit in what he describes as the experience of being in love in an unrestricted manner. Finally, he concludes by extending this view of the components of basic religious involvement even 'to the more elementary forms of religion'. In regard to these latter he asks:

Can one not discern in them the harvest of the Spirit that is love, joy, peace, kindness, goodness, fidelity, gentleness, and self-control (*Gal.* 5 :22)? As a theologian holding that God gives all men sufficient grace for salvation, I must expect an affirmative answer; but as a mere theologian, I must leave the factual answer to students of the history of religions.[90]

For Lonergan what is unique about Christianity is not its moral code or a particular philosophical *Weltanschauung*, but its

witness to a historical event—the raising of Jesus from the dead—
and the unique mediation of God's grace through Jesus Christ
the Lord. 'In the Christian, accordingly, God's gift of his love is
a love that is in Christ Jesus. From this fact flow the social,
historical, doctrinal aspects of Christianity.'[91]

Religious conversion as it occurs in an explicitly Christian
context, therefore, has two aspects. It involves (1) the state of
being in love with God which is common to all who undergo
religious conversion at any time and in any religio-cultural
context, and (2) commitment to God as revealed in his Son Jesus
Christ whom he raised from the dead and constituted unique
mediator of his love.

Lonergan, in his exploratory essay 'Faith and Beliefs', casts
light on the meaning of the conversion-event as it occurs respectively in Christian and non-Christian contexts through an analysis
of the different meanings 'belief' might have in the two contexts.[92] He hypothesises that 'belief' in a non-Christian context
might be said at least minimally to refer to the specific religio-
symbolic objectifications of the inner religious experience of the
members of the diverse non-Christian religions. Moreover, these
'beliefs', or objectifications of the interior religious experience of
the dynamic state of being in love with God in an unrestricted
fashion and of the transvaluation of values which is the operative
moment of 'universalist faith', will involve varying degrees of
adequacy or inadequacy. For the Christian the ultimate criterion
for judgments regarding the adequacy of 'beliefs' is the word of
God mediated through the Christ because in the context of
explicit Christian conversion belief is acceptance of God at work
in Christ. For the Christian the deepest meaning of religious
experience is manifested by God in history, and all objectifications of interior religious experience must ultimately be judged as
to their adequacy or inadequacy in terms of revelation. In the
case of conversion in an explicitly Christian context, then, there
is present not only the 'gift of God's love flooding our hearts' and
belief 'in what results from the objectification of that love'[93] but
more. For,

besides completing our personal self-transcendence in the secrecy
of our hearts, God would also address his people as a people,
announce to them his intentions, send to them his prophets, his
Messiah, his apostles. In that case religious beliefs would be objecti-

fications not only of internal experience but also of the externally uttered word of God.[94]

Religious conversion and the God problem

With the faith-belief distinction clearly in mind as regards its functioning in non-Christian as well as explicitly Christian conversion situations, we can now indicate in a more precise fashion in what way religious conversion operates as a *de facto* existential condition of possibility for correctly understanding Lonergan's approach to the problem of God in terms of his own hermeneutic principles. Our procedure here is interpretative and not evaluative. Lonergan is a Catholic philosopher-theologian who does his thinking within the basic horizon fixed by conversion within a Catholic context. His language accordingly is the language of one who lives within a Catholic world. This world involves a mixture of elements which are purely cultural and others which are of foundational religious importance. To operate consequently as an authentic interpreter of Lonergan's thought it is important to understand the function of various relative horizons in his thought. But it is the area of basic horizon—intellectual, moral, and religious—which is of greatest importance.

Lonergan distinguishes between absolute inauthenticity and relative inauthenticity. This distinction is most important in a negative sense, i.e., in the sense of removing false interpretations for understanding the hermeneutical task as it refers to Lonergan's works and specifically to his work on the God problem. For Lonergan, absolute inauthenticity means the absence of conversion. In the language of Heidegger's *Sein und Zeit*, Lonergan indicates that the absolutely inauthentic person is the one who refuses to think, decide, or act for himself. He simply follows the crowd and thinks, says and does what all the rest think, say and do. Here there is a basic absence of authentic 'human' functioning.[95]

Relative inauthenticity is something else. An individual or a whole group of individuals can be relatively inauthentic. In Lonergan's words: 'As Kierkegaard asked whether he was a Christian, so divers men can ask themselves whether or not they are genuine Catholics or Protestants, Moslems or Buddhists, Platonists or Aristotelians, Kantians or Hegelians.'[96] An individual is relatively inauthentic to the extent that he is not in existential accord with the ideals and norms of a given tradition or world. The individual may think that he is 100 per cent American because he happens to coincide in certain respects with what the ideals of the tradition demand, but still be relatively inauthentic because through 'selective inattention or a failure to understand or an undetected rationalisation'[97] he is not in accord with any given number of essential elements in a tradition. In like manner, a whole group may be relatively in-authentic and then, even though they continue, e.g., to use the hallowed language of the tradition, they actually 'devaluate, distort, water down, corrupt that language.'[98]

There is, of course, the more ultimate question of the validity of any tradition itself. To the extent that a religious tradition articulates itself in beliefs and conventions which actually distort and falsify religious experience, the religion itself is inauthentic. The same may be said as regards inauthentic ethical and philosophical *Weltanschauungen* which are the embodiment of false interpretations of the data of consciousness on the intellectual and ethical levels.

Religious conversion involves a certain complexity because it can occur in non-Christian as well as Christian contexts. This means that the manner in which religious conversion will function as a *de facto* existential condition of possibility for achieving a proper understanding of the God problem will differ to an extent in terms of the context in which it is operative. Lonergan conceives of religious conversion in an explicitly Christian context as involving implicitly a certain dogmatic realism which impels the believer to rise above naïve realism in a movement toward critical realism. As Lonergan states in *De Constitutione Christi*: 'He who professes the Catholic faith even as a child already learns that spiritual realities are real.' Likewise, 'he who adheres to Catholic doctrines through the *vera* reaches the *realia*.'[99] Religious conversion as operative in an explicitly Christian context enables man through his assent to God revealing himself in the historical reality of Christ to move at least implicitly toward a critical epistemology and metaphysics which can then ground a philosophy of God.

Lonergan, however, acknowledges the possibility—and, no doubt, actuality—of the operative presence of religious conversion in a non-Christian context.

For example, in *Insight*, he states that if an indivual 'is genuine in denouncing obscurantism and in demanding the unconditioned (i.e., is faithful to the exigencies of intelligence) either one already adores God without naming him or else one has not far to go to reach him.'[100] In the light of this comment and Lonergan's stress on the need of supernatural assistance in order to be faithful to the basic 'positions' of critical realism, it would seem clear that in *Insight* he did acknowledge in a certain fashion the operative presence of religious conversion in non-Christians. Likewise, in the light of his distinction between faith and belief it would seem correct to suggest that the non-Christian's experience of being in love in an unrestricted fashion and the transvaluation of values which flows from this would illumine the operational levels of human consciousness so that a fidelity to the exigences of understanding would be the result. Also, to the extent that the non-Christian correctly thematises his religious experience in terms of belief in God's immanence, transcendence and love, he would be within a horizon at least in principle open to such a thing as a philosophical approach to the existence of God.

Ideally, religious conversion should function most perfectly as a *de facto* condition of possibility where religious experience is most richly given in the depths of the spirit and where the objectification of the total meaning of this experience is most adequately realised. Christ is the revealer *par excellence* of the meaning of religious experience. He is its ground and end. So, ideally, the explicit Christian believer should find it most easy to come to grips with a philosophy of God. Yet, authentic traditions—even the most excellent—can be distorted and misinterpreted. In this case perhaps a highly moral and religious non-Christian whose beliefs include the seven qualities Heiler suggests as being operative in all the major religions may well be far better off and far more capable of thinking accurately about God than a Christian whose beliefs are distorted and maimed through false interpretations.

Finally, the authentic interpreter of any great classic will in Lonergan's view be one in whom all three conversions are operative in as total a fashion as possible. The operative presence in the subject of a living faith, hope and love is evidently more important—if a choice between the two must be made—than the mere adherence of the subject to certain objectively true beliefs. It is better to be a good Buddhist—one in whom at least the dynamic state of being in love with God is operative—than a bad Christian—one whose beliefs are correct but in whom love is lacking. Yet the ideal is to be both authentic as a subject and correct in one's beliefs or objectifications of one's religious subjectivity. The individual who embodies this combination will be the ideal interpreter in Lonergan's view and the most capable of grasping a truly valid philosophy of God.

PART II

THE INTERNAL DEVELOPMENT OF LONERGAN'S PHILOSOPHY OF GOD

3

Critical Self-affirmation as Breakthrough to Intellectual Conversion

MEN commonly acknowledge that they are knowers. Indeed, it is the fact of knowledge which gives rise to the seemingly endless queries in its regard. The strategic value of Lonergan's approach is that he aims to focus interest not so much on the fact of knowledge as on its nature. Accordingly, in the first ten chapters of *Insight* Lonergan prescinds entirely from the complex epistemological issues of the exact nature of knowledge, the notion of being and the problem of objectivity. He engages instead in a phenomenological exposition of the manner in which mathematicians, scientists and men of common sense in fact operate cognitionally. Gradually there emerges a certain invariant pattern of cognitive operations manifested in the operations of mathematicians, scientists and men of common sense. Lonergan speaks in global terms of these operations as experiencing, understanding and judging. But these terms and the relations which bind them together form a highly subtle complex which can only be fully understood as the result of a lengthy personal engagement.

In the chapter on the self-affirmation of the knower Lonergan invites the reader to ask and answer the question: Am I a knower? It is Lonergan's purpose to bring the reader to the point where through self-performance he will come to grasp and acknowledge the process of experiencing, understanding and judging as the immanent law of his own interiority which he must either obey or else lapse into incoherence or silence. The basic aim in the 'invitation to performance' in chapter XI is to bring the reader or, more properly, the performer to acknowledge that he is a knower precisely in the sense that he experiences, understands and judges and that he does not 'know' in any other way except by engaging in this particular process of interrelated operations. The whole affair then is a practical one. It is not a matter of whether or not the knowing process might be other than it is, but simply of what it *de facto* is here and now.

There is, however, a further dynamic element which must be systematically indicated at this point if the general lines of the process are to be synthetically understood and if the process is to be at least in a preliminary fashion properly situated within the context of transcendental method. The key to the dynamism of cognitional process as well as to the relationship of cognitional process to transcendental method (*à la* Lonergan) is 'transcendence'. Transcendence is in a sense the underlying theme of Lonergan's entire philosophical endeavour. Thus, in Part I of this work the stress was in large measure on the interrelationships of three forms of self-transcendence, namely, cognitive, moral and religious. Transcendence, however, is not only operative in the dynamic interrelationship of these three forms of self-transcendence but on a more fundamental level is the core constitutive impetus of the process as a whole.

In the opening section of chapter XIX on general transcendent knowledge Lonergan deals with the notion of transcendence as opposed to immanence. Very simply, for Lonergan transcendence means 'going beyond', or, in other words, 'the elementary matter of raising further questions.'[1] Lonergan roots man's basic orientation toward transcendence in 'his detached, disinterested, unrestricted desire to know.'[2] Lonergan thus, without explicitly noting it, links the opening section of his discussion of general transcendent knowledge or knowledge of God with the very first section of the first chapter of *Insight* where the act of insight is initially described as coming 'as a release to the tension of enquiry.'[3] And, this tension of enquiry is basically explicable in terms of man's 'drive to know, to understand, to see why, to discover the reason, to find the cause, to explain.'[4]

Lonergan assigns various names to man's fundamental drive towards transcendence. It is the pure desire to know; it is the Eros of the mind; it is a transcendental intending of the intelligible, the true and the good; it is the notion of being; it is the unifying intentionality dynamically operative and immanent within the diverse levels of human consciousness. Again, Lonergan speaks of the experiential, intelligent, rational and deliberative, or existential, levels of consciousness in terms of an unfolding of a single transcendental intending of a number of interchangeable objectives,[5] i.e., the intelligible, the true and the good. There is at the core of the human subject a drive toward transcendence or a conscious operational intending which promotes man from one level of consciousness to another and from one level of self-transcendence to another.

Now the affirmation of oneself as a knower in the precise sense indicated above is one instance (and a privileged one at that)[6] of cognitive self-transcendence. Cognitive self-transcendence, itself, however, involves a series of stages and before relating cognitional process to transcendental method it will be useful in the context of the notion of transcendence to indicate briefly these stages in terms of their dynamic interrelationship.

Cognitional process has a dynamic structure. It is a dynamic whole with parts. For human knowing involves such disparate yet interrelated activities as sensing, inquiring, imagining, understanding, conceiving, reflecting, judging. No one of these moments or parts constitutes the whole of human knowing. But, on the other hand, human knowing cannot exist apart from them.

Further, human knowing is a self-assembling, self-constituting whole. The pure desire to know—i.e., man's transcendental thrust towards the intelligible, the true and the real—initiates the process in terms of inquiry. Once insight into data occurs, the desire to understand is transformed into the desire to understand correctly. In other words, the desire for an idea becomes the desire for a correct idea. And so in human knowing one part summons forth the next until the whole is reached. Inquiry leads to insight; insight issues in concepts, theories, hypotheses; hypotheses stimulate critical reflection regarding their truth value; critical reflection leads either to judgment or to the doubt which in turn means renewal of inquiry. Throughout the entire process, of course, it is the one transcendental intentionality which is unfolding in the diverse sublations in levels of consciousness which occur as the individual moves from experience through understanding to judgment.

At this point the issue of method may properly be raised. Thus, Lonergan defines method in general as 'a normative pattern of related and recurrent operations with cumulative and progressive results.'[7] It is not difficult to see how this definition of method can be related to cognitional process as it has been thus far globally sketched.

In Lonergan's analysis of human cognition, as found in the first ten chapters of *Insight* and elsewhere, a pattern of related operations is seen to be involved in the cognitional procedures of mathematicians, scientists and men of common sense. Likewise, it becomes clear that this pattern of operations is recurrent and that in all fields of human endeavour (but very strikingly in the sciences) it yields cumulative and progressive results. Finally, in the chapter on the self-affirmation of the knower it becomes clear that this pattern of related and recurrent operations is normative as an immanent law of human consciousness and cannot be denied without contradiction on the level of performance.

Moreover, the method, which, as shall shortly be indicated, is *radically* identical with cognitional process itself, is transcendental. It is transcendental in the Kantian use of the term because it is not constituted by experience but is the necessary (though not sufficient) *a priori* condition of possibility for experience—i.e., data do not constitute the pure desire to know as such, although without data there will be no actual knowing. Likewise, the method which is cognitional process is transcendental in the scholastic sense because the transcendental intending of the intelligible, the true (being) and the good which is the core of cognitional process is not confined (in its intending) to any particular genus or category.

At this point a distinction should be drawn between the dynamic pattern of interrelated operations which constitute human knowing and the thematisation of these operations in conceptual accounts. The pattern of operations itself may be spoken of as 'radical' transcendental method since it is the ground of all attempts at thematisation and is the ultimate touchstone of the adequacy of any conceptual account. Accordingly, the unthematic—i.e., the process of cognition itself—always takes precedence over the thematic since accounts of cognitional activity can always be improved upon but the process itself remains invariant and untouched by thematic accounts of its nature. In a technical philosophical sense, however, transcendental method may be described as the process through which one heightens awareness of one's cognitional operations and so objectifies the process.

In *Insight* Lonergan speaks of metaphysics as latent, problematic and explicit.[8] In the context of the present analysis latent metaphysics would seem to be equivalent to what is here designated as 'radical' transcendental method. It is, in other words, the cognitional process itself, and all men—to the extent that they function intelligently, reasonably and responsibly—are, in fact, subject to its immanent norms and hence practitioners of transcendental method. Further, problematic metaphysics would appear to be an intermediate phase in which numerous attempts have been made to thematise radical transcendental method. Still, the epistemological bog of positions and counter-positions resulting from man's polymorphic consciousness has not yet been transcended in terms of an adequate thematisation. Finally, explicit metaphysics comes into being when, as Lonergan expresses it, 'latent metaphysics . . . succeeds in conceiving itself, in working out its implications and techniques.'[9] This last stage of explicit metaphyics would correspond to thematic transcendental method in its fully articulated phase.

In view of the preceding analysis, it seems correct to say that for Lonergan transcendental method is most radically the dynamism of cognitional process itself. Yet, man as the subject of cognitional activity is capable not only of spontaneously functioning according to the exigences of cognition but also of understanding and evaluating the nature of these exigences. Accordingly, radical transcendental method is intrinsically ordered towards an epistemological moment of correctly conceiving and verifying its own inner dynamism and metaphysical moment in which it heuristically grasps the nature of the known. Transcendental method thus finds its roots in the cognitive process itself and encompasses in its full development the territory of Lonergan's three basic philosophical questions as well.[10]

Our concern in the present chapter is mainly with the first of these questions, what am I doing when I am knowing?, with a view to touching more meaningfully on the question of self-affirmation. Accordingly, we will move immediately to treat of the basic phases of knowing. Our aim is not a summary presentation of the challenge of Part I of *Insight*, but to indicate elements relevant to the present context which, however, throw some light on that challenge.

Experiencing, understanding and judging, then, are global terms which stand for the three basic phases of cognitional process. As moments in a process, each is relationally defined in terms of the others. It is, however, legitimate to analyse each of the phases in turn as long as it is kept in mind from the beginning that experiencing, understanding and judging are not three independent types of fully human knowing but rather are three constitutive components of one fully human knowledge. Also, features of the interrelationship of the three components of the one human knowing are of necessity introduced to an extent in each stage of the analysis. Finally, any abstraction there may be is overcome by the discussion of the self-affirmation of the knower which concludes this chapter.

EXPERIENCE

Lonergan employs the term experience in a broad sense and in a more strictly delimited sense. Thus, experience in a general sense is defined as whatever data are presupposed and complemented by enquiry and all ulterior stages of the cognitive process. Experience in this sense may be said to apply to the total possible range of the data of sense and the data of consciousness. By the data of sense are meant the objects of sensation such as colours, odours, tastes, hard and soft, wet and dry, etc. By the data of consciousness are meant all the operations of either a sensitive or cognitive nature which are the conscious operations of a conscious subject. All of these data, whether of sense or of consciousness, provide material or data for enquiry, insight, reflection, judgment and decision.

In a more strictly delimited use of the term 'experience', Lonergan defines consciousness as the subject's internal experience of himself and of his acts. Here by experience Lonergan means awareness, an awareness immanent in the cognitional operations of the subject. This meaning becomes clearer in terms of Lonergan's analysis of the phenomenon of presence.

In regard to the phenomenon of presence there is first the presence of one object to another in which no knowing is involved. Such is the presence of the chair to the lamp in a room. Secondly, there is the cognitive presence of an object to a subject, e.g., the presence of the lamp in the mind of the knower (we prescind here from all the complex issues involved in the notion of the cognitive presence of an object in a subject and presume nothing more than the common-sense notion of this phenomenon). Thirdly, there is the presence of the subject to the subject. This presence is a unique type of presence: 'It is the presence in, as it were, another dimension, the presence concomitant and correlative and opposite to the presence of the object. Objects are present by being attended to; but subjects are present as subjects, not by being attended to, but by attending.'[11] This third type of presence involves the subject's awareness of himself sensing, wondering, understanding, judging, deciding. In this type of presence it is not the object of the sensing, etc., which is involved but the sensing itself is that of which one is aware.

Now it is easy enough to direct attention to the third type of presence just described but it is difficult to explain this phenomenon. This is so because, as Lonergan notes, the notion of subject and hence consciousness is recent and primitive.[12] Yet, the notion of consciousness is central to any analysis of knowledge and so every effort must be made to define the notion with as much precision as possible.

First, then, consciousness involves an awareness which may properly be spoken of as cognitive but it is not the objective type of cognition which is the result of enquiry, insight, formulations, critical reflection and judgment. Further, consciousness is not only cognitive in a non-objective sense but is also constitutive. An example may help here. Thus, for an individual to make the objective judgment, 'I have a toothache' he must be *aware* of the toothache and also *conscious* in making a judgment. Now, in fact, no one is ever unconscious of the fact that he is suffering pain (to suffer pain unconsciously makes no sense) nor is anyone ever *unaware* of the fact that he is critically reflecting, judging or responsibly deciding. Consciousness, accordingly, 'not merely reveals us as suffering but also makes us capable of suffering';[13] consciousness 'is cognitive, not of what exists without consciousness, but of what is constituted by consciousness.'[14] In like manner consciousness not only reveals us to ourselves as enquiring, judging, etc., but pertains to the very constitution of these activities. Thus, as Lonergan succinctly states it:

Indeed, since consciousness is of the acting subject *qua* acting, the experience of one's rationality is identical with one's rationality bringing itself to act; the experience of one's intelligence is identical with one's sensitivity coming to act.[15]

Certain further precisions regarding the nature of consciousness are in order at this point. Consciousness then is the condition of possibility *qua* constitutive of all intellective activity and is therefore not the product of any cognitive act or deliberative operation. It is possible to heighten one's awareness or consciousness by shifting one's attention to one's consciousness—e.g., I can either be peripherally aware of a toothache or maximally conscious of it. But what is most important to note is that a shifting of attention or heightening of awareness is not what constitutes consciousness as such. Likewise, heightening of awareness does not involve a qualitatively new cognition but simply a more intense awareness. Consciousness accordingly is not some sort of inward look; it is not a confrontation with any object; it is not an act to which one deliberately attends as such. It is very simply an awareness immanent in sensitive, affective and cognitional acts and indeed identical with them as activities of the subject.

Again, consciousness is not identical with the content of a given cognitive act. I not only see a coloured object but I am aware of my looking. Likewise, I not only hear sounds but I am conscious of my listening. If, however, consciousness or awareness were identical with the contents of given acts, then what would be the meaning of speaking of awareness in reference to such diverse acts as seeing, hearing, enquiring, judging, etc? As Lonergan puts it: 'If seeing is an awareness of nothing but colour and hearing is an awareness of nothing but sound, why are both named "awareness"?[16] Certainly, it is not because there is a similarity between colour and sound, much less between sounds and concepts or decisions. It remains then that 'within the cognitional act as it occurs . . . there is a factor or element or component over and above its content, and . . . this factor is what differentiates cognitional acts from unconscious occurrences.'[17]

A further fact about the nature of consciousness which should be indicated is that consciousness as the awareness immanent in cognitional acts differs inasmuch as the acts differ. Thus, the awareness immanent in intelligent operations is precisely awareness *of* intelligent operation and, as the intellectual activities involved in the process of knowing differ, so likewise will the consciousness. This does not mean, of course, that consciousness is some sort of introspective activity through which intelligence and reasonableness come up for inspection. It simply means that the individual has conscious states and acts which are intrinsically intelligent and reasonable and that consciousness is constitutive of their being so.

There is also the further problem of the unity of consciousness but this aspect can be more profitably handled in the last section of this chapter which will again touch upon the self-affirmation of the knower. Suffice it to state here that ultimately it is an abstraction to speak of acts as conscious. Rather it is the acting agent who is properly spoken of as the conscious subject of his operations.

A final note should be added about experience in general. For Lonergan, as noted above, experience in general is what is presupposed and complemented by enquiring, understanding, reflecting, etc. In this sense the data of sense are presupposed by any and all enquiry as a condition of its possibility. Likewise, the data of consciousness are presupposed by any enquiry regarding the data of consciousness. Enquiry into the nature of enquiry presupposes as its condition of possibility the experience of enquiry. 'One must begin from the performance, if one is to have the experience necessary for understanding what the performance is.'[18]

More specifically, in regard to the data of sensitive consciousness it should be noted that *as the given* these data are unquestionable and indubitable. They are indubitable because what can be doubted is the answer to a question. But they are prior to any questioning and independent of any answers. They are unquestionable because they are constituted apart from questioning and remain the same regardless of the results of questioning.

In similar fashion the data of intellectual consciousness involve a certain unquestionable ultimate. Thus, consciousness and not questioning questioning is constitutive of questioning. Likewise, consciousness and not insight into the nature of insight is constitutive of insight. Consciousness of an intellectual operation is therefore a condition of possibility for any enquiry into its nature.

Finally, the intellectual consciousness just spoken of is truly cognitive. But it is subjective—an immanent awareness of the subject and his acts—and not objective—a knowledge achieved through wonder, insight, reflection, etc. Thus, as Lonergan

D

observes, inasmuch as consciousness 'constitutes in act what it knows, it recalls Aquinas' remark that the light of agent intellect is known *per se ipsum* (*De verit.*, q.10, a.8, ad 10m, 2^{ae} ser.).'[19] Yet, although consciousness constitutes in act what it knows, it has the indistinctness of the preconceptual and hence 'cannot be preferred by man as intelligent and rational to what is known intelligently and rationally under the formalities of being, quiddity, truth.'[20]

UNDERSTANDING

The act of understanding or insight is central to the process of human knowing in Lonergan's analysis. Insight is the source not only of all theory but also of all its practical applications and indeed, 'of all intelligent activity'.[21] Insight is operative alike in mathematicians, scientists and men of common sense.

Aristotle's statement in his *De Anima* that 'understanding . . . understands the forms in the images'[22] is cited by Lonergan on the title page of *Insight* as a basic expression of the meaning of insight. The centrality of the act of understanding for Lonergan in the process of human knowing is brought out in his observation that all the other elements or operations involved in the process either prepare for the act or presuppose and complement it. Experience, wonder, enquiry, imagination, etc., prepare for the occurrence of insight. Conceiving, defining hypotheses and formulating theories, doubting, evaluating evidence and making judgments follow upon the act of understanding and complete it. This radical centrality of the act of understanding in Lonergan's philosophy may be indicated through a brief exposition of the way he situates it in relationship to angelic and divine knowledge viewed in the scholastic context of the Aristotelian theorem of knowledge by identity.[23] For Lonergan, the Aristotelian theorem of knowledge by identity as applied to human knowing is correct and incomplete. It is true, as Aquinas quoting Aristotle indicates, that 'the intelligible in act is the intellect in act.'[24] It does not necessarily follow, however, that the reality of the object understood is identical with the reality of the understanding intellect. Thus, Lonergan remarks that even in angelic knowledge—clearly the question regarding the existence or nonexistence of angels is not at issue in terms of the present context—there is not a perfect identity of being and knowing. One immaterial angel knows another immaterial angel 'without the former's knowledge being the latter's reality.'[25] In Lonergan's hypothesis angels do not require, as men do, a series of operations, e.g., experiences, questions, images, phantasms, etc., prior to and as a condition of possibility of the occurrence of an act of understanding. Angels do, however, have to judge in order to know that what they understand does, in fact, exist.[26] Only in God is there a perfect identity in every respect of the knowing with the known because in God 'the being and knowing . . . coincide.'[27]

The point of the above brief analysis is simply to indicate in a broad and general fashion the central importance which Lonergan assigns to the act of understanding in the process of human knowing. This is indicated through a certain comparison and a process of elimination to which this comparison gives rise. Thus in human knowing there is the triad of experiencing, understanding and judging. In angelic knowing there is only understanding and judging. In God there is simply the reality of an infinite act of understanding.

It is true, of course, that man needs phantasms or images in order to understand and he needs reflection and judgment in order to assure the correctness of his understanding. The act of understanding, however, is of central importance because in it a certain identity of knowing with the known is achieved. Yet, since reflection is required in order to know whether the understood is more than a mere hypothesis and does, in fact, exist as a reality distinct from the knower—we prescind here from the phenomenon of the subject's knowledge of himself as object—'and since reflection is not an identity, the Aristotelian theory of knowing by identity is incomplete.'[28] The Aristotelian theorem is, however, perfectly verified in divine knowing in Lonergan's analysis. This helps to make intelligible why for Lonergan it is the act of understanding which is the nucleus of human knowing. It is not by accident that *Insight* is named *Insight* rather than *Experience* or *Judgment*.

Human understanding pivots between the concrete and the abstract. Thus the content of the act of understanding is the intelligible; but it is the intelligible precisely as grasped in concrete data or in the image. The content of an insight is thus something above, beyond, and supervening upon the mere presentations of sense and imagination. The genesis of insight in conscious experience and in the context of the sensible is clearly indicated in the statement of Aquinas which Lonergan often cites: 'Anyone can experience this of himself that when he tries to understand something, he forms certain phantasms to serve him by way of examples, in which as it were he examines what he is desirous of understanding.'[29]

Insight is prior to concept and is the latter's ultimate ground.

Now this simple statement of what Lonergan claims is cognitional fact calls for a number of comments. The statement is an external expression of an inner word, a concept, which itself results from an introspective insight into one's personal efforts to understand and to formulate.[30] To make one capable of intelligently uttering such a statement is the goal of what Lonergan calls the 'five finger exercises' of the first part of *Insight*. This being the case, we must insist that the present short treatment of the act of direct understanding is no more than indicative. Instead then of briefly describing the main results of self-attentive cognitional enquiry, we content ourselves with some further points immediately relevant to the description of reflective understanding.

In Lonergan's analysis of cognition the senses 'know' the concrete singular existent but not under the formality of existence. Thus, for example, the eyes see a coloured existent but not under the formality of being but of colour. Further, the intellect does not intuitively grasp the individual existent as existent and present and unconsciously abstract concepts from the sense data. Rather, as a result of intellectual enquiry regarding the possible meaning of data, an insight occurs in which there is a conscious grasp of an intelligible unity or relationship in data. As a result of this insight, intellect utters what it has understood in the phantasm in inner words, i.e., concepts and definitions.

It is, moreover, of crucial importance to understand that for Lonergan the second level of knowing—insight and definition—involves formal intelligibility, hypothesis or grasp of possible being. It is only through an act of reflective understanding in which the formal intelligibility, grasped and articulated on the second level of knowing, is reduced to its principles in the data of sense and consciousness and understood to be verified in that data, that a judgment may be pronounced and hence an existent known.

For Lonergan, then, there is the experience of insight into phantasm and of the intelligent uttering of the inner word of definition as a result of insight. This cognitive experience itself grounds and makes possible intellectual knowledge of the singular and the relating of a universal to a 'this'. There is not yet knowledge of the individual as existing : it is only through the mediation of reflective understanding and judgment that the existent is known. Moreover, it should be emphasised that this analysis applies to each and every instance in which knowledge of an existent as truly existent is reached. Thus, even a perceptual statement such as 'I see an apple' can only be made by engaging in the total process of experiencing, understanding and judging. In like manner, the statement, 'I know that insight is into phantasm' is the result or product of the same process and the evidence for its validity does not lie in an appeal to an intellectual intuition of the individual existent as existing and present but rather simply in the conscious *experience* of any act of insight.

The point bears comment from another angle, even if it touches on a topic to be raised only in the following chapter. In Lonergan's cognitional analysis, one reaches knowledge of contingent existence only in judgment, and judgment is neither perception nor intuition but a matter of yes or no, of affirmation or negation. The 'notion of existence' for Lonergan is the crowning component in the notion of being. But knowledge of existence is achieved only in judgment. As Lonergan tersely expresses it :

The notion of being is our desire to know, our drive to ask questions. The crowning question is the question for reflection, *An sit?*, Is that so? An affirmative answer to that question posits a synthesis. Through the positing, the 'Yes,' the 'Est,' we know existence and, more generally, fact. Through the synthesis that is posited, we know what exists or, more generally, what exists or occurs.[31]

In his *Réalisme thomiste et critique de la connaissance*,[32] Etienne Gilson sets forth a position on the intuition or perception of the concept of being in sensible data which Lonergan has often referred to in lectures as an example of a fundamental counterposition and which he also criticised at length in his review of Coreth's *Metaphysik*.[33] No attempt will be made here to repeat in full either Gilson's position or Lonergan's critique, but certain crucial points of difference will be indicated in so far as they help to clarify Lonergan's position on the notion of being.[34]

In his *Réalisme thomiste*, Gilson asserts that over and above perceptions of sense and intellectual abstractions there exists an intellectual vision of the concept of being in every datum of sense.[35] It is, moreover, in Gilson's view the concept of being as apprehended in the datum of sense which is predicated in perceptual judgments of existence.[36] Gilson's position in *Réalisme thomiste* is that of an immediate realism which holds that it is through perception, or direct vision of the concept of being, that perceptual judgments of existence are made possible and true objectivity is achieved.

Lonergan, in his *De Methodo Theologiae*, describes Gilson's position as an 'intuitive realism'[37] which is similar to the Kantian position on knowledge in that it grants with Kant that man's only immediate relationship to an object is through intuition, but which is dissimilar to Kant in that it affirms an intellectual intuition through which man is able to have knowledge not merely of what appears but of what in fact is so. For Gilson idealism does not of necessity involve a contradiction,[38] and hence the only way to establish realism for him is to affirm the existence of an intellectual perception of the concept of being in sensible data.

Lonergan's basic response to the Gilson-type appeal to a perception of existence as the foundation of realism is that simply to postulate it is dogmatic and hence open to an equally dogmatic denial, and that to attempt to ground it through introspective analysis—an effort Gilson does not attempt and, in fact, considers unnecessary for the metaphysician[39]—is doomed to failure since consciousness reveals no such intuition.

In his '*Insight*: Preface to a Discussion',[40] Lonergan replies in a concrete fashion to those who would argue for the existence of some sort of intellectual intuition of actual existence as the necessary basis for perceptual judgments of existence, by offering an example of how the simple judgment of fact regarding the existence of a dog is reached and by showing that at no point in the process does any perception or intuition of being enter in.

Before concluding this section on direct understanding we offer some remarks bearing upon the notion of the infallibility of insight as regards data, the essentially enriching character of insight and yet the incompleteness of insight as far as knowledge of being is concerned.

First, Lonergan stresses that

The generalities of our knowledge are related to concrete reality in two distinct manners. There is the relation of the universal to the particular, of *man* to *this man*, of *circle* to *this circle*. There is also the far more important relation of the intelligible to the sensible, of the unity or pattern grasped by insight to the data in which the unity or pattern is grasped. Now this second relation, which parallels the relation of form to matter, is far more intimate than the first. The universal abstracts from the particular, but the intelligibility, grasped by insight, is immanent in the sensible and, when the sensible datum, image, symbol, is removed, the insight vanishes. But conceptualism ignores human understanding and so it overlooks the concrete mode of understanding that grasps intelligibility in the sensible.[41]

Insight accordingly provides the most crucial link—indeed *the link*—between the intelligible and the sensible. Insight is the core moment on the level of understanding and it is the condition of possibility for the later type of cognitional operation in which the abstract universal is related to the particular.

Now, it should be noted carefully that insight is always into phantasm, that insight is infallible in regard to phantasm, that insight is enriching because it adds to phantasm an *intelligible* unification or relation which phantasm as such does not possess and that the question of the relationship of what insight grasps in data to being cannot be resolved on the second level of the knowing process.

The fact, then, that insight is always into phantasm has already been indicated. Secondly, in the context of insight into phantasm it is important to note that the imagined object or the object of sense experience as presented to intellectual consciousness as something to be understood is as such not yet actually understood or intelligible in act. Moreover, when wonder and enquiry yield to insight and the phantasm becomes actually understood the change takes place not in the phantasm—which remains in itself simply phantasm—but in the intellect. Thirdly, as noted above, at the moment of insight the intellect in act or, in other words, the intellect actually understanding, is itself the intelligible in act.

Now, with the above distinction clearly in mind, certain further precisions are required if the exact nature of insight is to be clearly grasped. On the one hand, then, insight is *a priori* and synthetic because it goes beyond what is given to sense or to empirical consciousness and adds an *intelligible* unification or relationship to what is mere data.[42] On the other hand, however, insight is infallible in regard to phantasm and this point, too, must be considered. Thus, as Lonergan observes:

It is not merely that there is an act of understanding and simul-taneously an act of imagination, each with its respective object. But the two objects are intrinsically related: the imagined object is presented as something to be understood; and the insight or appre-hensive abstraction grasps the intelligibility of the imagined object in the imagined object; thus, insight grasps imagined equal radii in a plane surface as the necessary and sufficient condition of an imagined uniform curve; imagination presents terms which insight intelligibly relates or unifies.[43]

The further point, then, is that since one infallibly understands what one imagines, 'misunderstanding is the fault, not of intelli-gence, but of imagination which can exhibit what is not and can fail to exhibit all that is.'[44] The point here is that the correctness of one's insight cannot be solved on the level of direct, intros-pective, or inverse understanding alone. It can be adequately resolved on the level of reflective understanding and judgment. Thus, for example, it is one thing to grasp a possible law in data and another to verify the correctness or adequacy of the law. Likewise, it is one thing to grasp a unity-identity-whole in data but quite another to affirm the existence of the particular thing in question.[45]

The mention of unity-identity-whole leads us to echo our warn-ing regarding the avoidance of summary coverage of the varieties of understanding treated by Lonergan. So, for example, the distinction between 'body' and 'thing' elaborated in chapter VIII of *Insight* lays the axe to the root of a history of debate about 'substance'. It is a tricky topic of introspective analysis, central to intellectual conversion, which we pass over almost in silence.

JUDGMENT

Judgment is first used here to indicate globally what Lonergan refers to as rational consciousness or the third level of consciousness. In a more strictly delimited sense, however, judgment in Lonergan's usage designates the final term in the process which leads to cognitive self-transcendence.

It is helpful to draw a parallel between the process operative on the second level of consciousness—understanding—and that operative on the third in order to make intelligible in a preliminary fashion the type of intellectual performance involved on the third level of consciousness.

The level of understanding or intellectual consciousness involves three moments: (1) questions for intelligence,[46] (2) the insights resulting from questions for intelligence, and (3) the formulations or definitions which are the conscious intelligent products emanating from the insights. In similar fashion, the level of judgment or rational consciousness or, if you wish, reflection, involves three stages: (1) questions for reflection, (2) the act of reflective insight or reflective understanding which occurs as a result of questions for reflection, and (3) judgment, which terminates the process.

Judgment, then, is basically a matter of assent or dissent, of agreement or disagreement, of affirmation or negation, of yes or no, of 'it is' or 'it is not'. It is important to note, however, that the word 'is' is not used by an individual exclusively to affirm. It can be employed in a statement which simply reports what another individual holds, or in an expression of a hypothesis. Context is essential for determining whether a given use of the word 'is' pertains to a mere synthesis or to the positing of a synthesis. This may be expressed otherwise by characterising judgments in terms of propositions. In Lonergan's usage a proposition is a declarative sentence, e.g. 'The king is dead.' Further, propositions may be either simple objects of thought or consideration, or objects of agreement or disagreement as well. Thus, it is one thing to attempt to understand certain propositions in *Insight* or for that matter the whole of *Insight* but quite something else to deny or affirm, to agree or disagree with what is being said. In judgment the proposition or object of thought is transformed into an object of affirmation. The synthesis, then, of subject and predicate—e.g., 'Joe is intelligent'—already occurs on the level of understanding. Consequently it is not the proper task of judgment to effect a synthesis of subject and predicate but rather to posit or deny a synthesis already effected at an earlier stage of cognitional process.

Furthermore, judgment is not only a positing or negating of a synthesis achieved on the level of understanding but an *absolute* positing or negating. As Lonergan states in his *De Methodo Theologiae*[47] one does not judge in degrees, but simply and absolutely. This applies as much to judgments of probability as to certain judgments. In the former instance there is an 'absolute positing of probability'[48] whereas in the latter there is an absolute positing of an actual existent or happening. Thus, as Lonergan succinctly expresses it in *Insight*, 'the probability of a probable judgment is a certainty.'[49] Accordingly, every judgment, whether it regards a certain or only a probable content, involves in itself or precisely as *judgment* a certain and absolute positing.

Inevitably a consideration of judgment taken in the delimited sense of the term of the knowing process on the third level of consciousness must touch on the nature of reflective insight or understanding. Judgment and reflective understanding are intrinsically interrelated and though quite distinct are ultimately unintelligible in their inner workings apart from each other. At this point it will be more helpful to consider more directly, however, the nature of the act of reflective understanding, which stands to judgment as insight does to definition, and value judgment to decision.

Reflective insight, like direct or introspective insight, is more difficult to describe than the intelligible emanation which proceeds from it and on account of it. Just as direct insight is preconceptual and hence difficult to describe, so reflective insight involves a subtlety of operation which remains richer than any attempt to conceptualise it.

Basically, reflective understanding is an act which is prepared for by a question for reflection and followed by a judgment. Reflective insight encompasses within its scope three basic elements. These are : (1) a prospective judgment; (2) a link between the prospective judgment and the conditions required for making the judgment and (3) the fulfilment of the conditions. The act of reflective understanding itself is an act of insight which grasps the evidence or fulfilling conditions as indeed given and as sufficient for pronouncement of judgment.

It should be noted in regard to the prospective judgment that Lonergan refers to it as 'conditioned'. It is conditioned by the very fact that it is expressed in terms of a question for reflection. Thus, for example, the prospective judgment, 'It is Tuesday', is expressed in the question for reflection, 'Is it Tuesday?' The prospective judgment is accordingly conditioned because evidence is required if it is to be pronounced. Once the evidence is grasped to be sufficient, however, in the act of reflective understanding the prospective judgment becomes, in Lonergan's terminology, a virtually unconditioned. By a virtually unconditioned, then, Lonergan means a prospective judgment or conditioned whose conditions are understood to be fulfilled.

The act of reflective understanding is a most subtle and refined activity of spirit. Lonergan speaks of the act of reflective understanding as in some sense cognate with Pascal's *esprit de finesse* and Newman's illative sense.[50] Indeed, Lonergan explicitly states that reflective insight stands to judgment as Newman's illative sense stands to unconditional assent.[51] Lonergan, however, advances beyond Newman in that he explains on a scientific philosophical level what Newman only inchoatively grasped and discussed in a more descriptive frame of reference.

In the light of the above, Lonergan's analysis of reflective understanding involves certain paradoxical aspects. On the one hand, reflective understanding involves elements too subtle to be fully expressed in objective terms. Logic and methodology are concrete embodiments of the attempt to thematise the inner drive of the overall dynamics of cognitional process and of reflective understanding, but they in no wise exhaust through conceptual expression the richness and subtlety of spontaneous intelligence in act. On the other hand, however, introspective analysis of the act of reflective understanding in its genesis and term does reveal certain structural invariants operative in all instances of reflective insight and judgment. Accordingly, in Lonergan's cognitional analysis, intellectual performance always transcends any attempts at its full thematisation and yet careful introspection or self-appropriation does reveal its essential characteristics or operational features.

We may conclude this all too brief discussion of judgment with

some general comments. As early as the *Verbum* articles
Lonergan observed that both types of inner word, definition and
judgment, 'proceed from an *intelligere*, but a difference of
product postulates a difference of ground.'[52] In *Verbum* Lonergan
devotes forty-six pages to a chapter on understanding and definition, and forty-eight pages to a chapter on reflection and judgment. In these two chapters crucial differences are indicated
between insight, on the second level, and reflective insight, on the
third level. Likewise, in *Insight* the chapter on reflective understanding makes a unique advance beyond the earlier chapters
which dealt with insight on the level of understanding, and is as
highly differentiated and unique in its analysis of reflective insight
as are the earlier chapters in their exposition of the nature of
insight on the level of understanding.

Definition and judgment both proceed from acts of understanding but definition proceeds from insight into phantasm
whereas judgment proceeds from an act of reflective understanding which grasps a sufficient ground or evidence for judgment.
Again, both insight and reflective insight arise from the orientation of the pure desire to know. Insight, however, arises from
the pure desire as it expresses itself in a spirit of wonder and
enquiry. Reflective insight arises from the pure desire as spirit of
critical reflection. Finally, while direct insight has its instrumental
or material cause in a schematic image or phantasm, the reflective
insight regards not only imagination and sense experience but
also direct acts of understanding and definition in order to discover
in all taken together sufficient evidence for judgment. Lonergan
succinctly sums up in an explanatory statement the activities
involved on the levels of intellectual and rational consciousness
in the following manner :

There are two levels of activity, the direct and the reflective. On
the direct level there occur two types of events : there are insights
into phantasm which express themselves in definitions; there is the
coalescence or development of insights which provide the hypothetical syntheses of simple quiddities. On the reflective level these
hypothetical syntheses are known as hypothetical; they become
questions which are answered by the *resolutio in principia*. Thus
return to sources terminates in a reflective act of understanding,
which is the grasp of necessary connection between the sources and
the hypothetical synthesis; from this grasp there proceeds its self-

expression which is the *compositio vel divisio*, the judgment, the assent.[53]

This chapter has involved an exposition of the key factors involved in the basic process of human knowing as Lonergan understands and articulates it. *Insight*, however, is most fundamentally and profoundly an invitation to the reader to heighten awareness of his own cognitional activities and through the use of the introspective technique of self-appropriation to verify personally what it means to be a knower.

In the chapter on the self-affirmation of the knower Lonergan asks the reader to attempt to verify for himself whether or not he is a knower in the sense that he performs the operations Lonergan describes as constitutive of fully human knowing. At this point in *Insight* Lonergan still brackets the problems of being, objectivity, etc., and simply invites the reader to engage in a concrete cognitive performance.

In the concrete instance of the self-affirmation of the knower the question for reflection is, 'Am I a knower?' The link between the prospective judgment and its conditions is the statement of meaning, 'I am a knower, if I am an intelligible concrete unity-identity-whole, characterised by acts of sensing, perceiving, imagining, enquiring, understanding, formulating, reflecting, grasping the unconditioned and judging.' The fulfilment of the conditions is given in consciousness.

A first point should be made in reference to the 'I' or the concrete intelligible unity-identity-whole described as the subject of the prospective judgment, I am a knower. The 'I', then, or conscious centre of unity in diverse cognitional acts, would have to be postulated if it were not immediately given in consciousness because otherwise there would be no way of intelligibly relating to one another the cognitional acts or their contents. Thus, what is perceived is what is enquired about; what is enquired about is what is grasped by insight; what is understood is what is formulated; what is formulated is what is reflected upon, and what is reflected upon is what is judged. It would not be possible to make the above statements, however, if one enquired, another understood and a third judged. For it to be the case that what is perceived is what is enquired about it must be the same one who both perceives and enquires. The only way that contents on divers levels can combine into a single known is that there be a single knower or I or concrete, intelligible, unity-identity-whole which is the subject of the diverse cognitional operations through which the diverse contents are grasped. The only way an individual can utter a judgment for which he alone is wholly responsible is to be able to base it on experiences and insights, formulations and reflections which he can equally call his own. As Lonergan expresses it :

If there were no 'I', how could there be a 'my experience' with respect to which a 'my enquiry' occurred? . . . If there were not one consciousness, at once empirical, intelligent and rational, how could rational judgment proceed from an unconditioned grasped in the combination of thought and sensible experience?[54]

It is not necessary, however, to rely upon a merely postulated Kantian-type synthetic unity of apperception, for a rudimentary meaning of consciousness. Indeed, as Lonergan puts it :

Consciousness is much more obviously of this unity in diverse acts than of the diverse acts, for it is within the unity that the acts are found and distinguished, and it is to the unity that we appeal when we talk about a single field of consciousness and draw a distinction between conscious acts occurring within the field and unconscious acts occurring outside it.[55]

Consciousness thus supplies the fulfilling condition of at least one element in the conditions for affirming that 'I am a knower', namely the awareness of the 'I' as conscious centre of the cognitive acts. The terms 'concrete' and 'intelligible unity-identity-whole' are simply the conceptualised thematisation of this basic datum of consciousness.

Lonergan proceeds to show that the act of the self-affirmation of oneself as a knower in the sense specified above involves a concrete judgment of fact which can only be avoided at the price of total silence or self-contradiction. He engages in an Aristotelian type retortion whose aim is to demonstrate that self-affirmation is an immanent law of intelligence and that any attempt to deny that one is a knower in the sense specified is to involve oneself in a contradiction between statement and performance. In other words, more concretely put, to deny that one is a unity-identity-whole characterised by acts of sensing, perceiving, enquiring, understanding, reflecting and judging one must appeal to one's own experience, elucidate one's understanding, indicate sufficiency of evidence for judgment and claim personal responsibility for the judgment one makes. Self-affirmation accordingly, in Lonergan's analysis, cannot ultimately be avoided by anyone who endeavours to operate in full accord with the exigences of intelligence and rationality and on the basis of his own cognitive experience.

The fact, however, that self-affirmation is an immanent law does not imply a matter of absolute necessity. The immanent law of self-affirmation indicates that man does, in fact, know in a certain concrete way and that it is impossible to utilise this process of knowing in order to deny the process, without self-contradiction. The immanent law, however, does not imply that the particular way in which man does in fact know is a matter of absolute necessity—i.e., that it could not have been otherwise— nor that at some future date man's knowing might not become something other than it is.

The judgment, therefore, 'I am a knower', is a conditioned whose conditions happen to be fulfilled. In other words, the judgment involves the conditioned necessity of contingent fact. It is important to note, however, that this judgment is not subject to revision in the way that probable judgments of empirical science are subject to indefinite revision. The difference is that empirical science involves explanation on the basis of sense and this means that although the element of hypothesis can be reduced to a minimum it is always possible that new data will arise which could involve a shift in the fundamental terms and relations of a given hypothesis or explanatory system. In the case of cognitional theory, however, the explanation is based not on sense data but on the data of consciousness. This means that the terms and relations articulated in cognitional theory are not simply a matter of hypothesis but are in fact given in consciousness itself. Consciousness thus provides a rock foundation or ultimate ground for cognitional theory and, in Lonergan's view, once the basic terms and relations of cognition are introspectively discerned and explanatorily defined no major revision can occur.

In conclusion, it would seem correct to state in view of the above that if it could be shown that Lonergan has overlooked a basic term or relation in human knowing or if he has fundamentally misinterpreted one or other level of consciousness then his claim to have reached an explanatory account of human knowing subject only to minor revision would be proven false. This point is of crucial importance because Lonergan's explanation of objectivity and of the isomorphism of knowing and being are critically dependent on the assumption of the basic validity of his explanatory account of human knowing and its verifiability in terms of human consciousness. The same is also true of Lonergan's proof for the existence of God. The ultimate grounding of the proof rests on the correctness of Lonergan's identification of the intelligible with being. If, however, Lonergan is in basic error in regard to his interpretation of the nature of consciousness and of the two intelligible emanations, then his particular proof for the existence of God loses its cogency.

4

Confinement in Openness:
the Position on Being

IN chapter 3 the first of what Lonergan designates as the three
basic 'positions' was developed. The first position regards knowing
and is correctly understood and affirmed to the extent that it is
acknowledged that 'the subject becomes known when it affirms
itself intelligently and reasonably and so is not known yet in any
prior "existential" state.'[1] This first position is effectively reached
when an individual verifies for himself in terms of his own experience that he is subject to the exigences of experience, intelligent
enquiry, critical reflection and judgment, and that as subject
to these immanent intellectual dynamisms he must affirm himself
as an existing intelligible unity differentiated by capacities to
experience, to enquire, and to reflect.[2]

Lonergan's first basic position critically rests on the distinction
he draws between the conscious experience of oneself as an
experiencing, understanding, and judging subject and the self-
affirmation of oneself as a knower. For Lonergan, to be conscious
of oneself on the one hand, and to understand and critically
verify the meaning of self and consciousness, on the other, are
entirely different cognitive events. The difference between the
two is the difference between the simple experiential presence to
oneself as subject and proper human objective *knowledge* of oneself as conscious, achieved through insight, critical reflection and
judgment. Accordingly, the counter-position in regard to this
first position will be basically any view which confuses the
distinction between simple experience of oneself as subject and
objective *knowledge* of oneself achieved through understanding
and judgment, or which places *knowledge* of oneself *as existing*
in some sort of intuition or existential state prior to judgment.

Lonergan employs the military metaphor of breakthrough,
encirclement, and confinement to indicate dramatically and concretely the essentially dynamic character of his epistemological

enterprise. The three dynamic terms, of course, designate stages in what is radically one operation : the campaign to establish in an impregnable fashion the fortress of critical realism.

It is important to stress the unity of the operations of break-through, encirclement, and confinement. True enough, in *Insight* for what are very good pedagogical reasons, Lonergan is careful to distinguish from one another his discussions of knowing, being, and objectivity. In fact, he is at pains to emphasise the limited claims involved in his respective discussions of these three critical epistemological issues. It remains true, however, that the three basic positions which Lonergan develops in *Insight* are closely interrelated and are ultimately only intelligible in terms of one another. This unified quality of the three basic positions is most strikingly manifest in Lonergan's attempts to synthesise briefly the core foundation points of his philosophy of critical realism in such essays as 'Cognitional Structure'[3] and the unpublished Latin lecture, *De Notione Structurae*.[4]

Although the aim of this chapter is basically synthetic it will be useful to consider first the problem of being and then the closely related problematics of the isomorphism of knowing and being and of objectivity.

BEING

Lonergan affirms that the acknowledgment of the notion of being is implicit in the breakthrough.[5] It is necessary, however, at this point to attempt to make the implicit explicit.

Tersely expressed, Lonergan's basic position regarding being is that 'the real is the concrete universe of being and not a sub-division of the "already out there now" '[6] To establish fully this second basic position, what Lonergan terms 'confinement' must occur, in which the third basic position—i.e., the position on objectivity—is also thematised and firmly grounded. The analysis of being in terms of the notion of being, however, allows for what Lonergan terms an 'encirclement' because it radically delimits, from a critical viewpoint, what being can possibly mean and *eo ipso* excludes a whole range of false conceptions of being. The method to be employed here in effecting the encirclement will involve a brief preliminary conspectus of the overall problem area involved, a positive moment in which Lonergan's position on being is thematised, and a negative moment in which various counter-positions are dialectically studied in their relationship to the position.

First, Lonergan envisages *Insight* as involving primarily not a study of the fact of knowledge but 'a discrimination between two facts of knowledge'.[7] These two facts of knowledge involve respectively the type of knowing which Lonergan speaks of in terms of a certain biological or animal extroversion and the type which consists of understanding and judgment. It is Lonergan's view that both types of knowing have their own criteria and validity but that they must be carefully distinguished if the most profound sort of philosophical error is to be avoided. Unless one clearly distinguishes between the two facts and grasps the scope and limitations of each, one will doubt that properly human knowing is correct understanding and 'under the pressure of that doubt, either one will sink into the bog of a knowing that is without understanding, or else one will cling to understanding but sacrifice knowing on the altar of an immanentism, an idealism, a relativism.'[8]

Lonergan further indicates that one can only escape from the horns of the dilemma of idealism versus materialism by grasping that there are 'two quite different realisms, that there is an incoherent realism, half animal and half human, that poses as a half-way house between materialism and idealism and, on the other hand, that there is an intelligent and reasonable realism between which and materialism the half-way house is idealism.'[9]

In Lonergan's analysis an incoherent type of realism which would pose as a half-way house between materialism and idealism would be a type of position which would uphold the validity of man's knowledge but would rest its claim to certainty on one component in cognitional process or in an appeal to some form of extroverted or introverted 'look' at the real, an immediate intuition of being.

In contradistinction to the 'incoherent type of realism' just described, Lonergan's position involves in his words 'an intelligent and reasonable realism between which and materialism the half-way house is idealism.' This description by Lonergan of the type of realism he espouses is most significant not only because implicit in it is a clear break with all forms of intuitionism but also because it is an acknowledgment that if one advances only halfway toward his position one may end up in idealism. Indeed, not a few philosophers object to Lonergan's view precisely because they believe that idealism is not only a halfway house between materialism and Lonergan's position but is, in fact, despite the latter's denial, the ultimate meaning of his final position.

In the light of the above, certain fundamental questions naturally arise and the answers to these questions will serve to determine the fundamental validity of Lonergan's basic positions'. Thus, for example, what is meant by *being* and what is its relation to the *real*? Is the *real* known in some stage of cognition prior to judgment or is judgment the sole medium through which the real is apprehended? Is there or is there not a human intellectual intuition of concrete actual existence or being?

For Lonergan the answers to the above questions are already implicitly provided in terms of the occurrence of the self-affirmation of the knower. For, in the process of self affirming self as knower there is no appeal at any point to an intellectual intuition of concrete existence—in fact, the latter is implicitly excluded. Moreover, if, as Lonergan contends, 'this affirmation of oneself as a knower also is an affirmation of the general structure of any proportionate object of knowledge'[10] it follows that no appeal to any intuition of existence or being can be legitimately made either in scientific or common-sense enquiry or *a fortiori* in regard to the affirmation of the existence of God.

For Lonergan the breakthrough towards the establishment of critical realism occurs the moment the self-affirmation of the knower takes place. There is the necessity, of course, of passing from experience through understanding to judgment. And, if one cannot move beyond understanding to judgment, the result is idealism. In the self-affirmation of the knower, however, it is Lonergan's contention that one does move beyond the immanentism of understanding through the grasp of a virtually unconditioned to judgment and a knowledge of what in fact is.

It remains, however, through a more specific consideration of being, to attempt to move beyond the point of breakthrough to that of encirclement and finally confinement. The main point to be demonstrated in the following analysis of being, therefore, is that the real, or the concrete, universe of being is known only through correct understanding and that apart from correct understanding, knowledge of reality is not achieved.

The key element in Lonergan's approach to the problem of being is his identification of what he designates as the 'notion' of being with the pure desire to know as consciously operative. It is because of this identification of the notion of being with the desire to know that in Lonergan's analysis the radical solution to the problem of the relationship between knowing and being is by definition the opposite of nothing and hence includes spective psychology and epistemology rather than on that of metaphysics.

A first point, then, is that for Lonergan the objective of the knowing process is everything. It is for this reason that Lonergan defines the objective of the pure desire to know as being, since being is by definition the opposite of nothing and hence includes everything that is. The question at once arises, however, as to just how it can be established that the objective of the pure desire to know is, in fact, being or the all or everything.

It should be noted that it is not on the grounds that any man has achieved or for that matter ever will achieve a knowledge of everything about everything that Lonergan affirms that man's desire to know is a desire to know everything about everything. Rather, it is on the basis of a cognitional analysis of the conscious intentionality operative in the desire to know that Lonergan affirms the unrestricted character of man's noetic intending.

It would be helpful at this stage, with an eye also to chapter 5, to note Lonergan's distinctions between the notion of being, the concept of being, and the idea of being. This particular set of distinctions is, as a set, unique to Lonergan. The ground of these distinctions is cognitional and hence their ultimate validation rests on an appeal to man's experience of his intellectual and rational consciousness, and on the correctness of certain deductions which in Lonergan's analysis follow of necessity from a properly verified understanding of human understanding and the occurrence of certain basic judgments of fact.

First, then, for Lonergan the notion of being is identical with man's desire to know as it promotes man from enquiry to insight and conceptualisation, and from the latter to critical reflection and judgment and then beyond the infinitesimal increment in knowledge which one judgment represents towards the goal of pronouncing the totality of correct judgments. The notion of being then, as identical with the pure desire to know, is not any product of the knowing process but it is that knowing process in its pure heuristic intentionality. Lonergan points out that 'a heuristic notion, then, is the notion of an unknown content and it is determined by anticipating the type of act through which the unknown would become known.'[11] The notion of being or the pure desire to know, accordingly, is the supreme heuristic notion because the unknown content of which it is the notion is at root everything and this objective is to be reached to the extent that all possible correct judgments are made.

Secondly, Lonergan speaks of the concept of being. In Lonergan's view one does not have a concept of being in the sense that an act of understanding occurs in which the essence or nature of being is grasped and is then uttered in a definition, since the occurrence of such an act would be an understanding of everything about everything and no such occurrence is, in fact, given in human consciousness. Thus, as Lonergan indicates, we can interrogate each immediate individual datum of our experience in regard to its nature or quiddity but what is consequently understood is never the nature of being but the essence or quiddity or species of some particular being. In Lonergan's words :

Our intellectual knowledge of being cannot result from abstraction of essence. For if from a horse I abstract essence, what I abstract is the essence, not of being, but of horse; if from a man I abstract essence, what I abstract is the essence, not of being, but of man; and the same holds for every other immediate object of our present knowledge. No being by participation can yield us knowledge of the essence of being, because no being by participation has the essence of being; and what is true of essence, equally is true of quiddity, nature, species, and form. A being by participation no more has the quiddity of being, the nature of being, the species of being, the form of being, than it has the essence of being.[12]

If, however, it is true that we can have no quidditative knowledge of the essence of being in terms of the immediate objects of our experience, to what does one attribute man's talk about being and beings, and his employment of such terms as being, existence, reality, etc? In Lonergan's analysis, although it is not true that man at present enjoys an insight into the nature of being, man does experience the notion of being operative in himself in so far as he intelligently enquires and critically reflects, and on the basis of this conscious experience he can understand and define not what the essence or meaning of being is, but how its meaning is to be determined. Lonergan thus describes his definition of being as a second order definition. Other definitions determine what is meant but Lonergan's definition 'asserts that if you know, then you know being; it asserts that if you wish to know, then you wish to know being; but it does not settle whether you know or what you know, whether your wish will be fulfilled or what you will know when it is fulfilled.'[13]

Thirdly, in Lonergan's terminology the *idea* of being signifies the content of an act of understanding that grasps everything about everything. This means, as will be developed at greater length in chapter 5, that the idea of being is the content of the act of divine understanding that understands everything about everything.

It follows in accord with Lonergan's definition of the idea of being, that since the idea of being includes everything about everything, no finite or limited or participated being can contain in itself the essence or nature or idea of being. It is true that for Lonergan the quiddities or essences of existing material things are intrinsically intelligible. Yet, in Lonergan's analysis understanding of essence is never understanding of existence or of the essence or idea of being as long as the essence understood is not identical with its existence.

Finally, as will be indicated in a more critical fashion in chapter 5, while finite essence is in Lonergan's view intrinsically intelligible, contingent existence is not. Thus, it is not by *understanding* or *a fortiori* by a certain looking or intuition of either an extroverted or introverted nature that contingent existence is *known*. Rather, for Lonergan contingent existence is extrinsically intelligible and hence is not understood 'until it is reduced to a non-contingent cause extrinsic to itself.'[14] *Contingent existence* accordingly is first of all *known* by man not through an act of direct or introspective understanding but in judgment, and it can only be understood by man in so far as it is reduced to its extrinsic non-contingent cause. It is thus clear that Lonergan's position regarding knowledge of contingent existence stands in unalterable opposition to any viewpoint which would argue for the existence of some sort of perception, or intuition, of contingent existence, no matter how subtle or spiritual such an intuition might be.

Now that the basic Lonerganian distinctions between the notion of being, the concept of being, and the idea of being have been indicated, it would seem desirable to discuss at greater length the basic characteristics of the notion of being.

Such a discussion, however, to be genuinely helpful in the reader's effort to get to grips with Lonergan's view, would have to parallel his own treatment in *Insight*. We think it better then to simply refer the reader to Lonergan's own considerations.[15] Similarly, we pass over the possibility of clarification by contrast with other views on being. The notion of being, as a subject of thematic consideration within the field of interiority, is recent and difficult. In *Insight* Lonergan states that Aquinas did not explicitly distinguish between the notion of being and the concept of being and yet 'was remarkably aware of the implications of that distinction.'[16] Jean Langlois remarks that Lonergan's 'great originality' consists in his identification of the notion of being with the pure desire to know.[17] The point to these comments is that Lonergan's articulation of the notion of being is original and subtle and so the avoidance at present of summary treatment is warranted.

THE NOTION OF STRUCTURE

In his talk, *De Notione Structurae*, Lonergan, in the context of elaborating on a section of Aquinas's *In Boethium De Trinitate*[18] indicates that according to Thomas the intellect is able to abstract certain elements which are not in fact separated in the thing as long as the particular elements abstracted are not by nature intrinsically ordered to other elements and hence unintelligible apart from the other elements. Thus, for example, Lonergan indicates, in citing an example Aquinas employs, that it is possible to understand a letter apart from a syllable although the converse is not true. In like manner, it is possible to understand animal without foot or man without whiteness. The intellect, however, cannot abstract an element which has an intrinsic intelligible ordination to and dependence on another in separation from the other, but this type of element can only be *comprehended* or understood together with the other. As examples of this latter instance Lonergan, in following Aquinas, cites the part as ordered to the whole, the part in its relationship to its co-part, and the relative in relation to its correlative. Thus, for example, a foot is not intelligible apart from the whole which is the animal because it is, as part, intrinsically ordered to animal as whole. Again, the part cannot be understood apart from its co-part. Thus, Lonergan indicates that fundamental elements in the systems of Aristotle and Aquinas are defined not by a proper definition but through a certain mutual proportion. As specific examples of this type of element Lonergan indicates the matter-form relationship and likewise the relation of the organ of sight, the eye, to the power of sight—sight as form of the organ—and the power of sight to the act of seeing. As Lonergan puts it, the organ of sight is related to the power of sight as the body is related to the soul. Likewise, the power of sight is for the sake of actually seeing, and so there is an intrinsic relationship of the power of sight to the act of seeing. Again, the very intelligibility of an accident involves an intrinsic relationship to substance—*'accidentis esse est inesse.'*[19] Finally, the relative is not *understood* apart from its correlative, e.g., fatherhood cannot be understood apart from sonship and vice versa.

Lonergan proceeds to discuss structure not in an abstract and general fashion but concretely. He speaks in turn about three structures: the structure of the thing known, the structure in human knowing, and the structure involved in objectivity.

Lonergan is addressing himself to a group of scholastic philosophers in his talk on the notion of structure and so he begins not with the structure of the knowing, as he does in *Insight,* but with the structure of the known, with metaphysics rather than with cognitional analysis. He so proceeds not because he considers metaphysics a first but for the sake of his audience, who might perhaps be expected to find his examples from metaphysics more immediately meaningful than his cognitional and epistemological analyses. Thus, as he puts it:

(I wish to speak to you) first about the structure of the thing known . . . because it is the structure best known to you. Next, about the structure of cognition, which is similar to the structure of the thing known, and thirdly, about the structure of objectivity, which constitutes a conjunction between the first and second structures: we know the thing on account of the objectivity of knowledge.[20]

It is possible, then, in the light of the prior analyses of the structure of the knowing process as Lonergan envisages it to pass now to an analysis of the structure of the known. Actually, the structural elements of the object known through experiencing, understanding and judging have already been indicated in one fashion or another in preceding considerations, but here an attempt will be made to bring them together in a synthetic and explanatory fashion.

As a preliminary, however, to the specific discussion of the elements which together constitute the known object it will be helpful first to consider Lonergan's notion of the isomorphism of knowing and the known. This analysis will lead in turn to a consideration of the metaphysical elements constitutive of the known.

THE ISOMORPHISM OF KNOWING AND THE KNOWN

Lonergan defines isomorphism generically in the following manner :

Two sets of terms, say A, B, C . . ., and P, Q, R . . ., are said to be isomorphic if the relation of A to B is similar to the relation of P to Q, the relation of A to C is similar to the relation of P to R, the relation of B to C is similar to the relation of Q to R, etc., etc. Isomorphism, then, supposes different sets of terms; it neither affirms nor denies similarity between the terms of one set and those of other sets; but it does assert that the network of relations in one set of terms is similar to the networks of relations in other sets.[21]

Now, in the chapter in *Insight* on 'The Method of Metaphysics' Lonergan expresses the isomorphism of knowing and the known in the following proposition : 'If the knowing consists of a related set of acts and the known is the related set of contents of these acts, then the pattern of the relations between the acts is similar in form to the pattern of the relations between the contents of the acts.'[22] The isomorphic proposition as it stands is an analytical proposition. Lonergan explains that by an analytic proposition he means that particular instance of a virtually unconditioned where

(1) the conditioned is the proposition in question,

(2) the fulfilment of the conditions is the set of definitions of the terms contained in the proposition,

(3) the link between conditions and conditioned is the syn-

tactical structures in accord with which single terms in their defined sense coalesce to form a proposition.[23]

It should be noted, however, that analytic propositions can be transformed into analytic principles if certain conditions are fulfilled and Lonergan affirms that they are able to be fulfilled in regard to the isomorphism in question. Thus, by an analytic principle Lonergan means an analytic proposition whose terms, in their defined sense, occur in true judgments of fact. In other words, 'an analytic principle adds an existential reference to an analytic proposition, where existence is defined by its connection with factual truth.'[24]

The basic manner in which Lonergan's proposition of the isomorphism of knowing and the known is transformed into an analytic principle is through the performance or utterance of a series of affirmations of concrete and recurrent structures in the knowing of the self-affirming subject. The prime instance of this, of course, is in the performance of self-affirmation itself, and further instances are provided through the understanding and affirmation of the structure of knowing operative in common sense and scientific knowing. It becomes manifest that every instance of knowing proportionate being (proportionate being is contrasted with transcendent being and refers to whatever is able to be experienced by man as well as understood and judged by him) consists of a unification of experiencing, understanding and judging and it follows from the isomorphic principle that every instance of known proportionate being involves a parallel unification of a content of experience, a content of understanding and a content of judgment.[25]

To revert, for a moment, to a concrete instance, in the basic case mentioned above of the self-affirmation of the knower an example is clearly provided in which the analytic proposition of isomorphism is transformed into an analytic principle. The self which affirms experiences itself experiencing, understanding and judging, understands itself as experiencing, understanding and judging and judges its understanding of itself to be correct. In this case of self-affirmation we have an example in which the terms of the analytic proposition of isomorphism, in their defined sense, occur in a true judgment of fact. Further, a consideration of scientific method and the procedures common sense employs in making judgments of fact confirm Lonergan's view that the 'affirmation of oneself as a knower also is an affirmation of the general structure of any proportionate object of knowledge.'[26] Indeed, the only way to disprove the principle of the isomorphism of knowing and the known as here elucidated would be to prove that there exists in man a truly human knowing of being as being which does not coincide with the knowledge process as described in the chapter of *Insight* on self-affirmation.

Up to this point a detailed discussion of the 'general structure of any proportionate object of knowledge' has been postponed. This analysis will follow shortly but at this point, with the general notion of isomorphism in mind, it will be useful to consider briefly Lonergan's analysis of the object known as disclosed in Thomistic categories and in the procedures of science. These considerations will prepare the way for a synthetic statement on the metaphysical elements, a discussion of the structure of objectivity and, finally, a consideration of the metaphysical elements in their status as truly ontological principles of being.

In his *De Notione Structurae* Lonergan first considers the structure of the object known in terms of classical Thomistic categories and then in the light of modern scientific procedures. The approach here will be the same.

First, as Lonergan indicates, in Aristotle the material thing is considered to be composed of this matter and this form. The matter is matter through its relationship to form and the material form is material form because it is *per se* apt (*apta nata est*) to inform some matter.[27] Thus, the matter is not able to be understood apart from the form and vice versa, and the two together constitute a structure. Every finite act of existence is the act of existence of a certain essence and every essence is ordered to existence.[28] It is, of course, possible to discuss essence and existence separately but it is not possible to *understand* one apart from its intrinsic relation to the other.

Further, in Aquinas essence (we prescind here from angelic and divine essence) is the same as matter and form and so a more complicated structure is involved. Lonergan indicates that existence and essence constitute a structure but that essence is itself structured, composed of form and matter. It follows that structures are not limited to two elements. In the instance just discussed a structure is involved which includes three elements which can only be *understood* together.

Lonergan makes the further point that neither matter nor form nor existence are themselves things or beings but rather are the principles by which things or beings are constituted. Lonergan remarks : 'I insist on (this) difference, because we find the same difference in cognition and in objectivity.'[29]

Lonergan next turns to a discussion of science. He indicates that science basically involves the verification of theories in many individual instances. In brief, the scientist because he is seeking understanding adverts to problems. Because understanding involves the grasp of intelligibility in data, the scientist observes, experiments, measures. Because understanding involves the conceptualisation of what it grasps in data, the scientist formulates hypotheses. Finally, because insight is a grasp of the possibly relevant, hypotheses stand in need of verification and verification is in terms of data. Science accordingly, in Lonergan's view, basically involves the verification of theories or hypotheses in individual instances.[30]

Lonergan indicates the structural relationship between the objects known by science and the same objects as heuristically known through metaphysics thus : 'In so far as there is a *theory* there is had that through which *forma in rebus* is known, in so far as there is *verification* there exists that through which *esse in rebus* is known; and, in so far as there is a theory verified *in many individual instances* there is had that through which *materia* is known.'[31]

Now there is for Lonergan a difference between the metaphysician's mode of procedure and goal, and that of the scientist. Most fundamentally and simply put, the metaphysician proceeds according to the *intention* of the end but the scientist aims *to attain* the end to the extent he can. To express this in another way, metaphysics proceeds in a radically heuristic fashion and, as heuristic, it seeks not to come to know specific essences of objects but to anticipate the type of acts through which specific contents will be known and through the principle of isomorphism to indicate the structure of the object to be known. Thus, for example, the metaphysician 'defines' being not by specifying its essence but by stating that being is what is to be known through the totality of correct judgments. Likewise, in regard to proportionate being the metaphysician 'defines' it not by defining specific forms or essences of given proportionate realities but by

heuristically stating in accord with the isomorphic principle
that the knowing of proportionate being occurs through experiencing, understanding and judging and that the known as
content of these operations necessarily involves potential, formal
and actual constituent principles. Metaphysics thus in principle
regards proportionate being intentionally, or as to be understood,
rather than as understood in act.

In the light of the above it may properly be said that metaphysics stands in a certain heuristic relationship to science. Thus,
metaphysics assigns the general heuristic structure according to
which scientific discovery *de facto* does and will take place.
Metaphysics indicates that if science is to move toward its goal
of an ever more adequate knowledge of proportionate being, it
will do so by seeking through experiencing, understanding and
judging to verify theories in instances. Lonergan sums up his
basic understanding of the distinction and interrelationship
between metaphysics and science in the following manner :

> If one wants to know just what forms are, the proper procedure is
> to give up metaphysics and turn to the sciences; for forms become
> known inasmuch as the sciences approximate towards their ideal
> of complete explanation; and there is no method, apart from scien-
> tific method, by which one can reach such explanation. However,
> besides the specialised acts of understanding in which particular
> types of forms are grasped in their actual intelligibility, there also
> exist the more general acts of understanding in which one grasps
> the relations between experience, understanding and judgment, and
> the isomorphism of these activities with the constituents of what
> is to be known. If the metaphysician must leave to the physicist
> the understanding of physics and to the chemist the understanding
> of chemistry, he has the task of working out for the physicist and
> chemist, for the biologist and the psychologist, the dynamic structure
> that initiates and controls their respective enquiries, and no less,
> the general characteristics of the goal towards which they head.[32]

AN INITIAL DISCUSSION OF THE METAPHYSICAL ELEMENTS
In effecting the transition to a more detailed discussion of the
metaphysical elements, it will be useful to recapitulate briefly the
process which leads from an implicit to an explicit discussion of
metaphysics.

In the chapter in *Insight* dealing with the self-affirmation
of the knower, the shift is made from insight considered as activity

to insight envisaged as knowledge. In chapter XII of *Insight* being is heuristically defined as the objective of the pure desire to know, or as that which is to be known through the totality of correct judgments. It is, however, most properly in the deduction of isomorphism and the transformation of the analytic proposition of isomorphism into an analytic principle that explicit metaphysics is reached.[33]

A further point to be noted before discussing the metaphysical elements is that, although in *Insight* objectivity is discussed before the metaphysical elements, it seemed useful in the light of the procedure in *De Notione Structurae* first to discuss the metaphysical elements without considering their ontological status and then to use the discussion on objectivity as a bridge to the discussion of the metaphysical elements in their ontological status. This procedure is somewhat arbitrary but it seems helpful from a synthetic expository point of view. Moreover, the discussion of objectivity in this chapter, as is the case in *Insight*, precedes the analysis of the metaphysical elements in their ontological status.

Further, in the context of the above it is also important to note that the principle of isomorphism as it is elaborated in chapter XIV of *Insight* does not explicitly involve a consideration of the ontological status of the contents of the known. What the discussion does bring out, however, is that there is an intrinsic relational similarity between the structure operative in the knowing and the structure of the known. The two structures stand in a protracted analogy of proportion.

A final introductory point to be stressed is that the isomorphic principle does not necessarily imply a similarity or a dissimilarity between experiencing and potency, between understanding and form and between judgment and existence. It does indicate, however, that potency is related to form and act in a manner similar to the way experience is related to understanding and judgment. The implications, of course, of the isomorphic principle in regard to a proper understanding of the relationship between cognitional analysis and metaphysics, are radical and far-reaching.

Lonergan, then, enumerates and explains the six metaphysical elements: potency, form and act on what Lonergan calls the central and the conjugate levels. Potency, form and act on the central level mean the same thing for Lonergan as do the

Thomistic categories of prime potency or matter, substantial form and the act of existence. Thus, for example, the self-affirmed as a unity-identity-whole existing in data may be transposed through metaphysical equivalence into a central form or substantial form which is the first act of this prime matter and together with its matter is actualised on the level of existence through the second act, i.e., the act of existence.

Potency, form and act, however, on the conjugate level differ more than nominally from certain Aristotelian descriptions of accident. In Lonergan's view accidental forms of Aristotle's physical theory were perhaps sensible qualities as sensed, whereas for Lonergan conjugate forms are always grasped by understanding. Moreover, Lonergan dislikes the term 'accidental' since it suggests the merely incidental, and he insists on the relational-explanatory aspect of the conjugates which the term conjugate helps bring out.

In terms of each level of cognitional activity affirmed in the self-affirmation of the knower, a conjugate potency-form-act relationship can be discerned. Thus, on the level of experiencing, the eye or organ of sight may properly be described in the terms of metaphysical equivalence as a conjugate potency, sight as a conjugate form, and seeing as a conjugate act. Again, on the level of understanding, the possible intellect (the intellect in potency to the act of understanding) may be described as a conjugate potency, the habit of science or understanding as a conjugate form, and the act of understanding as a conjugate act. Finally, if one considers the fourth level of consciousness, i.e., that of decision, will may be described as a conjugate potency, willingness as a conjugate form, and willing as a conjugate act.[34]

The basic point to be noted in regard to each of the examples of conjugates just presented is that on each level of human operation there is a potential, formal and actual element and this is what is meant by the conjugate potency-form-act relationship. As Lonergan puts it in speaking of any and all instances of concrete proportionate being, 'their [concrete existing things] existing involves a central act, their natural unity a central form, their merely empirical individuality, a central potency, and their potential, habitual and actual behaviour conjugate potencies, forms and acts.'[35]

Now it is true that in his more recent writings Lonergan has ceased to employ faculty theory terminology and speaks rather in terms of intentionality analysis and levels of consciousness. Lonergan, however, does not now deny the basic validity of the type of examples of conjugates just given but would at present prefer to speak in what he considers the more relevant terms of intentionality analysis.

At this point it would certainly be helpful to consolidate further Lonergan's position by directly considering the six metaphysical elements in the context of scientific method, and by further considering the heuristic world view grounded on the position. Such considerations, however, take us too far afield.[36] We turn immediately, then, to a consideration of the structure involved in objectivity. This will lead to a discussion of the ontological status of the metaphysical elements.

OBJECTIVITY

In his 'Natural Knowledge of God' Lonergan defines objects as 'what are intended in questioning and what become better known as our answers to questions become fuller and more accurate.'[37] In various public lectures in the last few years Lonergan has spoken of objectivity as a matter of authentic subjectivity. By this latter paradoxical statement Lonergan intends to emphasise that since 'the intrinsic objectivity of human cognitional activity is its intentionality'[38] it is in an authentic fidelity to the exigencies of intelligence that objects are known and objectivity achieved.

In *Insight* Lonergan distinguishes between a principal notion of objectivity and components of objectivity emergent within cognitional process. In *De Notione Structurae* and in his 'Cognitional Structure' Lonergan does not explicitly deal with the principal notion of objectivity but concentrates on the three components of objectivity emergent within the process of cognition. In the present analysis first a brief exposition of Lonergan's principal notion of objectivity will be offered. Then the threefold structure operative in achieving the objectivity involved in the making of any correct judgment or authentic act of cognitive self-transcendence will be handled.

Lonergan's exposition of the principal notion of objectivity involves the use of an explanatory device or implicit definition. For Lonergan the principal notion of objectivity is contained in a patterned context of judgments. Thus, as Lonergan puts it,

E

One may define as object any A, B, C, D, . . . where, in turn, A, B, C, D . . . are defined by the correctness of the set of judgments :
   A is; B is; C is; D is; . . .
   A is neither B nor C nor D nor . . .
   B is neither C nor D nor . . .
   C is neither D nor. . . .

Again, one may define a subject as any object, say A, where it is true that A affirms himself as a knower in the sense explained in the chapter on Self-affirmation.

The bare essentials of this notion of objectivity are reached if we add to the judgments already discussed, viz., I am the knower; this is a typewriter, the further judgment that I am not this typewriter.[39]

The principal notion of objectivity, then, resides in a context of judgments, and without the occurrence of a plurality of judgments satisfying the above pattern, the notion does not emerge. Moreover, the validity of the principal notion of objectivity is the same as the validity of the set of judgments that contain it for, 'if the judgments are correct, then it is correct that there are objects and subjects in the sense defined, for the sense defined is simply the correctness of the appropriate pattern of judgments.'[40]

Now people commonly know objects and subjects although they may not be able to engage in the recondite art of implicitly defining them. It suffices, however, for ordinary knowledge of subjects and objects that individuals make the proper set of judgments in the appropriate pattern. Objectivity, then, in the principal sense is reached when distinct beings are affirmed—e.g., A is, B is; the beings are clearly distinguished from one another—e.g., A is not B; and one object, A, is understood and affirmed to be a knower.

Objectivity in its principal sense obviates the so-called problem of the bridge between subject and object. The subject does not first know himself as a knower and then ask how he can know anything else. Rather, the subject makes a set of judgments in a certain pattern in which knowledge of the distinction between subjects and objects emerges. Thus, there is objectivity 'if there are distinct beings, some of which both know themselves and know others as others.'[41] It should thus be stressed that the distinctions between subject and object as developed in the principal notion of objectivity are within being. This means that the positing, distinguishing and relating of A, B, C, etc., are the result of answering the existential questions : Does A exist? Does B exist? Is A B? etc. It is through experiencing, enquiring, reflecting and judging that there arises knowledge of objects, some of which are also understood and affirmed to be subjects. Objectivity accordingly does not consist in going beyond a known knower to a known, but 'in heading for being (Does A exist? Does B exist?) within which there are positive differences and, among such differences, the difference between object and subject.'⁴²

Now, in *De Notione Structurae* and elsewhere Lonergan indicates that just as knowing and the known involve three interrelated elements which together constitute one knowing and one known, so objectivity, as used in the non-principal sense referred to earlier, involves three interrelated stages or moments which together enable an individual to utter a correct judgment or, in other words, to achieve true cognitive self-transcendence. Thus, whereas the principal notion of objectivity is constituted only by a suitable constellation of judgments, the three elements of objectivity which are isomorphic to the threefold structure of knowing and the known pertain to the stages involved in reaching any individual correct judgment.

Lonergan sums up the non-principal notion of objectivity in the following manner :

The objectivity of human knowing is a triple cord; there is an experiential component that resides in the givenness of relevant data; there is a normative component that resides in the exigences of intelligence and rationality guiding the process of knowing from data to judging; there finally is an absolute component that is reached when reflective understanding combines the normative and the experiential elements into a virtually unconditioned, i.e., a conditioned whose conditions are fulfilled.⁴³

Empirical objectivity consists in the givenness of the given, in the givenness of relevant data either of sense or consciousness. Empirical objectivity is had accordingly if truly relevant data are, in fact, given. Thus, for example, in order to reach the virtually unconditioned 'My hand is white', certain fulfilling conditions on the empirical level are required. If they are in fact given on the empirical level, empirical objectivity is achieved. Lonergan, in *De Notione Structurae*, points out that empirical objectivity is of maximal import in the empirical sciences, since if questions can be raised in such fashion that their answers depend on the givenness of certain sense data, the scientists are then satisfied.[44]

Secondly, there is normative objectivity. It regards the proper use of intelligence and reason. There are faulty and correct ways of moving from data to judgment. Thus, for example, the exigences of intelligence require one not to contradict oneself in the process of uttering hypotheses. If a contradiction occurs normative objectivity is not achieved. Again, if an individual yields in his enquiring and reflecting to any influence prejudicial to the proper unfolding of the desire to know, normative objectivity is violated. Moreover, it is ultimately on normative intelligence that the validity of all logics and methods depends. Indeed, logic and method are at root a partial objectification of the normative exigences of the unrestricted, detached, disinterested desire to know. Normative objectivity differs accordingly from empirical objectivity in the same way as understanding differs from experience. It also differs from rational or absolute objectivity because, as Lonergan indicates in *De Notione Structurae*, 'everything which pertains to normative objectivity has a certain intrinsic universality; but . . . absolute (objectivity) is found in the particular and the contingent.'[45]

Thirdly, there is absolute objectivity, the third component in the non-principal notion of objectivity. Absolute objectivity is rooted in the virtually unconditioned grasped by reflective understanding and affirmed in judgment. Absolute objectivity is reached to the extent that one achieves cognitional self-transcendence in the utterance of a correct judgment. If one correctly grasps and affirms, for example, the virtually unconditioned, 'Caesar crossed the Rubicon', then the conditioned becomes a conditioned whose conditions are fulfilled and it is a *de facto* absolute. Indeed, it is in virtue of absolute objectivity that such principles as those of identity and contradiction are formulated. 'The principle of identity is the immutable and definitive validity of the true. The principle of contradiction is the exclusiveness of that validity. It is, and what is opposed to it, is not.'[46] It is crucial, however, to observe that the absolute objectivity described here arises from a grasp of a 'virtually' unconditioned and not a 'formally unconditioned', and hence involves not the intrinsically but the *de facto* absolute.

The formally unconditioned (God), which has no conditions at all, stands outside the interlocked field of conditioning and conditioned; it is intrinsically absolute. The virtually unconditioned stands within that field; it has conditions; it itself is among the conditions of other instances of the conditioned; still its conditions are fulfilled; it is a *de facto* absolute.[47]

Finally, we again stress that empirical, formal and absolute objectivity are components emergent within cognitional process and, as is the case with the elements involved in the process of knowing and the object known, together constitute a unity.

In Lonergan's view objectivity in the threefold sense just discussed is constitutive of the nexus between knowing and the known. Objectivity is the *known* relationship between knowing and the known. There is, however, a distinction between being objective, and correctly understanding and judging the nature of objectivity. Men commonly make many correct judgments each day, and hence are empirically, normatively and absolutely objective. Yet, it is possible to be objective without understanding the nature of objectivity. As Lonergan expresses it in *The Subject*, although 'these three components (empirical, normative and absolute objectivity) all function in the objectivity of adult human knowing, still it is one thing for them to function and it is quite another to become explicitly aware that they function.'[48] It is thus the aim of intentionality analysis to effect an understanding of understanding, and hence also an explicit and correct thematisation of the nature of objectivity.

For Lonergan objectivity is properly understood if and only if 'objectivity is conceived as a consequence of intelligent enquiry and critical reflection, and not as a property of vital anticipation, extroversion and satisfaction.'[49] His 'positions' on objectivity complement and crown his 'positions' on knowing and being. Truly human knowing is not a matter of any single cognitive operation or of taking any kind of intuitional look, but of experiencing, understanding and judging, of intelligent grasp and reasonable affirmation. Again, being which is identical with the real is what is known only through correct judgments and is not 'a subdivision of the "already-out-there-now" or of the "already-in-here-now" '. In like manner for Lonergan objectivity is not a matter of extroversion or fidelity to 'picture-thinking',[50] but a process involving experiential, normative and absolute moments which together enable a man to transcend appearances and simple possibilities, and to know what really and truly is so.

THE ONTOLOGICAL STATUS OF THE METAPHYSICAL ELEMENTS

The final issue to be considered in this chapter is the precise status of the metaphysical elements. Do the metaphysical elements constitute an extrinsic or an intrinsic structure of proportionate being? In other words, do potency, form and act, on the central and conjugate levels, merely assign the structure in which an understanding of proportionate being occurs, or do they also constitute the structure immanent in the very reality of proportionate being itself? For Lonergan and for anyone who accepts his basic positions on knowing, being and objectivity, the only possible position is that the metaphysical elements are truly ontological and are the structure immanent in the reality of proportionate being.

The first point and basic issue is that of the intrinsic intelligibility of being. In Lonergan's position on being, the 'Parmenidean' view—that what can be is identical with what can be thought—is acknowledged without reservation. Intelligibility is the ground of possibility, and possibility is possibility of being. Obversely, what is unintelligible cannot be understood or consequently affirmed to exist. 'By intelligibility is meant what is to be known by understanding. By the intrinsic intelligibility of being is meant that being is precisely what is so known or, in negative terms, that being is neither beyond the intelligible nor apart from it nor different from it.'[51]

If, further, one acknowledges that the real or reality is properly to be identified with being or with that which is known through correct judgments and is not to be envisaged as a subdivision of the 'already-out-there-now', then one necessarily grants that the real as identical with being is intrinsically intelligible.

A second point is that intelligibility is of different kinds. There is the potential intelligibility of presentations, or materials, for enquiry. Such presentations are in some sense intelligible, since as the focus of enquiry they are what is to be understood, and once enquiry terminates in insight they become understood. The intelligibility of the presentations as such, however, is potential and not formal. Formal intelligibility is the intelligibility of the idea, of what is grasped inasmuch as the individual is understanding something. Potential intelligibility, on the other hand, is the intelligibility of the materials in which the idea is emergent and which the idea unifies and relates. Finally, there is actual intelligibility. It is the intelligibility which is known inasmuch as one grasps a virtually unconditioned. Thus, whereas the potentially intelligible is what can be understood and the formally intelligible is what may or may be, the actually intelligible is limited to what *de facto* is.

Thirdly, just as intelligibility is intrinsic to being, so likewise the differences of intelligibility are intrinsic to being. For existing proportionate beings are known through not one but three cognitive operations. The differences of intelligibility are consequently intrinsic to being because being is known only in judgment, and judgment presupposes as its conditions of possibility the prior stages of experiencing and understanding with their potential and formal intelligible contents.

Fourthly and lastly, just as intelligibility is intrinsic to being and reality, and the intelligibility is of three different kinds, further differentiations arise, and so are likewise to be acknowledged as intelligible differentiations immanent in proportionate being. As Lonergan expresses it :

There are different formal intelligibilities; conjugate forms are of different kinds; central forms are defined differently from conjugate forms and they differ from one another by the different conjugates they unite; and potencies and acts share the definitions of the forms with which they constitute unities. For every difference in intelligibility there is a difference intrinsic to the reality of known proportionate being.[52]

In conclusion, this chapter has involved the consideration of Lonergan's basic 'positions' on being and objectivity in a manner which complements rather than repeats or summarises Lonergan's own exposition. The presentation of the position is obviously a variable dependent on the person to whom the presentation is made. It is hoped, however, that this and the previous chapter provide an added general orientation towards a personal basic critical foundation for a comprehending approach to the problem of God as it is dealt with in the final chapter.

5

The Affirmation of God

AFTER some introductory remarks relating again to context we
will proceed to an analysis of key elements in Lonergan's proof
for God's existence. We conclude the chapter with some dialectical considerations.

There is no need here to recapitulate our earlier discussion of
context. It would be helpful to note, however, that Lonergan,
in his 'Dublin Lectures on *Method in Theology*',[1] offered solid
corroboration of the general validity and importance of the stress
on context in this present work. In this regard a few specific
points may be noted.

First, Lonergan made it clear both in his lectures in Dublin
and in the question periods which followed the lectures that the
separation between the two theologies, i.e., natural and systematic, has been a mistake and that natural theology, while retaining
a certain legitimate distinctness, should be done within systematic
theology. In earlier writings, as has already been noted, Lonergan
stressed that the distinction between philosophy and theology
should most certainly be maintained but not the separation of
the two. In the Dublin lectures, however, Lonergan developed
this point more specifically in emphasising that natural theology
should be done as a moment—a distinct moment, to be sure—
within systematic theology. Here Lonergan, at least in an
implicit fashion, enters into substantial agreement with Karl
Rahner on the point that natural theology should not be carried
out alongside revelation theology but rather as an element within
it.[2]

It is important for the present discussion to understand more
precisely why Lonergan at present emphasises that natural
theology should be done within systematic theology. One key
reason became quite evident in Dublin : for Lonergan it is conversion and not proof which is at the heart of the matter in
regard to the God problem. In Lonergan's view proofs are
usually worked out by believers who wish to provide certain

grounds in reason for the faith that is in them. It is not that believers engage in a futile attempt to demonstrate their faith, but rather that they attempt to show that it is a reasonable commitment; and one way of doing this is by reflecting on man's natural capacity to know the existence of God and his success in doing so.

Lonergan does not deny that a man, by way of exception, may be led to conversion by reasoning about the God hypothesis, and whether or not it can be proven. Yet, for Lonergan, this is an exception and it should not be used as a reason for separating natural theology from systematic theology. Thus, if proofs for God's existence are emphasised or handled in such a way that the significance of conversion in the process of coming to know God is played down or overlooked, there is a real danger of lapsing into an abstract, non-existential mode of envisaging reality. On the other hand, when a proof for God's existence is worked out as a distinct moment within systematic theology, the primacy of conversion is clearly acknowledged and all danger of abstractionism is eliminated.

The recent stress placed by Lonergan on the conversion-proof problematic highlights the importance of our emphasis on the context in which Lonergan has worked out and is still working out his philosophy of God. It is precisely in stressing the fact that Lonergan is a Christan philosopher, and that in his view moral and religious conversion are *de facto* existential conditions of possibility for 'doing' an authentic philosophy of God, that one achieves a proper hermeneutical perspective in regard to Lonergan's procedures in general and his most recent developments.

Again, for Lonergan, as we have already seen in chapter 1, the highest level of human operation is the fourth level, the level of value. Moreover, Lonergan is increasingly re-emphasising the operative significance of value judgments in all fields of human cultural and intellectual endeavour. In his 'Theology and Man's Future', for example, Lonergan remarks:

Not even the natural sciences can prescind from the question of value, for the very pursuit of science is the pursuit of a value, and the contention that science should be value-free, *wertfrei*, if taken literally, implies that science should be worthless. Theology has long been aware of conflicting judgments of value, even with radical conflicts, and a successful method of theology will have a technique for dealing competently, respectfully, and honestly with this issue.[3]

Now it is clear that if value judgments are operative even in the context of the natural sciences, *a fortiori* they are involved on the level of the human sciences and above all in such an enterprise as natural theology or systematic theology.

In the light of the above comments on value it seems correct to affirm that men do not seriously reflect on the problem of God unless they consider it a value to do so. Moreover, reflection on the problem of God is intimately connected with ethics, since one is dealing here in principle with the supposed ultimate ground of all meaning *and* value. It is consequently an abstraction to attempt to consider the problem of God entirely apart from the context of value judgments. Lonergan's placing of natural theology within systematic theology thus makes sense from this perspective.

In Lonergan's formulation of what he calls 'functional specialties' in theology, systematic theology follows upon six prior specialties including dialectic and foundations, as well as doctrine. In dialectic an attempt is made to understand the 'character, the oppositions and the relations of the many viewpoints exhibited in conflicting Christian movements, their conflicting histories, and their conflicting interpretations.'[4] In foundations an attempt is made to objectify conversion, which is basic to Christian living, and to make it thematic. It follows that if one does natural theology within systematics, one does so with open eyes in regard to the role and supreme importance of value judgments and of conversion in one's existential reflection on the God problem.

It is not, however, relevant here to enter further into a discussion of the exact significance of Lonergan's inclusion of natural theology as a distinct moment within systematic theology. It has been broached as an issue because it indicates how important it is to consider the new context of Lonergan's philosophy of God and because it casts still further light on the significance Lonergan assigns to moral and religious conversion in the process of reflecting about God in so far as he is knowable by human reason.

The relevance of the cognitional underpinning for a consideration of Lonergan's proof for the existence of God is evident from intellectual conversion's position as the *de jure* existential condition of possibility for any possible personal validation of that proof. Lonergan's formal proof itself reads simply : 'If the real is completely intelligible, God exists. But the real is completely intelligible. Therefore, God exists.'[5] The point to be noted is that for Lonergan the most important element in the development leading up to and culminating in the formal proof is the '*process that identifies the real with being, then identifies being with complete intelligibility, and finally identifies complete intelligibility with the unrestricted act of understanding that possesses the properties of God and accounts for everything else*' (my italics).[6] Lonergan's formal proof for God's existence, accordingly, as worked out in section 10 of chapter XIX of *Insight*, is the natural culmination of a highly subtle and complex process. This process has its roots in cognitional analysis, its key breakthrough in the occurrence of intellectual conversion, and its full development in the intelligent grasp and reasonable affirmation of transcendent being. It is a highly dynamic process, involving a series of shifts from lower to higher viewpoints until the extrapolation from proportionate to transcendent being, from restricted acts of understanding to the unrestricted act of understanding, becomes not only possible but necessary if one is to remain perfectly faithful to the exigences of the pure desire to know. Clearly, it is only if one intelligently, critically and wholeheartedly commits oneself to the positions—the cognitional foundation stones of Lonergan's entire intellectual enterprise—that it will ultimately be possible critically to validate for oneself the legitimacy of Lonergan's formal proof for the existence of God. Indeed, to use Lonergan's expression, nothing less is required of the individual than an 'unrestricted commitment to complete intelligibility'.[7]

LONERGAN'S APPROACH TO THE PROOF FOR GOD'S EXISTENCE

This section will involve a series of preliminary observations regarding Lonergan's explicit approach to the God problem and then an exposition of key elements involved in the process leading up to and including the affirmation of God.

It is clear that chapter XIX of *Insight*, which consists of fifty-two pages of highly compact and subtle reasonings about human knowledge of transcendent being, could itself easily be the subject of a lengthy study. This latter study, however, would presuppose as its condition of possibility the type of analysis carried out in the present work.

Again, Lonergan in the interview given at the Florida Congress, pointed out that the 'fundamental thrust'[8] of *Insight* in its initial conception was a study of human understanding, and that as further questions arose chapters were added, including chapter XIX. Lonergan likewise indicates in this same interview that chapter XIX was written prior to his concern with the existentialists and is the product of a type of thinking different from his more recent writings on moral and religious conversion, etc.[9] Lonergan further states that he would be quite ready to drop chapter XIX out of *Insight* and put it inside theology. As we have seen, this is precisely what Lonergan formally proposed in the 'Dublin Lectures on *Method in Theology*'.

In *Insight*, however, Lonergan affirms that there is an intrinsic relationship between the argument in chapter XIX and the positions developed in earlier chapters. Thus, in the introductory remarks of chapter XIX Lonergan states that four main stages may be discerned in the development of *Insight*. First, attention is centred on cognitional activity as activity. Secondly, cognitional activity is studied as cognitional. Thirdly, the general case of knowledge of proportionate being and the possibility of setting up a metaphysics of proportionate being and a consequent ethics are handled. Fourthly, the last stage in the argument of the book 'is concerned with human knowledge of transcendent being'.[10]

With an eye to the relationship between the four stages of *Insight* just described, Lonergan is at pains to emphasise in chapter XIX that his discussion of human knowledge of transcendent being is not only 'continuous with all that has gone before but also is its culmination'.[11] Elsewhere, Lonergan indicates that the fourth stage of the argument in *Insight* proves to be the inevitable fulfilment of the entire account in *Insight* of understanding and judgment.[12]

The question then arises as to how Lonergan's statements about his treatment of general transcendent knowledge as being the inevitable culmination of the movement in *Insight* square with his more recent acknowledgment of the need to place chapter XIX of *Insight* within systematic theology. At first sight, it would not seem that Lonergan's acknowledgment of the need to situate natural theology within systematic theology and to envisage natural theology today in terms 'of the concrete person in a concrete context' in which the person is either becoming 'religious or is finally discovering that he has become religious and wants to know whether he is crazy or not',[13] implies a denial of the fact that chapter XIX is the inevitable culmination of the cognitional, epistemological, metaphysical and ethical considerations of *Insight*. Thus, if natural theology is done within systematic theology, it will be required of the systematic theologian who does natural theology that he be intellectually converted in the full and rigorous sense of this term. Traditionally the systematic theologian has employed philosophic tools, and the systematic theologian who does natural theology from a Lonerganian perspective should most certainly do likewise. He should do so because the argument in chapter XIX, which will be retained in systematic theology as a distinct moment, requires as the condition of possibility for understanding it the personal self-appropriation of the positions on knowing, being and objectivity. Accordingly, Lonergan, in stressing that chapter XIX should be put into systematic theology, is in no way denying that the chapter is the inevitable culmination of reflection on the implications of the positions and the expression of the ultimate condition of possibility of the positions. Rather, his concern is simply to establish the most appropriate context in which a contemporary natural theology can be fruitfully worked out.

A key point in Lonergan's entire discussion of human knowledge of transcendent being is the need to avoid assiduously any and every form of obscurantism. Basically, obscurantism may be viewed as either total or partial. 'The rejection of total obscurantism is the demand that *some* questions, at least, are not to be met with an arbitrary exclamation, Let's forget it' (my italics).[14] Further, man desires to understand completely, he wishes to know everything about everything, and this desire to understand completely is the opposite of any and every partial form of obscurantism however slight. Thus, 'the rejection of any and every partial obscurantism is the demand that no question whatever is to be met arbitrarily, that every question is to be submitted to the process of intelligent grasp and critical reflection.'[15]

Now this stress on the need for man to renounce both total and partial obscurantism is especially relevant to the contemporary scene in natural theology, since today the issue is not so much the relative merits of various proofs for the existence of God, but the very legitimacy of the question of God itself.

In this context Lonergan, in his 'The Absence of God in Modern Culture',[16] and in other recent writings as well, indicates that as a result of the shift from a classicist mentality to historical-mindedness and of man's comparatively recent discovery of his tremendous creative potential in the technological, scientific, social, and cultural spheres, God has become increasingly irrelevant to many, and is frequently viewed as a positive threat to human autonomy. In modern science, for example, precisely because it is highly specialised and methodically geared to achieving knowledge of this world and of this world only, the God hypothesis is viewed as superfluous. Likewise, as the human sciences engage in a reinterpretation of man and his world and as this reinterpretation is popularised, the agnostic world views underlying various interpretations of man—e.g., the Freudian, the Darwinian, the Marxist—enter into the life-stream and expression of the average man, and God appears to be absent even in the everyday domain of feeling, insight, judgment, decision and action. Lonergan's stress on the need to renounce obscurantism in every form thus takes on a sense of added urgency in the light of current emphases on the irrelevancy of God or even on the need to proclaim his death in order to assure the development of the potentialities of man.

Further, Lonergan's denunciation of all obscurantist tendencies is the negative side of his constant emphasis throughout *Insight* on the need to be faithful to the exigences of the detached, disinterested desire to know. Thus, the pure desire to know is of itself unbiased and open. Obscurantism, however, is either a total or partial blocking of the proper unfolding of that desire. It arbitrarily brushes aside at least some questions and to act thus is to corrupt the desire to know in its root orientation. Thus, for example, it has been stressed that the questions, 'What am I doing when I am knowing?', 'Why is doing that knowing?', 'What do I know when I do it?', are questions too basic to be dodged and also questions to which basic answers can be given. The obscurantist, however, frequently dismisses one or two, or even all three of these questions as simply beside the point. It remains, however, that the three questions are intelligent, and the fact that intelligent answers can be and are given is the proof of the legitimacy and intelligibility of the questions.

Furthermore, there is a fourth type of question which spontaneously arises, and does so within the context of the unrestricted character of the pure desire to know and reflection upon the unrestricted character of the proportionate objects of human intelligence. This fourth type of question asks about ultimate meaning, carries man beyond the realm of proportionate being into that of transcendent being, and is expressed in a rich variety of ways: 'What is the ultimate meaning of reality?', 'What is being?', 'What is the ultimate explanation of the correspondence which exists between our knowing and the known?', 'Why does anything exist?', 'Why does anything occur?', 'What is the explanation of the contingent, of the virtually unconditioned whose conditions happen to be fulfilled, of what simply happens to be the case?'.

Now, the obscurantist is quick to dismiss such questions as metaphysical and hence meaningless, or in principle unanswerable. Nor is this propensity for obscurantism absent even in the most cultured minds. As Lonergan has remarked:

Just as the misuse of the notion of nature makes it ridiculous in the eyes of those most eager to know what is to be known by understanding, so too misconception and misuse of the notion of God lead to its rejection by the very men that are most insistent in denouncing obscurantism, in demanding judgments to rest on the unconditioned, and in calling for consistency between knowing and doing.[17]

Lonergan, however, in his insistence on the need to recognise obscurantist tendencies for what they are and to purify one's consciousness from any taint of these intellectual diseases, proves himself to be quite contemporary and to offer a most striking challenge to intellectuals who, as uncritical inheritors of a Kantian or positivist attitude, are quick to lapse from a clearcut denunciation of obscurantism in scientific procedures into an evident practice of obscurantism when it comes to ultimate questions.

In his most recent lectures on God and religion, Lonergan meets contemporary opposition to the God hypothesis head-on by shifting attention for the moment from the subtleties of various proofs for God's existence to the more foundational issue of the very worthwhileness and meaningfulness of the God question itself. Lonergan thus inquires about inquiry itself. He asks, for example, why it is that acts of understanding satisfy inquiry; why it is that the grasp of the virtually unconditioned leads to judgment and yet beyond judgment to new inquiries; finally, whether it is really worth while to deliberate about whether a given course of action is truly a value and worth while. In raising such elemental and yet unavoidable questions about the meaningfulness and value of intentionality itself, Lonergan broaches the question of God and underlines its singular importance. For, inquiry about the very meaning and value of inquiry itself forces the intellectually honest individual to face the issue of ultimate meaning and value or, in a word, the question of God. The only alternative to asking the ultimate questions is a lapse into total or partial obscurantism.

One final point should be made in regard to the general matter of obscurantism. It might be objected that although no question should be arbitrarily brushed aside, certain questions are simply too difficult or so beyond the scope of the human mind that it is not only useless but indeed arrogant to attempt to find an answer to them. Such, for example, would be the attitude of a certain type of agnostic towards the question of God.

An initial response to the issue just raised is that the 'pure desire of the mind is a desire of God'.[18] As has already been noted, Lonergan, in 'The Natural Desire to See God',[19] in his 'Openness and Religious Experience',[20] in *Insight* and other writings as well, consistently develops the position that man by nature desires to know the essence of God. This unrestricted character of the pure desire to know in its orientation has already been described in chapter 4 above. Accordingly, the points to be emphasised here in response to the agnostic's implicitly obscurantist attitude are: (1) man's basic intellectual dynamism is a desire for God; (2) this natural orientation of man's intentionality towards total meaning and value justifies (indeed impels) man to attempt to think and to speak about God—that is, to make the effort to thematise his initially unobjectified orientation towards him.

It is, of course, true that 'because it is difficult to know what our knowing is, it is also difficult to know what our knowledge of God is.'[21] Yet, it is also true that 'just as our knowing is prior to an analysis of knowledge and far easier than it, so too our knowledge of God is both earlier and easier than any attempt to give it formal expression.'[22]

What Lonergan attempts in his discussion of God in *Insight* is more than the agnostic would believe possible, yet in no sense is it a blasphemous attempt at the complete explanation of God. For Lonergan God 'is not some datum to be explained. . . . He is absolute explanation, pure intelligibility in himself, and the first cause and last end of everything else.'[23]

What Lonergan aims at in chapter XIX of *Insight* is the exploration of the 'power and of the limitations of the human mind,'[24] in the context of possible human knowledge of transcendent being. Moreover, in his view, it is within the natural power of the human mind to arrive at natural knowledge of the truth of the proposition, 'God exists'. Thus, 'the notion and affirmation of God pertain to the positions, not in any incidental fashion, but as necessary answers to the inevitable questions about the idea of being and the identity of being with the real.'[25] Yet, Lonergan also recognises the limitations of human knowledge of transcendent being in its present state:

The present chapter on general transcendent knowledge is concerned to determine what we can and do know about transcendent being prior to the attainment of an act of understanding that grasps what any transcendent being is. To employ the terms that will be more familiar to many, the present chapter is concerned with the knowledge of God that, according to St Thomas Aquinas, consists in knowing that he is but not what he is.[26]

In his brief outline, 'The Natural Theology of *Insight*',[27] Lonergan asserts that his argument for the existence of God differs from the old proofs for the existence of God in two ways, and in each case it does so to meet later needs. The first difference involves a variant on the principle of causality which is considered here in the elaboration of the proof itself. The second difference involves the 'matter of taking a precise philosophic position.'[28] This difference has already been noted but it is brought up here to serve as a bridge to the discussion of the proof itself and because Lonergan considers it one of the two significant factors differentiating his approach from the more traditional elaborations of a natural theology.

Summarily expressed, Lonergan's proof for the existence of God presupposes the acceptance of critical realism. As Lonergan puts it : 'One cannot prove the existence of God to a Kantian without first breaking his allegiance to Kant. One cannot prove the existence of God to a positivist without first converting him from positivism. A valid proof has philosophic presuppositions, and the argument set forth in *Insight* is indicated in the antecedent (if the real is completely intelligible, God exists) the real is completely intelligible.'[29] Here we are at the heart of the matter. One cannot really accept the positions and hold that being is only incompletely intelligible. Thus, in a response to an enquiry by this writer regarding certain basic objections of David Burrell's to Lonergan's argument for God's existence, Lonergan wrote 'I think he [Burrell] overlooks the possibility of someone affirming the positions and rejecting the counter-positions'.[30] For Lonergan the pure desire to know is not a desire for incomplete intelligibility—questions never cease and to ask if there might be some horizon beyond which man cannot question is already to go beyond—but a desire for complete intelligibility.

Finally, and this point is absolutely crucial, it is Lonergan's view that if one confines human knowing within the domain of proportionate being—the realm of mere matter of fact—one strips it 'of knowledge not only of transcendent but also of proportionate being'.[31] The issue here is sharp and clear. Radical fidelity to the positions requires the affirmation of the existence of God. Refusal to affirm the existence of complete intelligibility (that is, God) means that one has slipped into some form of obscurantism and an implicit denial of the position which identifies being with the intelligible and the real with being.

LONERGAN'S PROOF FOR THE EXISTENCE OF GOD[32]

The approach in this section will involve an initial outline of structural elements in chapter XIX of *Insight* and then an analysis of the premises of Lonergan's formal proof. No attempt will be made to indicate every nuance developed in chapter XIX or in other writings of Lonergan, where the God problem is discussed. Rather the aim will be to highlight crucial elements in Lonergan's treatment in the hope that the reader will be led to a more thorough analysis of Lonergan's writings.

Now in Lonergan's view there are in a sense as many proofs for the existence of God as there are 'aspects of incomplete intelligibility in the universe of proportionate being'.[33] Lonergan thus refers to the well-known five ways of Aquinas as five particular instances in which the incomplete intelligibility of proportionate being leads one to the affirmation of the existence of the complete intelligibility, commonly named God. Lonergan, however, maintains that while there are many arguments for the existence of God 'all of them . . . are included in the following general form : "If the real is completely intelligible, God exists. But the real is completely intelligible. Therefore, God exists." '[34]

Lonergan's formal statement of his proof for God's existence occurs in section 10 of chapter XIX of *Insight*. This formal proof, however, has presuppositions worked out at length in the earlier chapters of *Insight* and is itself the culminating moment in the reflections which unfold in sections 2-9 of chapter XIX. More specifically, the minor premise of Lonergan's formal proof presupposes the complete acceptance of the positions on knowing, being and objectivity. The major, for its part, achieves its intelligible and probative character especially in the light of the discussion of sections 1-9 in chapter XIX.

Our approach to Lonergan's formal proof for the existence of God will involve three basic stages : (1) an initial outlining of the basic structural features of sections 1-10 of chapter XIX; (2) an analysis of the meaning and validity of the minor premise in Lonergan's formal proof of God, i.e., 'But the real is completely intelligible', and (3) a consideration of the major premise of Lonergan's formal proof—i.e., 'If the real is completely intelligible, God exists'—ending in the explicit articulation of its implicit stages of argumentation as elaborated by Lonergan in section 10 of chapter XIX. In regard to this stage, it should be noted that the major premise of Lonergan's formal proof for the existence of God is basically a statement of the full implications of the development operative in sections 1-9 of chapter XIX and so an analysis of key points in these sections will in a sense be the constitutive core of our analysis of the major premise.

We turn now to the first of the three stages in our approach to Lonergan's formal proof of the existence of God. For the sake of clarity it will be helpful first to indicate in schematic fashion basic structural features of sections 1-10 of chapter XIX of *Insight*. Sections 1-3, then, involve general considerations about the notion of transcendence in its relation to transcendent knowledge. Section 4 includes preliminary observations regarding man's ability to extrapolate from proportionate being to transcendent being.[35] Sections 5-7 treat of the idea of being in what Lonergan terms its primary and secondary components. Section 8 deals with the nature of causality and its universal applicability. Section 9 explicitly takes up the notion of God and section 10 asks whether the existence of God can be affirmed. In these sections 1-10 two basic movements in the central argument can be discerned. They involve respectively sections 4-8, and sections 9 and 10.

In the first of these movements it can be noted that in sections 4-7 Lonergan is working on the level of hypothesis and asking what being is, whereas in section 8, on causality, he moves from the level of understanding to the level of judgment and affirmation. As Lonergan puts it : 'By asking what being is [in sections 4-7], we have been led to conceive an unrestricted act of understanding. If now we ask what causality is [in section 8], we shall be led to affirm that there is such an unrestricted act.'[36] This first of the two movements, then, in sections 1-10 of chapter XIX, involves a hypothetical and a judgmental moment. The idea of being is first conceived as the content of an unrestricted act of understanding and then the consideration of the universal applicability of the principle of causality reveals that it is possible to affirm the existence of an unrestricted act of understanding.

In the second movement section 9, like sections 4-7, is on the level of hypothesis, whereas section 10, like section 8 of the first movement, is on the level of judgment and affirmation. A parallel structure is apparent in the second movement : section 9 raises the question what is God in a way that leads to an elaborate hypothesis; section 10 finds the grounds for affirming that hypothesis compelling. Although both of the movements may be spoken of as 'proofs' of God, technically it is only in the second movement that the God hypothesis is explicitly formulated as such, and then verified. It remains true, however, that the God hypothesis, which is raised as a question for understanding in section 9 and transformed into a question for reflection in section 10, presupposes and includes the first movement of hypothesis and verification regarding the unrestricted act of understanding worked out in sections 4-8.

As the final element in section 10, the formal statement of the proof is worked out in the form indicated earlier : 'If the real is completely intelligible, God exists. But . . . Therefore.'

So much for our initial outlining of the basic structural features of sections 1-10 of chapter XIX. The second and third stages in our approach involve the consideration of the minor and major premises of the proof respectively.

Before we begin our discussion of the minor premise, however, it will be helpful to make four general observations about the presuppositions, nature and intent of this proof.

First, since grasping the proof requires as a condition of possibility an acceptance of the positions and a complete rejection of the counter-positions, it will lack meaning for anyone who has not made a complete break with various currents of modern thought such as positivism, empiricism or Kantianism. As Lonergan expresses it : 'There would have to be some fallacy in the argument, if it did not presuppose a complete break with the various currents of modern thought that insist on atheism or agnosticism. But such a complete break does exist in the rejection, root and branch, of the counter-positions and in a complete acceptance of the positions.'[37]

Secondly, Lonergan's proof for the existence of God not only presupposes a complete acceptance of the positions but also concrete affirmations, within the positions, of the existence of various realities. Thus, in *Insight* there is the affirmation of the self, the affirmation of the existence of something else, indeed the affirmation of the existence of the universe of proportionate being. It is clear in the context of these diverse affirmations that Lonergan's proof is not *a priori* nor Anselmian but *a posteriori*. Thus, Lonergan's proof is not *a priori*, i.e., it is not an argument from cause to effect, but rather the converse. Again, it is not a new expression of the Anselmian argument, i.e., it does not argue simply from the conception of God to his existence, but requires that the God hypothesis be reasonably affirmed through the grasp of a virtually unconditioned. To express this in another way, Lonergan's approach to the existence of God involves going beyond a merely analytic proposition, in which God's existence is so conceived that the denial of his existence would be a contradiction in terms, to the analytic principle, in which the terms and relations of the proposition occur in a concrete judgment of fact.

Thirdly, the formal proof for the existence of God encompasses the first as well as the second of the two hypothesis-verification developments in chapter XIX as described above. Indeed, implicit in the affirmation of the existence of the unrestricted act of understanding (section 8 on causality) is the affirmation of the existence of God since, as Lonergan points out in section 10, 'our concept of an unrestricted act of understanding has a number of implications and, when they are worked out, it becomes manifest that it is one and the same thing to understand what being is and to understand what God is.'[38] Moreover, since the analysis of causality leads one to affirm that the unrestricted act of understanding exists and since it is shown in section 9 that what is meant by God is identical with the unrestricted act of understanding, it is clear that in section 8 the grounds for the affirmation of God are established. It remains true, however, that it is in sections 9 and 10 that Lonergan's formal proof for the existence of God achieves its plenitude.

Fourthly, although Lonergan presents a God hypothesis which he considers verifiable, he would be the first to acknowledge that his proof is not the last word, that the extrapolations and verifications it involves can be filled out and enriched indefinitely. It remains true, however, that in his opinion the fact of knowledge always proves its possibility, and he believes that he has shown in his discussion of God in *Insight* that man can and does arrive at natural knowledge of God.[39]

We may turn now to stage two of our approach to the formal proof, namely to the discussion of the minor premise of the proof. The minor premise is discussed before the major premise in accord with Lonergan's own procedure in *Insight*.

Lonergan's procedure in regard to the minor premise is to argue that 'being is completely intelligible, that the real is being, and that therefore the real is completely intelligible.'[40]

In chapter 4 above, it was indicated that for Lonergan being is the objective of the pure desire to know, that being is what is to be known through the totality of correct judgments, that being is intelligible because it is what is to be known through correct understanding, and what is not intelligible cannot even be understood, let alone be judged to be true and to exist. The intention of being is thus the intention of the intelligible and also the intention of the real. It is the intention of the real because by the real is meant not merely an object of thought but an object of affirmation, and being is precisely what is known through affirmation. The real accordingly is being, and since being is intelligible, the real is intelligible. This argumentation is succinct but these points have already been developed at length in earlier chapters and need not be repeated here.

Lonergan, however, not only speaks of the real as being intelligible but as being completely intelligible. The step from the affirmation of the real as intelligible to the affirmation of the real as completely intelligible is necessarily implied in the affirmation that being (with which the real is identified) is what is to be known completely only when all intelligent questions are answered correctly. As Lonergan expresses it, 'Being, then, is intelligible, for it is what is to be known by correct understanding; and it is completely intelligible, for being is known completely only when all intelligent questions are answered correctly.'[41]

The crux of this whole matter of the complete intelligibility of being, and hence also of the real, is the need to be absolutely faithful to the exigences of the pure desire to know, and to resist each and every tendency toward obscurantism. An obscurantist can believe that being is only partially intelligible. On the 'position', either being, and so the real, is completely intelligible, or else it is simply unintelligible. No middle ground is possible here. As Lonergan puts it in *Insight*:

If the real is being, the real is the objective of an unrestricted desire to understand correctly; to be such an objective, the real has to be completely intelligible, for what is not intelligible is not the objective of a desire to understand, and what is not completely intelligible is the objective, not of an unrestricted desire to understand correctly, but of such a desire judiciously blended with an obscurantist refusal to understand.[42]

There remains the analysis of the major premise—i.e., 'If the real is completely intelligible, God exists.' Its understanding requires a grasp of the four main issues of the development through sections 1-9 of chapter XIX. These are, first, the extrapolation from proportionate to transcendent being; secondly, the idea of being in its primary and secondary components; thirdly, the notion of causality, and fourthly, the identification of the unrestricted act of understanding with the notion of God as developed in section 9.

First, then, as regards the proposed extrapolation from proportionate to transcendent being one should note Lonergan's insistence that the fact proves the possibility. Indeed, the fundamental tactic throughout *Insight* is to proceed not from the conditions of the possibility of knowledge to the fact of knowledge but conversely. Thus, it is ultimately the fact of the individual's performance of self-affirmation that *proves* in a critical fashion the possibility of human knowledge. Likewise, as will be indicated, it is Lonergan's argument that an individual can perform the extrapolation from proportionate to transcendent being and that this performance *proves* the possibility of such an extrapolation.[43]

Lonergan, then, after discussing the pure desire to know as the dynamic source of man's orientation toward cognitive self-transcendence, asks if man can extrapolate not only horizontally but also vertically. Horizontal extrapolation means looking from the past to the future and anticipating future recurrence of past events. Vertical extrapolation, however, at its deepest level involves the possibility of moving 'on the side of the subject from restricted to unrestricted understanding and on the side of the object from the structure of proportionate being to the transcendent idea of being.'[44]

The question leading to the extrapolation, as Lonergan remarks here, has been raised already through the identification of the real with being—that identification which leads to the venture of asking, 'What, then is being?'.[45] In answering this question Lonergan distinguishes between (1) the pure notion of being, (2) the heuristic notion of being, (3) restricted acts of understanding, conceiving and affirming being, and (4) the unrestricted act of understanding being. The pure notion of being is simply the pure desire to know considered as the dynamic ground of all intelligent enquiry and critical reflection. Further, since the pure notion of being unfolds through acts of understanding and judging, there can be formulated a heuristic notion of being as whatever is to be grasped intelligently and affirmed reasonably. Again, although the pure desire to know is as such unrestricted in its orientation, still it can only handle one question at a time and hence must prescind from other questions while working toward a solution of the particular issue at hand.

'The pure notion of being raises all questions but answers none. The heuristic notion envisages all answers but determines none. Particular enquiries solve some questions but not all.'[46] Lonergan concludes accordingly that 'only an unrestricted act of understanding can meet the issue'[47] regarding the question, 'What is being?'

The extrapolation from restricted acts of understanding to an unrestricted act of understanding follows with a certain understandable necessity once the proper position on being is established. Thus, as was indicated in chapter 4 above, the objective of the pure desire to know is being, the totality of what is. Being, then, is at once completely universal since it includes everything—and completely concrete since it primarily refers to what in fact exists and only secondarily to what might exist. Restricted acts of understanding, however, cannot as such be an understanding of everything about everything. Restricted acts of understanding involve the grasp in some fashion of the essences of particular existents, e.g., the essence of horse, of a particular molecule, but not the grasp of the essence of being itself. Restricted acts of understanding, accordingly, have ideas as their contents. The idea as opposed to the concept is what is immediately grasped by insight prior to its utterance in concepts. The idea of being, however, can only be the content of an unrestricted act of understanding.

The extrapolation from restricted acts of understanding to the unrestricted act of understanding, and correlatively from proportionate being to transcendent being, is valid because it follows with a certain intelligible necessity from an exploration of the notion of being in terms of its objective, the totality of what is. Lonergan shows that the extrapolation is possible in the last analysis by effecting the extrapolation. Thus, the question 'What is being?' naturally arises and must be at least heuristically answered if one is to avoid a lapse into obscurantism. Lonergan does not claim that man can answer the question here and now by enjoying an unrestricted act of understanding, for then his capacity to know would not be limited, as he experiences it to be. He does claim, however, that man can heuristically answer the question, 'What is being?' by 'working out the conclusion that the idea of being is the content of an unrestricted act of understanding.'[48] Moreover, he effectively works out his conclusion, strategically excludes all other alternatives, and accordingly demonstrates the possibility of the extrapolation through concrete factual performance.

Now in pursuing the question, 'What is being?' one is led to conceive of the idea of being as the content of an unrestricted act of understanding. To conceive of such, however, and to affirm its existence are quite distinct matters. Before considering the affirmation let us pause to consider the conception by some detailed analysis of the primary and secondary components of the idea of being.

Lonergan's notion of the idea of being is perhaps the single most important notion in chapter XIX of *Insight*. Moreover, it is impossible to grasp clearly and accurately what is meant by the idea of being unless one has already arrived at a highly diversified and personally verified understanding of the nature of restricted acts of understanding. Indeed, the extrapolation from restricted acts of understanding to the unrestricted act of understanding is a subtle and refined intellectual accomplishment doomed to failure from the outset unless attempted by one who is operating from the basis of fully developed intellectual conversion.

In Lonergan's analysis, then, an idea is the content of an act of understanding and the idea of being is the content of an unrestricted act of understanding. Now, as the content of an unrestricted act of understanding, the idea of being is the idea of everything about everything. Likewise, since being is intrinsically intelligible, the idea of being is the idea of the total range of intelligibility. Again, the idea of being is one idea since it is the content of an unrestricted act of understanding and, as the act is necessarily one and not an aggregate or a succession of acts—this would be to deny its unrestricted character—so the idea is one. Again, the idea of being, though one, is of many and, though immaterial, non-temporal and non-spatial, includes the intelligibilities of the material, the temporal and the spatial. Moreover, 'there is no paradox in affirming that the idea of being is one, immaterial, non-temporal, and non-spatial, yet of the many, the material, the temporal and the spatial.'[49] There is no paradox because what is possible in regard to the content of restricted acts of understanding is *a fortiori* not impossible in terms of an unrestricted act of understanding.

In chapter 3, we indicated that although insight is always a grasp of the intelligible in the image or phantasm, the content of the insight is something above, beyond and supervening upon the mere presentations of sense and imagination. The act of insight is a grasp of *intelligible* unities and/or relationships in data. As intelligible the content of the insight is not imaginable nor is it intrinsically conditioned by the spatio-temporal domain of the material residue. This same transcendence towards the material, the temporal and the spatial is also evident on the level of reflective understanding. As Lonergan points out :

Our enquiry and insight demand something apart from themselves into which we enquire and attain insight; initially and commonly that other is sensible experience, and in it is found the empirical residue. But if sensible experience and so the empirical residue condition enquiry and insight, it is no less plain that that conditioning is extrinsic. Seeing is seeing colour, and colour is spatial, so that seeing is conditioned intrinsically by the spatial continuum. But insight is an act of understanding, and so far from being conditioned intrinsically by the empirical residue, understanding abstracts from it. Again, to grasp the unconditioned, there is a prerequisite of a known fulfilment of conditions; commonly this fulfilment lies in sensible experience; still the fulfilment is anything but unconditioned; and it is the unconditioned that intrinsically conditions a grasp of the unconditioned.[50]

The discusion of insight as intelligent grasp of the intelligible in data leads to Lonergan's distinction between the primary and secondary components in the idea of being. To understand precisely what Lonergan means by the idea of being and most especially the significance of the distinction between its primary and secondary components, one must transcend any view of knowing as essentially a dualistic, confrontational process involving an intuiting, a looking at, a beholding of and a corresponding to something else that is intuited, looked at, beheld.

In the Aristotelian-Thomistic perspective, knowing is primarily and essentially perfection, act, identity. For both Aristotle and Aquinas, sense in act is the sensible in act and intellect in act is the intelligible in act. It is true, of course, for both Aristotle and

Aquinas, that in this present world 'besides the knower in act and the known in act, there are also the knower in potency and the known in potency; and while the former are identical, still the latter are distinct.'[51] Yet, in the view of Aristotle, Aquinas and Lonergan, in the pure instance of knowledge, potency is not essential and therefore neither is distinction.

It follows that in immaterial substances, as one negates potency, so also one negates distinctions : '*In his quae sunt sine materia, idem est intelligens et intellectum* (Arist. *De Anima*, III, 4, 430a 3ff; Met., L, 9, 1075a 3 ff.). A Platonist subsistent idea of Being would have to sacrifice immobility to have knowledge; but Aristotle, because he conceived knowing as primarily not confrontation but identity in act, was able to affirm the intelligence in act of his immovable mover.[52]

Lonergan's conception of God as the unrestricted act of understanding is coincident with Aristotle's conception of the unmoved mover as νόησις νοήσεως, if νοησις has the same denotation as νοέω in the text on insight in the *De Anima* where Aristotle states that understanding grasps the forms in images.[53] Lonergan here allies himself with the medieval translation of the Aristotelian νόησις νοήσεως, as *intelligentia intelligentiae* instead of with what he terms the later conceptualist translation of the expression as 'thinking thought'.[54]

For Lonergan, then, the idea of being is the content of an unrestricted act of understanding. There are, however, three distinct ways in which the term 'intelligible' may be used in relation to the act of understanding as envisaged in the present context, and it is the second of these which is the key to our grasp of what Lonergan means by the primary component in the idea of being. First, there is in the universe of proportionate being the potential intelligibility of empirical objects. Lonergan refers to this type of intelligibility as material intelligibility.[55] Secondly, there is the intelligibility grasped inasmuch as one is actually understanding. This is the type of intelligibility which Lonergan designates not only as spiritual intelligibility—it is spiritual because it is intrinsically independent of the empirical residue—but also as intelligent intelligibility. It is intelligent intelligibility because the act of insight is intelligent. It is the intelligible content of the act of insight and in the act of insight the

Aristotelian-Thomistic theorem of knowledge by identity is verified. In the act of insight the intellect in act is the intelligible in act. Thirdly, there is the intelligible which is the definition, essence or concept. It is a spiritual intelligible because it is abstracted from the empirical residue and results from a spiritual act—the act of insight—but it is not an intelligent intelligible. Lonergan refers to the concept as the intelligible in the ordinary sense but designates the intelligible which is the content of the act of understanding as the intelligible in the profounder sense, or as the intelligent intelligible.

In Lonergan's view the primary component of any idea 'is what is grasped inasmuch as one is understanding; it is the intelligible ground or root or key from which results intelligibility in the ordinary sense.'[56] It follows, therefore, that in Lonergan's extrapolation from human to transcendent knowledge the primary component in the idea of being must be the intelligible in the profounder sense, or the intelligent intelligible.

We should recall that Lonergan defines being in terms of knowing, and so the ultimate is not being but intelligence. Consequently, for Lonergan the primary component in the idea of being is nothing other than the unrestricted act of understanding itself. In this perfect instance of knowing there is a complete identity of the intelligible and the intelligence in act.[57]

It should be clear that to understand the meaning in Lonergan's usage of 'primary intelligible' one needs to grasp the nature of the restricted act of understanding. For, it is this act which serves as the analogical basis for Lonergan's extrapolation to the unrestricted act of understanding.

There is, however, a further matter of the secondary component in the idea of being. The analogical basis in human knowledge for extrapolating to the secondary component lies in the distinction between insight and conception. In insight the intellect in act is the intelligible in act. Indeed, so total is the identity of understanding and the understood in the human act of understanding that at this level the distinction between meaning and meant, between subject and object, have not yet emerged. At this level the subject in act and the understood in act are one. The subject, however, is carried on by the inner nisus of the pure desire to know as it unfolds to utter in definitions what he has preconceptually grasped in insight. And it is this further cognitional dimension which provides an analogical basis for extrapolating to a secondary component in the idea of being. Thus, just as it is because of, and in virtue of, the act of insight that the definition is uttered, so it is because of and in virtue of the unrestricted act's understanding of itself that it understands everything of everything else.

It is crucial, of course, to avoid every form of dualistic thinking in attempting to grasp precisely the distinction between the primary and secondary intelligibles. The unrestricted act of understanding does not consist of successive moments or an intrinsic multiplicity of acts since this would mean the negation of its unrestricted character. The secondary intelligibles, however, must be truly distinguished from the primary intelligible though not necessarily as distinct realities.

The meaning of the distinction between the ordinary and profounder use of the term 'intelligible' may be grasped in terms of a test which Lonergan proposes: 'The intelligible in the ordinary sense can be understood without understanding what it is to understand; but the intelligible in the profounder sense is identical with the understanding, and so it cannot be understood without understanding what understanding is.'[58] Thus, for example, a person may be able to get an insight into a poem or an equation or marriage without understanding what understanding is. But a person cannot understand method in science or method in theology in the full sense unless he understands understanding, i.e., unless he grasps what he is doing when he makes use of phantasms, achieves insight, formulates definitions etc. Accordingly, it is in the understanding of understanding that the proper analogue is found for the primary component in the idea of being, and it is from one's understanding of understanding as grounding conception that an analogue is found for extrapolating to the secondary component in the idea of being.

In the light of the above comments it will be helpful briefly to discuss here in a preliminary fashion the secondary intelligibles in terms of God's knowledge of possible and/or actual world orders. This procedure is not in strict methodological accord with the development in *Insight* which prescinds from this problem until section 9 of chapter XIX. But, in view of the synthetic approach in the present work and the need for a certain economy in discussion, the issue of God's knowledge of the secondary intelligibles is introduced here. It should be kept in mind, of course, that it is not until section 9 of chapter XIX that Lonergan indicates that the unrestricted act of understanding is identical with God.

God as the unrestricted act of understanding primarily understands himself and secondarily everything else. Traditionally, the 'everything else' has been discussed under the rubric of possibles, actuals, etc. In the context of the classical terminology in Lonergan's analysis, the unrestricted act's understanding of everything other than itself is because of and in virtue of its understanding of itself. In other words, the primary object of the divine understanding is the divine essence and the secondary objects—the total series of possible and/or actual world orders— are what are understood in virtue of the unrestricted act's understanding of itself.

For Lonergan the secondary objects may be viewed in connection with the divine essence, or primary object, in three ways. First, as Lonergan points out in *De Deo Trino*, the secondary objects may be viewed *sub ratione entis*.[59] The secondary objects thus considered are nothing other than the divine active power, which is able to create or constitute the secondary objects. Thus, in understanding his power God understands everything which he is able to effect through his power, namely, the entire series of possible worlds. Secondly, the secondary objects viewed *sub ratione possibilis* are the total series of possible world orders viewed in their inner intelligibility and as able to be realised precisely in the fashion God understands them through transcendent divine power. Lonergan says that the secondary objects, or possibles, viewed *sub ratione possibilis* are known in the manner of 'beings of reason' because their total reality as possibles is the divine active power.[60] Thirdly, among the secondary objects are the actuals—past, present or future—and God knows them as actually existing in so far as he chooses to create them and does so.

The above distinctions in their fuller implications will be discussed at greater length in later considerations of God's efficiency, exemplarity, and final causality. Although the discussion of possibles, actuals, etc., might appear to some as irrevelant in the context of contemporary philosophising, the obverse is actually the case. Thus, for example, it is impossible to engage in dialogue with the proponents of process philosophy unless one has clearly worked out the relationship of divine knowledge, efficiency and will, to contingent realities.

In summary, then, the key point to be grasped in the discussion of the primary and secondary intelligibles is that the former is what is grasped in so far as the unrestricted act's understanding of itself is envisaged as the intelligent intelligible and the latter is what is understood in so far as the divine essence is understood to be contingently imitable and/or, in fact, imitated through the exercise of transcendent divine power. To express this in another way, the secondary intelligibles in the idea of being are what is understood in so far as the unrestricted act of understanding understands itself. The secondary intelligibles are conditioned in that they are understood because of and in virtue of the unrestricted act of understanding's understanding of itself. The primary intelligible, however, is the formally unconditioned, or the unrestricted act's primal grasp of itself considered apart from whatever is also understood in virtue of this primal understanding.

Our third basic issue preliminary to focusing on Lonergan's formal proof regards the nature of causality. Lonergan's notion of it differs from both scientific and classical metaphysical notions. In the scientific perspective a notion of causality is envisaged which relates effects to causes only within the observable world of empirical phenomena. Again, within the scholastic tradition causality has generally been formulated in metaphysical terms. Lonergan's formulation of causality, however, is in cognitional terms. It speaks of the complete intelligibility of the real, thus involving a shift from scientific and metaphysical formulations of causality 'to a transcendental formulation in terms of the manner in which . . . (man's) apprehension of the universe is to be constructed, namely, with an exigence for complete intelligibility.'[61]

The basic issue in Lonergan's treatment of causality is whether or not the three external causes—efficient, exemplary and final—may be understood and affirmed to be generally valid principles which in their fullness imply a first agent, last end, and primary exemplar of the universe of proportionate being. The approach here will be first to indicate briefly the meaning of efficient, exemplary and final causality as Lonergan understands them. Then the question will be raised regarding the issue of the universal applicability of the causes and the possibility of using them to go beyond the world of proportionate being. Finally, each of the three causes will be discussed in the context of their transcendental applicability.

The external causes may be considered in concrete instances, in principle, and in the fullness that results from applying the principles.

The three external causes, for example, may be exemplified in the concrete instance of America's endeavour to get a man to the moon and back again. In this instance the final cause is the value for America of getting a man to the moon. The exemplary cause is the design of the space ship etc. The efficient cause involves the actual work of building the space ship etc.

Now the question arises, is it possible to move from the three types of causality just exemplified, which are constantly operative in multiple human endeavours, to a consideration of the universe of proportionate being itself in terms of these causes? For Lonergan the answer is definitely yes, and it follows necessarily from two basic facts which he critically establishes. First, being is intelligible. Secondly, the universe of proportionate being is of itself incompletely intelligible.

It is important to grasp the critical moment of Lonergan's analysis of external causality in terms of its possible transcendent applicability. To begin with, then, Lonergan's reliance on the position regarding the intelligibility of being and the identity of the real with being is all-important. It is this reliance that ultimately makes it possible and necessary, if one is to remain faithful to the exigences of intelligence, to move from a limited to a transcendent exercise of causality. Further, this reliance differentiates Lonergan's approach from that of classical metaphysics. Thus, Lonergan does not basically argue from a metaphysical viewpoint but from a cognitional exigence. It is, of course, also true that he argues from the fact that the universe of proportionate being reveals itself to be incompletely intelligible and that consequently it must have a transcendent explanation. Yet, it is in virtue of the position on being as the intelligible that this latter argumentation and extrapolation can take place.

It is not necessary here to enter once again into the analysis

F

which leads to the affirmation of the positions. Quite simply, on the position being is the intelligible, and what is not intelligible cannot be. Most radically, this implies that to talk of mere matters of fact that admit no explanation is to talk about nothing. 'If existence is mere matter of fact, it is nothing. If occurrence is mere matter of fact, it is nothing.'[62] Such conclusions are 'rude and harsh'.[63] Yet, there is no reason for surprise, since they constitute the nerve of the entire approach within the position and its basic strength. Thus, if the universe of proportionate being is not in itself completely intelligible, then, either one must seek complete explanation beyond the universe of proportionate being, or else one must deny the existence of the universe of proportionate being.

Is the universe of proportionate being completely intelligible in itself? Lonergan's response is a decided no, and his reasons for his response are ultimately reducible to the fact that the questions of existence and occurrence. i.e., 'Why does the universe of proportionate being exist?', 'Why do occurrences occur?', cannot be answered within the domain of proportionate being. These questions are legitimate if one acknowledges the position on being. From them empirical science prescinds, and it cannot in principle answer them. There is no method for deriving from physics or chemistry or biology or any other similar science answers to questions of existence and occurrence. As far as empirical science is concerned existence and occurrences are simply matters of fact. The empirical scientist can, of course, explain the existence of things provisionally, in that he can say that 'B is because of A' etc. But as long as he remains within the world of empirical phenomena, he never gets beyond the virtually unconditioned, that which simply happens to be so because its conditions happen to be fulfilled.

Again, the scientist may explain one occurrence or set of occurrences in terms of others within the world of observable phenomena. So, certain events may be said to occur in virtue of a settled scheme of recurrence, e.g., eclipses of the moon or any other events which occur within the planetary system. Yet, the further question arises, 'Why the planetary system?'. Again, there are explanations of the emergence of planetary systems and these explanations lead into probabilities, etc. Yet, as Lonergan remarks, 'there is, I believe, no overarching scheme of recurrence that accounts for the emergence of schemes of recurrence.'[64]

Again, one may conclude to the existence of a certain hierarchy of being, e.g., inorganic, botanical, sensitive and rational. But the questions arise, 'Why this particular hierarchy of being? Why not another?' Probabilities may afford some response, but the very fact that one is using probabilities means that a battery of other alternatives is possible. And so, the question remains, 'Why this particular hierarchy of being?'

Finally, a whole set of questions arises which are too basic to be dodged and yet are unanswerable on the level of proportionate being alone. Thus, for example, one can ask: 'Why should the real be being? Why should the real be intelligible? What is the ultimate ground of the intelligibility of being? Why should there be a correspondence between the structure of our knowing and the known?' Reflection upon these questions reveals that although it is through the structure of our minds and cognitional intentionality that we *de facto* know that the real is being, still it is equally clear that it is not our minds which ontologically constitute being as intelligible. To put this another way, just as we know that the moon is a sphere because it has phases, even though it is not the phases which are the ontological cause of the sphericity of the moon, so also we know that being is intelligible because of the dynamic intentionality of our minds, even though it is not the structure of our minds which accounts for the fact that being is intelligible and that the real is being.

The universe of proportionate being, then, is shot through with contingency, or incomplete intelligibility, both as regards our knowing of the universe of proportionate being, and as regards what is known. Man happens to be a knower, and he happens to know in a certain fashion. But his knowing is a matter of fact and not of necessity. Moreover, man's intelligence is an enquiring intelligence, seeking its own completion through successive stages of cognitive self-transcendence and in its very quest proclaiming its own incompleteness. Human intelligence is limited and does not contain in itself the intelligible explanation of its own existence or of its isomorphism with the known. Intelligence, nevertheless, demands an explanation of its own meaning, and this explanation would not seem to lie either in itself or in the universe of proportionate being to which it is to an extent correlative.

The discussion up to this point serves to unveil a certain paradox. Human intelligence is limited and incomplete in intelligibility; so is the universe of proportionate being, since it is isomorphic to intelligence's triadic operational structure. Yet, it is only through the exercise of human knowing that the truth of the proposition 'An unrestricted act of understanding exists' can be critically validated. This paradox, of course, is at the root of the dispute between the idealists and the critical realists. The idealist might agree with Lonergan that 'our own unrestricted desire to know defines for us what we must mean when we speak of being.'[65] Yet, the idealist will conclude that man for this very reason is imprisoned within himself and incapable of knowing the noumenon, or what really and truly is. Again, the idealist might concede that the idea of an unrestricted act of understanding or of a certain formally unconditioned might serve, or indeed, must serve, as an ultimate unifying factor in our knowing. But again he would perhaps argue that this factor of unification is a category of mind which thus prevents us from knowing the thing in itself as it is in itself. For Lonergan, however, such objections are invalid. In his view the idealist overlooks the fact that it is only in virtue of the intelligent and reasonable unfolding of the pure desire to know that man can reach any intelligent grasp and reasonable affirmation at all. Consequently, for the idealist to speak of a reality distinct from the reality known through intelligent grasp and reasonable affirmation is performatively incoherent and essentially unintelligible.

In Lonergan's analysis being, or reality, is what is to be reached through intelligent grasp and reasonable affirmation. Any attempt to speak of reality in any other fashion is to deny the position on being. If, however, one grants the position on being, then one must yield to the exigence for complete intelligibility and this exigence leads through reflection on the incomplete intelligibility of human knowing and the universe of proportionate being to extrapolate to an unrestricted act of understanding and to affirm its existence. Accordingly, it is necessary to affirm the existence of an unrestricted act of understanding, an ultimate and perfect identity of knowing and known, if one is to ground in the ultimate sense the possibility of human knowledge. The ultimate condition of the possibility of human knowing and of

the positions is the existence of the unrestricted act of understanding. Though 'our knowing is possible only if ultimately
there is an identity of *Denken* and *Sein*' it does not follow 'that
in our knowledge such an identity must be genetically first.'[66]
Rather, man must first establish that he does, in fact, know and
that as a matter of fact there is some reality proportionate to
his knowing. Only after these facts are established is there 'any
hope of reaching an explanation of the possibility of a correspondence between our enquiry and understanding, our reflection and judgment, and on the other hand the real as it really
is.'[67]

Now to reach the affirmation of the existence of the unrestricted act of understanding, one must effect 'the transition from
efficient, exemplary and final causality as facts within the
domain of proportionate being to universal principles that bear
our knowing into the domain of transcendent being.'[68] Only in
successfully effecting this transition in a critical manner may we
meet the exigence for complete intelligibility, since this exigence
requires that the ultimate explanation of the universe of proportionate being be self-explanatory, in no way contingent, and the
intelligible and intelligent ground of all that is. But this is the
same thing as to say that the unrestricted act of understanding
as grasped in its full implications must be the efficient, exemplary
and final cause of the universe of proportionate being. A more
lengthy discussion of the three external causes in their transcendent applicability will shortly follow in the analysis of the notion
of God, but let us spell out the last statement briefly here. Needless to say we cannot do justice to the lengthier development of
the related part of section 9 of chapter XIX, which itself in turn,
as Lonergan notes, 'may seem too rapid'.[69] Perhaps, however,
our own remarks, stressing the presupposition of intellectual conversion, will aid towards a grasp of Lonergan's point. The basic
problem, indeed, is that the conception of causality in any of its
types must be the fruit of interiority. Thus, just as the internal
causes are conceived in relation to experience, understanding
and judgment,[70] so final, efficient and exemplary causes must
be conceived in similar fashion : final cause in relation to the
conditionedness of judgment of value, efficient cause in relation
to the conditionedness of judgments of existence and occurrence,
exemplary cause in relation to conditioned intelligibility. Within

such a heuristic conception there remains in the realms of proportionate being a three-sided incompleteness of intelligibility which
is lifted only in so far as the proportionate universe is conceived
of and judged as a reasonably realised possibility. The proportionate universe cannot be truly so judged without there being
a self-explanatory transcendent being.

We now come to the third basic preliminary issue we wished
to deal with. Up to this point the question, 'What is God?' has
not yet been formally raised. In sections 4-7 of chapter XIX the
question, 'What is being?' is raised and the answer is reached
that the idea of being is the content of an unrestricted act of
understanding, and indeed identical with such an act. In section
8 the question is asked, 'Does an unrestricted act of understanding exist?' and a consideration of the transcendent applicability
of the three causes leads to the inevitable conclusion that the
unrestricted act of understanding does exist and indeed must
exist if the exigence for complete intelligibility is to be critically
met and the ultimate condition of the possibility of the positions
affirmed.

Sections 9 and 10 in chapter XIX in a sense involve a further
expansion of sections 4-8. In section 9 the question is broached,
'What is God?' and it is concluded that when the implications
of the unrestricted act of understanding are worked out it is
seen to be identical with God. Finally, in section 10 the issue of
the verification of the notion of God is raised and a formal proof
is proposed.

Philip McShane suggests a certain rough parallel between
Lonergan's approach to the existence of God in two stages in
chapter XIX and Aquinas's treatment of the same problem in
questions 1-26 in the first part of the *Summa Theologiae*.[71]
McShane observes that just as Aquinas first offers a brief proof
for the existence of God in question 2 and then proceeds in the
next 24 questions to elaborate a much fuller hypothesis of what
God is, so Lonergan first offers an initial proof in sections 4-8 of
chapter XIX of *Insight*, but then proceeds to elaborate a much
fuller hypothesis of what God is in section 9 and a consequent
verification in section 10. Again, McShane notes the further
parallel with the procedures of modern science—he instances the
history of the neutrino—an initial suspicion or partially descriptive hypothesis is verified, grounding the search for a more

elaborate and all-embracing hypothesis which can be verified.

The chief point to the above comparison of Aquinas, Lonergan and natural science, is to highlight the fact that investigating the nature of God and proving his existence is a complex affair, and that it is always possible for a thinker to improve his God hypothesis and its consequent verification.

There are differences—indeed, very crucial ones—between the hypotheses and verifications of the natural scientist, and those of the natural theologian. For the scientist, it is not true and certain knowledge but highly probable knowledge which is the aim. For the natural theologian, however, it is possible to arrive at true and certain knowledge of the existence of God. None the less, because God is not an immediate datum of either sense or consciousness but is only analogically known, man can forever improve his understanding of the divine.

Man's knowledge of God, however, is analogical. It is of such a nature because man understands directly and, in this sense, properly only what he can first imagine, and so the proportionate object of the human intellect in this life is the essence of a material thing.[72] If, however, man can have a proper knowledge only of the essence of material things, still he can have an analogical knowledge of higher realities.

Analogical knowledge of a thing is gained in so far as something like it in some way is known. Thus, for example, although man cannot have proper knowledge of God in this life, still he can gain some understanding of human understanding and human understanding bears some resemblance to divine understanding. Yet, since human understanding only bears some resemblance to divine understanding, one must qualify the affirmation, 'God is understanding', with the negation, 'God is not understanding in identically the same way that man is said to understand.' Finally, one should affirm that God is understanding in an eminent, transcendent fashion. The technical expression for this analogous knowledge is that it is knowledge by way of affirmation, negation and eminence.[73]

Two extremes, then, are to be avoided in treating of the knowledge of God. One extreme is to anthropomorphise God, to strip him of transcendence, to reduce him to the level of man. The other extreme is to deny that there is anything in man that speaks of God, that God is in any manner immanent in his creation.

In the approach to God through analogy, acknowledgment of God in both his transcendent and immanent characteristics is operative. God is at once acknowledged to be Mystery and yet in some way knowable. God is understood to be in some sense like man and yet it is at once acknowledged that for every similarity he may share with man a greater dissimilarity is to be proclaimed.

Lonergan's entire God hypothesis, as worked out in section 9, develops the supposition that there is an unrestricted act of understanding. That development is expansive, not in the strictly deductive sense of modern mathematics but rather, in the manner of an older style of mathematics' tolerance of 'casual insights'[74] as accumulating further understanding. The development, however, has its meaning within the field of interiority defined by intellectual conversion. Within this horizon, Lonergan, in his formulation of the God hypothesis, enunciates one after another what might be called the classical philosophical attributes of God as they are catalogued in various textbooks of natural theology. What differentiates his treatment from various classical treatises is the cognitional context in which the attributes of God are articulated. Thus, just as the exigence for complete intelligibility underpinned Lonergan's whole approach in sections 4-8, so in section 9 it is in the light of the conception of God as the unrestricted act of understanding that the transcendent being is said to be self-explanatory, without conditions, either necessary or impossible, one, simple, spiritual, good, timeless, eternal, omnipotent efficient cause, omnipotent exemplary cause, free, immutable, unlimited in perfection, creator, conserver, first agent of every event, the one who applies every contingent agent in its operation, ultimate final cause of any universe and ground of its value.

It is neither practicable nor necessary to discuss individually and at length each of the attributes of God enumerated. Rather, the most significant ones will be considered here.

Basically it is in the transcendental objectives of man's self-transcending intending that the key attributes of God are proleptically revealed. Man thus intends the intelligible, not half or incomplete intelligibility, but complete intelligibility. Again, man intends the true and the real, not just knowledge of some truths, but of all truth, of the real in its every part and aspect. Finally, man intends the good, not just this or that limited good, but ultimately a goodness that is beyond all imperfections. Man, in other words, radically intends the formally unconditioned intelligible, true, real, good God.

In treating of the attributes of God, therefore, it is most in accord with the analysis of human intentionality seen in the light of its transcendental objectives, to speak of God in terms of intelligence, existence and goodness, where these are cognitionally defined. It is thus not surprising to find that the logically first attribute of God in Lonergan's definition is intelligence and not being; the latter has been defined in terms of the former.[75]

Lonergan proceeds to develop his God hypothesis from the basis of the unrestricted act of understanding. First, he indicates that as unrestricted the act would admit of no development, alteration or duality. It thus follows of necessity that for the act of understanding to understand itself as the formally unconditioned and for it to know itself as the formally unconditioned would be one and the same thing. Thus, in the primary being which is identically the unrestricted act of understanding there would be no need for or possibility of a real distinction between understanding, reflection and judgment. For God to understand himself would be precisely for him to grasp himself as formally unconditioned and to affirm himself.

Again, the primary being would be not only intelligible and intelligent in an unrestricted fashion but also unconditioned goodness and love. The pure desire to know is also the pure desire for value. The primary being, accordingly, as the objective of the notion or intention of being which is transformed into a notion of value, would be unrestricted intelligibility and goodness or, in more ultimate terms, unrestricted understanding and love. The primary being would, of course, of necessity be identically unrestricted understanding and love.[76]

Further, as already noted, the primary intelligible would be self-explanatory, unconditional, either necessary or impossible, only one, simple and without any composition. While these attributes are individually treated by Lonergan, here it will suffice to note briefly that once the unrestricted character of the primary intelligible is acknowledged in its full implications, each of these attributes is seen to belong to God. Thus, there could only be one primary being since if there were several unrestricted acts of understanding similar in all respects they would differ merely empirically and the merely empirical is not self-explanatory.[77]

Now, Lonergan, in the first 13 considerations of section 9 of chapter XIX, hypothesises about the attributes of the primary being considered in itself. Later, in considerations 14-22, however Lonergan hypothesises about the unrestricted act of understanding in its relationship to everything other than itself. This involves an analysis of the unrestricted act of understanding in so far as it is conceived as grasping everything about everything other than itself and as the exemplary, efficient, and final cause of all that exists.

As a preliminary to considering in the manner of a hypothesis the primary being as exemplary cause of the universe of proportionate being, we first develop in rather more detail certain aspects of Lonergan's understanding of the nature of the unrestricted act of understanding.

First, then, in Lonergan's view the unrestricted act of understanding or primary being would be absolute in every respect. This is brought out clearly in the designation of God as the formally unconditioned.

A virtually unconditioned is a conditioned whose conditions happen to be fulfilled and which as such is *de facto* absolute. Thus, if it is true that Caesar at one time crossed the Rubicon, it will never be true that Caesar did not cross the Rubicon at the time in question. God, however, in Lonergan's hypothesis, is a *de jure* absolute. Thus, whereas the universe of proportionate being involves an interlocking field of conditioning and conditioned elements, God—the formally unconditioned—has no conditions and 'stands outside the interlocked field of conditioning and conditioned: [he] . . . is intrinsically absolute.'[78] It follows that God is immutable and that consequently his 'knowledge or will or production of the created universe adds only a *relatio rationis* to the *actus purus*.'[79] This is a position which Lonergan first enunciated in his doctoral dissertation on operative grace in Aquinas, and which is clearly his own position in *Insight*. God is in no way passive but rather totally active. God's knowledge would be the cause of the created term of his knowledge and in no way the result of the created existent's action upon him. In this view Lonergan stands in absolute opposition to any position which would hold that in some way God is acted upon by his creatures or learns from them what they freely choose to do. For Lonergan it would be a contradiction in terms for God, as the formally unconditioned unrestricted act of understanding, to be in any sense in intelligible dependence on anything else.

Again, and here we move more proximately into a discussion of the unrestricted act of understanding as exemplar-cause of the universe of proportionate being, God's knowledge of a world order would be prior to his knowledge of the individual parts of the order. In other words, Lonergan, because of his dynamic intellectualist view of knowing, cannot grant that God first, so to speak, grasps isolated things such as electrons, cats, men, grace, etc., and only secondarily and derivatively world orders. Here lies the error of the conceptualism which 'places conception before understanding and things before their orders.'[80] For Lonergan, however, just as insight is an understanding of many through one, e.g., 'the infinity of positive integers is grasped by us in the insight that is the generative principle of the relations and the terms of the series,'[81] so it is in virtue of God's simple grasp of himself that he grasps all else and in the grasp of all else the order of any universe is prior to its parts and understood as such. The unrestricted act of understanding in so far as it understands itself, understands everything else as well—the totality of possible or actual world orders—and is thus exemplary cause of whatever world order might be creatively realised.

To indicate God's exemplary causality from the reference point of the exigence for complete intelligibility and the incomplete intelligibility of the universe of proportionate being, the existing universe is seen to be conditioned in its intelligibility as well as in its existence and goodness. It is constituted of an interlocking field of conditioned beings mutually conditioning and being conditioned. According to the exigence for complete intelligibility, however, no conditions can be fulfilled simply at random—what is fulfilled simply at random is a mere matter of fact and the ultimately unexplainable mere matter of fact cannot be—and this means that all conditions must be fulfilled according to some exemplar existing outside the field of conditioning and conditioned which intelligibly grounds the entire order in its immanent internal unity. It thus emerges that because the immanent order of the universe of proportionate being is not unconditioned and self-explanatory, it must be viewed as exemplarily grounded in an unrestricted act of understanding which in understanding itself grasps all possible and actual world orders as well.

This discussion of the unrestricted act of understanding envisaged hypothetically as exemplary cause of the immanent order of the universe leads to its consideration as identically omnipotent efficient cause of the created universe. Lonergan's analysis of God as omnipotent efficient cause of the universe constitutes the basis of his consideration of the primary being as creator, conserver, first agent of every event, and the one who applies every agent to its operation. Accordingly, Lonergan's analysis of the nature of efficient causality must be precisely understood, since upon it depends his view of God as creator, conserver and first agent.

Lonergan has, in fact, formulated his understanding of the nature of efficient causality in a major book review,[82] in various Latin treatises,[83] and in *Insight*. It is not possible here to enter into all the nuances involved, but it must suffice to indicate Lonergan's basic position and the fundamental counter-positions which must, in his view, be avoided.

For Lonergan the metaphysical condition of the truth of the proposition that A causes B is the reality of a relation of dependence in B with respect to A. The key points to be grasped in regard to this definition are the following: (1) efficient causality, as such, in no sense involves a change in the agent as agent. As Lonergan expresses it in a homely but pointed example: 'The fire does not change when it ceases to cook the potatoes and begins to cook the steak.'[84] (2) Efficient causality in no sense is to be thought of as an influx going out from the agent to the patient which, so to speak, occupies the space intermediate between the agent and that which is acted upon. Lonergan refutes this counter-position by pointing out that if efficient causality is an influx, then 'it would seem that there must be an infinity of influences for each case of efficient causality. For if the influx is a reality, it must be produced itself; that production would involve a further influx, and that influx a further production.'[85] In other words, efficient causality cannot involve the exercise of an influx so that efficient causality as such would be a reality added to the agent as agent. The reality is, in fact, the effect itself as intelligibly dependent on the agent, as possessing a real relation of dependence in regard to the agent, and so the action as action is predicated of the agent as agent by extrinsic denomination.

Further, Lonergan claims that his analysis of the nature of efficient causality is in accord with the most refined positions of Aristotle and Thomas. As he notes in *Grace and Freedom*:

> The fundamental point in the theory of operation is that operation involves no change in the cause as cause. On Thomist analysis it involves a formal content between cause and effect; this is the procession, *ut ab agente in aliud procedens*. On Aristotelian analysis it involves a real relation of dependence in the effect. The two analyses are really identical though terminologically different. The consequent difficulty in terminology is heightened by the large variety of senses in which St Thomas employs the word, *actio*.[86]

God as efficient cause would be creator, conserver, first agent of every event and the one who applies every agent to its operation. First, God would be creator since as formally unconditioned he can presuppose nothing other than his own actuality for creating. He must then cause the total reality of what is. Likewise, since the metaphysical condition of the truth of God's creating of the universe of proportionate being is the reality of a relation of dependence in the universe with respect to God, he must also be the conserver of the universe since if the universe were to cease to be in a relation of dependence in regard to God, it would no longer exist.

Further, God would of necessity be the first agent of every event in the universe. Thus, since God alone can create, he alone is the proportionate cause of all existence and occurrence. All finite causes, accordingly, are causes in the essential rather than in the existential sense, that is, they are not causes of existence as such but of specific types of effects. As Lonergan expresses it: 'All finite causes are instruments naturally proportionate to producing effects as of a given kind, but not naturally proportionate to producing effects as actual occurrences.'[87] God, then, is of necessity the first agent of every event, for he alone is capable of producing existence and actual occurrences as such.

Again, God would apply every contingent agent to its operation. This is so because the finite agent cannot create, it must presuppose an object on which it may act, the proper constellation of suitable relations between itself and that on which it acts, and non-interference on the part of other causes. It is clear that the finite agent has no control over these conditions, since they must all be fulfilled in order that it may function as agent. Moreover, it is no solution to appeal to other finite causes, since they are equally finite and conditioned. The only solution, as Lonergan notes, 'is to postulate a master-plan that envisages all finite causes at all instants throughout all time, that so orders all that each in due course has the conditions of its operation fulfilled and so fulfils conditions of the operation of others.'[88] The only subject of such a master-plan would be the divine mind, and so God must be the principal agent in the execution of such a plan.

God, then, is not only the cause of all finite causes in their being, but he is also the principal cause of whatever finite causes cause, for it is God who orders it so that the conditions for each and every finite causal operation are fulfilled. Thus, just as it is the typist and not the typewriter who is the chief cause of the typed page, so it is God who uses the universe of finite causes as his instruments in applying each cause to its operation and who is, therefore, the principal cause of each and every agent.

Here the close connection between God's exemplary and efficient causality emerges most clearly. God creates through the exercise of his omnipotent efficient causality but he operates in accord with an intelligible plan and hence his intellect may truly be called the cause of things. Thus, in Lonergan's analysis, it is in virtue of his intelligence that God moves all things to their ends. For 'God causes every event and applies every agent and uses every operation inasmuch as he is the cause of the order of the universe.'[89] Accordingly, it is not by a peculiar activity that God controls each event. Rather it is because he controls all that he controls each, and he does so because he alone can be the cause of the order of the universe on which every event depends.

As for God's final causality, it is intrinsically related to his exemplary and efficient causality. For if it is in virtue of the divine plan that God moves all created things to their proper ends, it is because he grasps the order of the universe as a possibility *worth* realising creatively that he brings it into being.

The universe of proportionate being is not unconditioned in its goodness any more than it is in its intelligibility or its existence. Man, however, is unrestricted in his intention of the good, just as he is in his intention of the intelligible, the true, and the real. As Lonergan notes, 'Implicit in human enquiry is a natural desire to know God by his essence; implicit in human judgment about contingent things there is the formally unconditioned that is God; implicit in human choice of values is the absolute good that is God.'[90] It is thus in virtue of his orientation toward the good beyond criticism that man asks for an explanation of the existence of partial goods and of the limited good that is the order of the universe.

If the limited value that is the existing universe is to be intelligible, it must be grounded in unlimited goodness and value since as a limited good it is not self-explanatory. The value, then, that is the universe of proportionate being, as a *reasonably* realised possibility, must be the object of a free rational choice. The choice cannot be necessitated for this would introduce limitation into the rational consciousness which chooses and hence would not provide an ultimate intelligible explanation. Nor can the free choice be arbitrary for the arbitrary as an ultimate is unintelligible and hence could not be.

It follows that the unrestricted act of understanding, identically the perfect good, would be the source of the value that is the universe of proportionate being. So, just as an individual human being can reasonably choose to realise a particular good or order as a value, so God as identically unrestricted intelligence and goodness can freely choose to realise a particular world order. Of course, it is because of God's unrestricted love for the primary value and goodness which he himself is that he freely chooses to realise a finite instance of the good. God, then, chooses to realise a particular world order out of love for his own excellence and goodness, not in order to gain anything, but to share. God's free realisation of the universe of proportionate being is the result of a love of the value (himself) which overflows. 'God did not create the world to obtain something for himself, but rather overflowed from love of the infinite to loving even the finite.'[91]

It is then, above all, in his final causality that God overcomes contingency at its deepest level and is revealed as personal. Final cause is the cause of causes. This is properly understood only in a personalist context since final causality is only operative when the end is apprehended as good. The universe of proportionate being is then most properly viewed not as the actualisation of some plan or blueprint such as might be drawn up by some architect or engineer, but rather as the work of infinite love-intelligence originating in a freely espoused act of creative self-transcendence the value that is the universe.

Two issues which Lonergan treats in section 9 of chapter XIX remain for our brief consideration. These are the relationship between divine transcendence and human freedom, and the problem of evil and sin.

To understand Lonergan's position on the relationship between God's infallible knowing, his irresistible willing, and his absolute efficacy in creating, we should briefly examine his position on God's timelessness and eternity.

The main strategy of Lonergan's treatment of God's timelessness and eternity is to strike at the root of fallacious thinking in this area by making clear that eternity is nothing like time. Questions such as 'Does God know today what I shall do to-morrow?' or 'Does God's knowledge of tomorrow's affairs necessitate their happening?' are typical expressions of the pseudo-problems which arise when God's eternity is not properly grasped.[92] As Lonergan notes in commenting on Aquinas's view:

To a temporal being our four-dimensional universe has three sections: past, present and future. To an eternal 'now' this division is meaningless. On this point St Thomas never had the slightest doubt: he was always above the pre-Einsteinian illusions that still are maintained by our cosmology manuals; strenuously and consistently he maintained that all events are present to God.[93]

The 'now' of the primary being is timeless, eternal. There is no continuous time in God, for he is spiritual, and continuous time presupposes the empirical residue and the material. Nor is there ordinal time in God because there is no development in God. God, accordingly, is in his eternity without beginning or end, and without any succession. Lonergan would thus concur with Boethius that God's eternity is 'the simultaneously whole and perfect possession of interminable life.'[94]

It is a fallacy, then, to ask such questions as, 'Does God know today what I shall do tomorrow?', etc. The eternal 'now' of God is completely outside the network of temporal relations. Thus, in the case of the eternal 'now', 'all instants are one and the same instant; and so what is true at any instant is true at every instant.'[95] It is then simply an illusory figment of the imagination to speak of a before or an after, forethoughts or afterthoughts, in the context of God's eternal 'now'. God simply cannot be said to know something before it happens, not because he is not all-knowing, but because he knows nothing before or after, but in an eternal 'now' to which everything is present.[96]

There is a further problem regarding the relationship between God's infallible knowing, irresistible willing, and absolutely efficacious realising of the human act of choice and the integrity of the free choice. How, in a word, is it possible to reconcile the existence of the divine transcendence and human freedom? Does not God's infallible knowledge necessitate human choice? Is not this especially the case since God's knowledge is the cause of creation and in no way determined by it?

Lonergan makes no attempt to explain the divine being itself in so far as it transcends by its very nature the order of contingence and necessity. In his view, such an attempt would be a yielding to the fallacious idea that God is, in the last analysis, a datum to be explained by man, rather than the absolute explanation of all the data man possesses. Rather, he engages in an analysis of what metaphysical conditions are necessary and sufficient for the truth of the judgments that God understands, affirms, wills and effects the universe. It emerges in the course of the analysis that there is no contradiction in saying that God infallibly knows, irresistibly wills and efficaciously brings it about that a certain contingent event, e.g. a free choice on the part of a man, occurs contingently.

First, Lonergan points out that, in the light of God's immutability as agent of creation and the truth that he remains entitatively the same whether he creates or not, whatever is said contingently of God requires as condition of its truth the existence of an appropriate contingent reality. Lonergan further indicates that it necessarily follows that two propositions which require for their proper verification the same existential reality or appropriate term cannot necessitate each other except by a conditioned necessity. In the present case, the proposition, 'God knows, wills and effects that this created free act be', and the proposition, 'This created free act exists', are both verified in the same reality, namely the created free act itself. And even though if God knows, wills and effects that a created reality exists, it is impossible for it not to be, still the existence of the free act itself is a metaphysical condition of the truth of the proposition that God knows, wills and effects that the free act exists, and so the divine efficacy does not impose any more than a conditioned necessity upon this consequent.

The argumentation just elaborated is negative in that it does not attempt to explain how it is possible for God through his transcendent activity to know infallibly, will irresistibly and bring about efficaciously—in total causal independence of the created realities—the existence of truly free acts. On the other hand, it does clearly establish that no argumentation which claims that there is a contradiction between the affirmation of the absolute divine transcendence and that of the reality of human freedom is valid.

The last problem which Lonergan discusses in section 9 of chapter XIX is the problem of evil and sin. This problem, highly complex, touches man most profoundly. It might be objected consequently that to handle evil in the highly rational way Lonergan does here is not adequate. Suffice it to remark that it is only in a theological context that the problem of evil in its full existential dimensions can be adequately handled. Yet, it remains true that within a theological context even a discussion of evil in its more philosophical aspects will still occupy a valid and important place. And so Lonergan raises the problem of evil in the context of God's efficient causality of everything that is. If God is omnipotent efficient cause, first agent of every event, the one who applies every agent to its operation, is he not also the cause of sin and evil?

Lonergan's basic response to the problem of evil is to distinguish between basic sin, moral evil and physical evil. Basic sin is 'the failure of free will to choose a morally obligatory course of action or its failure to reject a morally reprehensible course of action.'[97] By moral evils Lonergan means the consequences of basic sins—e.g., moral evils of omission, the execution of illicit proposals. Finally, by physical evils Lonergan means the shortcomings of a world order which consists in what he calls a generalised emergent probability. In such an order neither physical nor moral evil presents a fundamental problem, and so we omit further discussion of their intelligibility.[98]

Now as regards basic sin, the point to grasp is that there is no point : in other words, that in basic sin there is no intelligibility to be grasped. It is simply the irrational. But as the simply irrational or the unintelligible, sin cannot be in intelligible dependence on anything else. Sin, in other words, cannot have a cause, for a cause is correlative with its effect and an effect is what is in intelligible dependence on something else. Since basic sins therefore have no cause, God cannot be their cause. Nor is this contradicted by the proposition that God is the cause of every event. For basic sin is not an event but rather consists 'in a failure of occurrence, in the absence in the will of a reasonable response to an obligatory motive.'[99] Lonergan further indicates that when a problem contains the irrational it can only be dealt with in a highly complex fashion. Thus, because of the irrationality of basic sin, one is led to distinguish between what God wills to happen, what he wills not to happen, and what he permits to happen. 'Besides the being that God causes, and the non-being that God does not cause, there is the irrational that God neither causes nor does not cause, but permits others to perpetrate.'[100] And why does God permit basic sin? In essence because it is not an evil but a good to create a being so excellent that it possesses rational self-consciousness and freedom of choice, and to allow it room to operate freely.

After this lengthy digression on basic preliminaries we return to section 10 with its focal syllogistic argument. The section raises the question 'Does God exist?' where now one ought to mean by God that understanding which one has achieved through the preliminaries. The existence of God will be known, like any other existence, through the grasp of a virtually unconditioned and a rationally posited 'Yes'. It is true that what is affirmed to exist is the formally unconditioned that is God. But, in the process of reaching the affirmation of the existence of the formally unconditioned that is God, what reflective understanding grasps is 'not the formally unconditioned that God is and that unrestricted understanding grasps, but the virtually unconditioned that consists in inferring God's existence from premises that are true.'[101]

It is true, of course, that in God's case 'it is one and the same thing for him to know what he is and whether he is.' His knowledge of himself consists 'in a grasp of the formally unconditioned and as the grasp answers the question, What? so the unconditioned answers the question, Whether?'[102] It is not true, however, that the two questions have a simple answer in our knowledge. We must first ask 'What is God?' and only after we have extrapolated from the restricted act to some hypothesis on the transent can we ask whether the extrapolation and its implications are valid and true.

Let us return to the major premise of Lonergan's formal proof : 'If the real is completely intelligible, God exists.' The manner in which the antecedent is both intelligible and true has been indicated in our treatment of the minor. The source of meaning of the consequent has been indicated by the immediately previous discussion.

Lonergan now proceeds in the following manner. First he affirms that if the real is completely intelligible, then complete intelligibility exists. Secondly, he adds that if complete intelligibility exists, the idea of being exists. Finally, he concludes that if the idea of being exists, God exists for

If the idea of being exists, at least its primary component exists. But the primary component has been shown to possess all the attributes of God. Therefore, if the idea of being exists, God exists.[103]

As regards the first stage (namely, the existence of complete intelligibility) it has already been shown in the analysis of the minor premise that being is completely intelligible and that the real is being and, therefore, completely intelligible. It thus follows that just as the real could not be intelligible if intelligibility were non-existent (since the real is not merely an object of thought but an object of affirmation), so in similar fashion the real could not be completely intelligible unless complete intelligibility exists. This argument, of course, presupposes the acceptance of the complete coincidence of the real and being. It is neither possible nor necessary here to enter once again into an analysis of the process which leads to the acceptance of the positions. It must suffice to state that in the minor premise the complete intelligibility of the real is demonstrated and that it follows with analytic necessity that if the complete intelligibility of the real requires that complete intelligibility exist, then if the minor is correct it must be affirmed that complete intelligibility exists.

Lonergan next states that if complete intelligibility exists, the idea of being exists. For, there are three types of intelligibility: material, abstract and spiritual. Intelligibility is material in the objects of physics, chemistry, biology and sensitive psychology. Intelligibility is abstract as uttered in concepts—e.g., in concepts of unities and laws. Intelligibility is spiritual when it is identical with the act of understanding. Material intelligibility is incomplete for it is contingent in its existence and occurrence, and includes a merely empirical residue of individuality. Abstract intelligibility is incomplete because it occurs only in the self-expression of spiritual intelligibility. Finally, spiritual intelligibility is incomplete as long as it can enquire. It follows that the only possibility of complete intelligibility is a spiritual intelligibility which cannot enquire because it already understands everything. And such an unrestricted understanding is the idea of being.

Lonergan concludes by stating that if the idea of being exists, God exists since the idea of being in its primary component has been shown to possess all the attributes of God.

The core of the argument is the process which identifies the real with being, being with complete intelligibility, and complete intelligibility with the unrestricted act of understanding that possesses the attributes of God and explains everything else. The argument, of course, presumes the affirmation of some reality— the critical affirmations of the self, the typewriter and the universe of proportionate being are presumed to have been mediated by earlier sections of *Insight*—but it is in the unfolding of the positions in their ultimate implications that the expansive moment in the argument consists and from which the rest follows.[104]

DIALECTICAL CONSIDERATIONS AND CONCLUSION

The following dialectical considerations are intended to highlight key aspects of Lonergan's position on general transcendent knowledge, to aid in the reversal of various counter-positions and to serve as a conclusion to this work. We begin these dialectical considerations with a brief analysis of and reply to certain difficulties recently raised by David Tracy regarding the context-content problematic in Lonergan's approach to the problem of

God in *Insight*. This confrontation with Tracy is an appropriate
way to begin the conclusion of the present work because throughout we have maintained both that it is essential to distinguish
clearly between context and content in Lonergan's treatment of
the God problem, and that moral and religious conversion must
be viewed as *de facto* and not *de jure* existential conditions of
possibility for critically verifying the correctness of Lonergan's
approach to the divine.

David Tracy, in a paper prepared for Ongoing Collaboration :
The International Lonergan Congress, in an initial criticism of
Lonergan's approach to the God problem, states that it is
necessary in the contemporary context to critically ground moral
and religious conversion before entering into a discussion of the
question of God.[105] In Tracy's view, however, Lonergan does
not effect this critical grounding in *Insight*. Consequently chapter
XIX is not related in the same degree of adequacy to the first
eighteen chapters of *Insight* as each of the earlier chapters is
related to what precedes it.

Furthermore, for Tracy the problem of the relationship of
moral and religious conversion to the question of God is not
simply a contextual problem. As Tracy himself puts it :

One could reply . . . I realise, that it is *merely* a contextual task,
i.e., that desirable as such critical explicitation of religious meaning
may be for the discussion of God-language, it is not necessary
precisely because the religious meaning is an existential condition
of the possibility of successfully responding to the question of the
existence of God but not necessarily a transcendental condition of
possibility. But this response would, I believe, be inadequate.[106]

For Tracy the critical grounding of moral and religious conversion is not simply a matter of providing a suitable context for an
adequate contemporary discussion of the question of God, but
is required 'as essential to the explicit argumentation'.[107] In
Tracy's view the critical enquirer needs to be morally and religiously converted prior to his engagement in any adequate demons-
tration of the existence of God and he must also be capable of
explicating the meaning of the two conversions and of critically
grounding them prior to any discussion of the God question.
Finally, Tracy does acknowledge that the argument in chapter
XIX could be critically re-expressed 'in the critical context of
the historically conscious, intellectually, morally and religiously

converted men'[108] but, until this is done Tracy submits that one is not discussing contemporary man and the problem of God but rather one is discussing a crucial aspect of contemporary man's contemporaneity (viz., intellectual 'conversion' and its metaphysical implications) and then reinterpreting the traditional argument from contingency in terms of that intelligibility. In short until such explicitations are made, chapter XIX is not related intrinsically to the first eighteen chapters of *Insight* in the exact manner that each of these eighteen chapters is related to the previous ones.[109]

Tracy's objections involve a number of issues which bear on the present work in one fashion or another and so we will undertake to respond to some of them. On the positive side and in agreement with Tracy, in the light of Lonergan's own development and current emphases, we would allow that it would be advisable to develop a natural theology within systematic theology. In this approach, of course, moral and religious conversion would be explicitly thematised prior to the development of a natural theology. Moreover, as already noted, Lonergan in recent discussions has acknowledged that the writing of *Insight* took place before he turned seriously to the existentialists and that no doubt he could write *Insight* quite differently now. Lonergan, accordingly, would be quite willing to admit that any number of nuances and improvements could be added to the original text of *Insight* and most especially so in the case of the later chapters.

None the less, a number of questions remain. Is a critical grounding of moral conversion required, as Tracy suggests, in order to ground critically Lonergan's argument in chapter XIX? An initial answer is that in Lonergan's view a consideration of the moral not only does not enter into the intrinsic argument of chapter XIX, but it could not be introduced into the process of argumentation as developed there. Thus, in a written response to certain questions submitted to him by this writer Lonergan replied that man's transcendental openness to value is not part of the objective process presented in *Insight*.[110] Lonergan acknowledged that 'man's openness to value and to God's grace are conditions of his being open to a religious interpretation of the universe as a concretely possible-to-him option.' But, at the same time, he insisted that 'the proof is a matter of experience, understanding and factual judgment.'[111] For Lonergan, then, the fourth level of consciousness is not involved as an *intrinsic moment* of the proof itself, but 'value, specifically religious value, and a religious *Weltanschauung*, and the option for these are needed on the existential level of consciousness for the others (experience, understanding and judgment) to function without hindrance.'[112]

Thus, Lonergan would not admit that a critical grounding of moral conversion is required in order to ground critically his proof for God's existence. He therefore still considers his proof valid.[113] And, although he acknowledges the need of moral and religious conversion in the subject to enable him to demonstrate God's existence without hindrance, still it is through an analysis of the positions on knowing, being and objectivity in their full implications that the proof as worked out in *Insight* is articulated and critically grounded.

Here we are not of course, taking any position on the possibility of working out a proof for God's existence based on moral consciousness. We simply maintain that Lonergan's proof of God as worked out in *Insight* is critically established and valid, and that even if chapter XIX is transposed into systematic theology, a critical grounding of moral conversion need not—indeed cannot—be introduced into the objective process of the proof. In other words, a critical grounding of moral conversion is not a *de jure* but *at most* a *de facto* existential condition of possibility for verifying the proof of God's existence as Lonergan works it out.

There is, moreover, the further question regarding the very meaning of a 'critical grounding' of moral conversion. There would seem to be indications in *Insight* itself that Lonergan does invite the reader to a certain 'critical grounding' of ethical consciousness inasmuch as he invites the reader to self-appropriate his moral or rational self-consciousness. In the performance of this process of self-appropriation the individual comes to an existential understanding that his doing ought to be in accord with his knowing. So, if by a critical grounding of moral conversion is meant the self-appropriation of rational self-consciousness, then it would be necessary to insist that at least in principle Lonergan even in *Insight* has already offered a critical grounding of moral conversion in an incipient fashion. Granted that the critical grounding is germinal, it is no less truly operative in

Insight. Finally, it would also appear that Tracy's objection to
the effect that chapter XIX is not related to the earlier chapters
in the same way in which the earlier ones are related to those
that precede them is open to question. It would be more accurate
to say that the analysis of the fourth level of consciousness in
Insight is not nearly as developed as are the analyses of the first
three levels of consciousness, even though the basic structure of
the level of decision is in its essential traits elucidated.

There is, however, the further issue of the 'critical grounding'
of religious conversion. On this issue we should make certain
distinctions clear. First of all, the 'critical grounding' of religious
conversion must not and cannot in principle ever be construed
as being a *de jure* or transcendental condition of possibility for
arriving at true and certain natural knowledge of God. Indeed,
whatever the value may be in doing natural theology within
systematic theology—and it is considerable—still the distinction
between nature and grace, and more specifically between natural
and supernatural knowledge of God, must be maintained.
Lonergan rigorously upholds the validity and relevance of this
distinction for contemporary discussion.[114] In like manner,
Lonergan continues to uphold the possibility and, in fact, the
contemporary achievement of natural knowledge of God.[115]

To speak of critically grounding religious conversion, indeed
to speak of religious conversion, as a prior essential step to the
God argument is incompatible with the position. It shows a
failure to preserve the distinction between nature and grace and
the distinction between natural and supernatural knowledge of
God. These distinctions require that religious conversion be at
most a *de facto*, certainly not a *de jure*, condition of possibility
for natural knowledge of God.

Moreover, one must be most cautious in speaking of 'critically
grounding' religious conversion. It is true that apologetics continues to enjoy a certain validity. It is retained in a certain refined
and ecumenically oriented fashion in the fourth functional
specialty, Dialectic. It is also true that the act of faith must be
reasonable. It is not true, however, that one can rationally
demonstrate the necessity of the faith commitment. Accordingly,
no critical grounding of religious conversion could ever be made
part of the objective process of affirming through reason the
existence of God. Moreover, as Lonergan continues to emphasise,

the gift of love which is the core of religious conversion is so foundational that it needs no critical justification. It is the first principle from which flows all that the Christian believes and says and does.

The next stage of these brief dialectical considerations will involve a discussion of certain objections.

Edward MacKinnon's basic objection to Lonergan's proof for the existence of God is that Lonergan 'has not succeeded in establishing the complete intelligibility of being'.[116] It becomes clear upon analysis, however, that MacKinnon's objection is based upon a fundamental rejection of Lonergan's 'position' on being. Thus, early in the article in which MacKinnon explicitly takes up Lonergan's proof for the existence of God he states the following:

Lonergan's methodology precludes any recourse to the divine mind at this stage of the development [the development in *Insight* prior to Lonergan's explicit discussion of the God question in chapter XIX]. He has not, accordingly, excluded the possibility of some thing or some aspect of a thing existing which is not intelligible. This unintelligible 'thing' would not be a being according to Lonergan's definition of being. Yet, it would be a being in the more customary sense of the term, 'that which exists,' and, apart from terminological quibbles, would be an aspect of reality which is unintelligible.[117]

Now the issue here is really quite a simple one. Either Lonergan's position on being is valid or it is not. If it is valid, then it makes no sense to speak of the existence of beings in a more customary sense of the word which would be unintelligible. But if it is not valid, then the issue of whether or not there might exist beings which are not intelligible is completely open. It is not possible, however, at this stage of the present work, to return once again to an analysis and defence of Lonergan's basic position on being. The 'position' has already been adequately exposed and defended and this being the case, MacKinnon's objection has already been met.

Two further comments about MacKinnon's objections are in order. First, he objects that in failing to distinguish between intrinsic and projected intelligibilities Lonergan overlooks the fact that 'there are cases in which one understands correctly, and yet the intelligibility grasped is not primarily the intelligibility intrinsic to being, but the intelligibility intrinsic to a man-made explanatory system which is used to systematise the pertinent data',[118] and in overlooking this fact Lonergan fails to establish the complete intelligibility of being. Now, the objection of MacKinnon just cited was basically met in chapter 4 of this work. There it was indicated that all understanding involves a grasp of intelligibility or possibility of being prior to reflective understanding and judgment and that, accordingly, the proper distinction is not between immanent and projected intelligibility but between understanding and judgment.

It may prove illuminating at this point to introduce briefly certain comments on 'spheres of being' made by Lonergan in various lectures on meaning during the past few years. For Lonergan, then, it is one thing to say that the moon exists and quite another to affirm that the logarithm of the square root of minus one exists. In both instances the verb 'exist' is used but in quite different senses and these different senses indicate different spheres of being. Thus, to say that there exists the logarithm of the square root of minus one means that you can find the logarithm of the square root of minus one by deriving it within an appropriate mathematical system, but it does not mean that such a mathematical entity exists in the same way as the moon exists. A distinction accordingly must be drawn between the restricted spheres of the merely mathematical, the merely logical, the merely hypothetical, the merely figurative, the merely mythical, etc., and the sphere of real being. There is, of course, a similarity between the spheres in that the contents of the different spheres are rationally affirmed, but they differ vastly because the conditions to be fulfilled for the rational affirmation to occur differ so much in each case. Thus, the fulfilling conditions for affirming real being have to be the data of sense or consciousness, whereas the fulfilling condition for proposing a hypothesis is a possible relevance to data, and for an analytic proposition mere logical coherence is enough. The point is to indicate that the verb 'is' is employed in different senses, and that these different senses reveal different spheres of being. This does not mean, however, that it is legitimate to distinguish between an intelligibility intrinsic to being, but diverse spheres of being must be distinguished according to the type of intelligibility involved.

Further, the drive of the mind is beyond the merely intelligible, the merely hypothetical, towards what can be verified in the data of sense or consciousness. Moreover, at the core of all intentionality is the desire for the transcendent sphere of being. Indeed, it is in virtue of the unrestricted desire to know everything about everything that all particular queries are initiated and their ultimate legitimacy upheld. Thus, just as the desire to know carries one beyond understanding to reflection and judgment and beyond knowledge of the merely logical, the merely hypothetical, the merely mathematical to what can be certainly verified in the data of sense or consciousness, so the desire to understand completely carries one beyond not only the restricted spheres of hypothetical being, etc., to the sphere of real proportionate being but beyond that sphere to the sphere of transcendent being.

What is most important to grasp, however, is that the whole process just described is of a part and that what is ultimate in intentionality is what sets the whole process in motion and ultimately authenticates it. This means that to remain on the level of mere sense experience, as do empiricists, or on the level of understanding, as do idealists, or on the level of the sphere of the real as opposed to the sphere of transcendent being, as do atheists, is to lapse into one form or other of obscurantism and to fail to understand the real meaning of knowing. In other words, implicit in the rejection of the transcendent sphere of being or God as the ultimate condition of the possibility of knowing is a rejection of the positions on knowing, being and objectivity and hence radically a denial of the possibility of human knowledge as such.

A second comment which should be made in the context of MacKinnon's objections, especially in the light of the immediately preceding analysis, regards what might appear to be a vicious circle in Lonergan's approach to the complete intelligibility of being. Thus, briefly expressed, for Lonergan the ultimate condition of the possibility of the 'positions' is the existence of the formally unconditioned, the completely intelligible intelligent intelligible that is God. Yet, it is precisely in view of and in the light of the 'position' on the intelligibility of being that the inference of God's existence is worked out. The vicious circle, however, is only apparent. Thus, while it is true that God or the formally unconditioned is what ultimately explains the intelligibility of being and the correspondence between our knowing and the known, still in our knowledge it is first critically established that we do, in fact, know and that intelligibility is an essential condition of possibility for affirming any existent. Only then is it inferred that the ultimate explanation of the possibility of our knowing is the unrestricted act of understanding that is God. In other words, God is the ultimate explanation of the intelligibility of being, but in our knowledge what are first critically known are the immediate conditions required for an intelligent affirmation. Only subsequently is there inferred the ultimate condition of the possibility of human knowledge itself.

A further objection to Lonergan's approach to the God problem is raised by David Burrell. Like David Tracy, Burrell too has problems with chapter XIX of *Insight* and its relationship to the preceding chapters. But Burrell's objections are of a far more serious nature than those of Tracy. Thus, whereas Tracy grants that it would be possible to rework the critical foundations of chapter XIX in such a way that its basic approach would still be viable, Burrell envisages Lonergan's basic attempt to extrapolate from the restricted to the unrestricted act of understanding as an impossible endeavour.

Burrell has two objections. His first objection is basically that since we have no direct acquaintance with or knowledge of complete intelligibility we cannot know that the real is completely intelligible. Thus, Burrell argues that 'we simply cannot affirm that being is completely intelligible because we cannot conceive what the judgment would be like which affirmed that all intelligent questions were in and all answered correctly.'[119]

In response to this objection of Burrell's Lonergan himself points out that one must advert to the fact that besides knowing there is intending.[120] In other words, although we may not experience an act of unrestricted understanding and in this fashion grasp the complete intelligibility of being, still we can and do experience the unrestricted character of our intending and hence the desire for complete intelligibility. Our intentionality accordingly is not blind but is in between not-knowing and knowing, and involves, as Lonergan puts it, 'a conscious intending of an unknown that is to be known'.[121] Moreover, the intending is not merely the intending of this or that particular intelligibility or the intending of the partially or half intelligible, but of total or complete intelligibility. As Lonergan expresses it :

It follows that our intending intends, not incomplete, but complete intelligibility. If it intended no more than an incomplete intelligibility, there would be a point where further questions could arise but did not, where the half-answer appeared not a half-answer but as much an answer as human intelligence could dream of seeking. If the dynamism of human intellect intended no more than incomplete intelligibility, the horizon not merely of human knowledge but also of possible human enquiry would be bounded. Whether or not there were anything beyond that horizon, would be a question that could not even arise.[122]

Further, Lonergan points out that there is a strategy in asking questions so that one cannot object that there is an infinity of possible questions and no way of putting any order into them. Thus, one can and does ask such strategically important questions as, 'What is being?', 'Does the idea of being exist?'. These questions which go right to the heart of the matter are both too fundamental and too ultimate to ignore without lapsing into obscurantism.

In Lonergan's view, then, fact proves possibility and it can be shown (1) than man intends complete intelligibility, (2) that the intention of complete intelligibility is 'at the root of all our attempts to mean anything at all,'[123] (3) that to impugn the unrestricted character of our intending is to undermine at its core the source of all human knowing, and (4) that man can and does ask strategic questions about the meaning of being, etc., and does arrive at critically validated heuristic answers.

A second objection of Burrell's is to the effect that Lonergan's extrapolation from a restricted to the unrestricted act of understanding is ineffectual and non-probative because, in Burrell's words, 'it is the act of judgment which provides us the key to what we mean when we say that being is real and intelligible' and yet, 'the unrestricted act does not proceed by way of judgment, since it does not proceed at all but understands everything "in a single view inasmuch as it understands itself".'[124] Burrell thus enquires: 'How then, when the unrestricted act lacks this very focal point, the judgment, can we pretend to extrapolate to it from the properties of a restricted act?'[125]

In response we might assemble the following points already discussed: (1) reflection and judgment are required in order to verify the correctness of our understanding; (2) isomorphic to our knowing is an object which involves a potential, a formal and an actual component or, in other words, an object in which matter, form and act are distinct principles of being; (3) the pure desire to know is a desire for complete understanding or a desire to know the essence of being and no proportionate object of our knowing can reveal the essence of being since in the proportionate objects essence and existence are distinct principles; (4) only a being whose essence it is to exist could provide an answer to the question, 'What is being?'; (5) in terms of the definition of being through knowing, the ultimate answer to the question, 'What is being?' can only be that it is an idea whose primary component is the unrestricted act of understanding.

Burrell objects that in our knowing it is only in judgment that being is reached and that accordingly the extrapolation to the idea of being as the content of an unrestricted act of understanding is inadequate. What should be noted, however, is that judgment is required in our knowing in order to affirm correctness of understanding. If, then, a perfect instance of knowing could be realised in which the knower and the known were identical not only intentionally but in being, then understanding alone would suffice for knowledge of the reality of the known and the addition of judgment would be simply superfluous. In other words, in this perfect instance of knowing, the act of understanding in the very act of its grasping itself would suffice to fulfil the functions of both understanding and judging as they occur in human knowing. In conclusion, then, the response to this second argument of Burrell most fundamentally is that the fact proves the possibility. Further, it is possible to extrapolate from human knowing to the divine in such a fashion that although God is described most properly not as an infinite act of judging but as an unrestricted act of understanding, still all that judgment positively implies in human knowing is eminently realised in God as the unrestricted act of understanding. It is in this context that Lonergan, in chapter XIX, can speak of the act of understanding as identically reflection and judgment.[126] In so doing he is simply indicating that the functions of reflection and judgment are realised in an eminent fashion in the unrestricted act of understanding itself.

Now in these dialectical considerations we could very profitably take up certain aspects of process philosophy and its relationship to Lonergan's philosophy of God. Process philosophy, as developed by Alfred North Whitehead, Charles Hartshorne, John Cobb, Schubert Ogden, and many others, offers perhaps the most powerful opposition to the type of philosophy of God Lonergan articulates. In point of fact, Schubert Ogden has already addressed himself explicitly to Lonergan's approach to God,[127] but for the most part there has not yet been any prolonged exchange between Lonergan and the representatives of process philosophy.

Clearly it is not possible here to analyse in any depth the diverse issues which divide process philosophy from the philosophy of Bernard Lonergan. Ogden's explicit critique of Lonergan, for example, involves a fundamental disagreement regarding the nature of cognition, and it is too basic and all-encompassing to be handled here. Ogden does, however, in his *The Reality of God*[128] implicitly criticise Lonergan's philosophy of God on two closely related issues and it will be helpful to take up these criticisms.

First, Ogden implicitly criticises a key point in Lonergan when he indicates that classical theism is involved in what he terms a 'hopeless contradiction'[129] in attempting to hold at the same time both that God's act of creation is free, and yet that it is one with his essence, which is in every respect necessary. If Ogden is correct that a contradiction is involved in the attempt to hold both God's immutability and his freedom in creating, then Lonergan's philosophy of God has a fundamental flaw. Yet, Lonergan's analysis of efficient causality reveals that the agent as agent is not changed in causing. It reveals that the reality of efficient causality is a relation of intelligible dependence of the effect on the cause. On this analysis God can truly cause and yet remain immutable. Further, Lonergan, through the use of an analogy based on human willing, shows that God in freely choosing to create is not changed.[130] Briefly, Lonergan's development is as follows. In human willing, to will a given end—e.g., to get well—is to cause the willing of a given means, e.g., to take medicine. It is in virtue of the willing of the end that the willing of the means takes place. The point to note, however, is that although it is the willing of the end that causes the willing of the means, still the willing of the means does not add any change or intrinsic entity to the willing of the end. Analogously, in God there is his infinite love of his own goodness and it is in virtue of this willing of the end, namely his own goodness, that he is able either freely to create or not to create. Furthermore, if God creates, this does not mean any change in God since the agent as agent is not changed in acting. It is in the same contingent term that both God's producing the world in act and God's actual willing the world are verified, and so just as God is not changed in his producing, he is not changed in his willing. For God to will the existence of the created term is for him to cause it, and so just as God as agent is not intrinsically changed in causing, God as willing is not subject to any intrinsic change.

Ogden raises yet another difficulty against 'classical theism' which he says involves an antinomy even more important than the one just considered. Ogden points out that in classical Christian theism men are asked to serve and glorify a God who, as pure act, is completely indifferent to what men do. In Ogden's own words: 'As *actus purus*, and thus a statically complete perfection incapable in any respect of further self-realisation, God can be neither increased nor diminished by what we do, and our action, like our suffering, must be in the strictest sense wholly indifferent to him.'[131] For Ogden this view involves great existential repugnance and is a more important antinomy than the metaphysical one regarding the divine immutability and God's freedom in creating.

The second objection of Ogden's is simply the expression on a more existential or psychological level of the first metaphysical difficulty. We might meet the difficulty regarding the supposed antinomy in the following manner. Just as the fact that God is not changed entitatively in creating does not in any way diminish the reality of his efficient causality, so the fact that God's knowing and willing of creation do not involve intrinsic internal changes in God, does not in any way deny that God truly knows and loves his creation, and in particular his rational creatures. Consequently, in Lonergan's analysis, God is not in any manner indifferent to man's choices and actions. Rather, in his divine transcendence God is able to understand, will and effect that the contingent events of man's free choices occur contingently and yet in irresistible accord with his divine plan. God is thus supremely operative and involved in his creation.

G

Between Lonergan and Ogden there is a radical disagreement in regard to the basic conception of God to the extent that Ogden would insist that unless God is envisaged philosophically as subject in his divinity to change, suffering and self-realisation, he cannot be reconciled with the God of Abraham, Isaac and Jacob, and the God of Jesus Christ. Lonergan, however, would argue that in Scripture itself the absolute transcendence of God is revealed and that in the light of this transcendence the anthropomorphisms which speak of God as angry, repentant or changing in mood, must be demythologised. This problem area, however, is beyond the scope of the present work and it must suffice simply to have indicated its general lines.

No doubt there exist various explicit objections to Lonergan's approach to the God problem which we have not considered here and, of course, the list of possible objections is as endless as the guises which counter-positions might assume. We hope, however, that in this brief dialectic most of the major explicit objections which have been raised against Lonergan's philosophy of God have been at least briefly touched upon. Actually, up to the present time, most of the objections to Lonergan's approach have centred upon diverse aspects of his cognitional analysis and epistemology. The argument throughout this present work has been precisely that failure to accept Lonergan's position on general transcendent knowledge is almost inevitably rooted in a failure to accept fully the positions on knowing, being and objectivity.

Before concluding however, there is one general objection to Lonergan's approach to God which we should touch upon. This objection regards the appropriateness or indeed the validity of speaking of God as an 'object'. In what sense, in other words, if any, is it proper to speak of God as an object and in what senses is it not proper to do so?

In Lonergan's view there are a number of current uses of the term 'object' which are invalidly applied to God. First of all, etymologically ' "object" connotes something sensible, localised, locally related presumably to a spectator or sensitive subject.'[132] In Lonergan's view it is obviously not correct to speak of God as an object in this sense. Again, in the Kantian sense in which the only immediate relation of our cognitional activities to objects is by *Anschauung*, or intuition, God is not an object. Further,

God is not an object in the sense that he is immediately given in the data of consciousness.

On the positive side, however, God may be spoken of as an object in the sense that an object may be said to be whatever is intended in questioning. For, inasmuch as intending is comprehensive, a desire to know everything about everything, God may most properly be described as the transcendental object, or objective, of the pure desire to know.

The designation of God as object in the sense that an object may be said to be whatever is intended in questioning in no way violates the personalist stress on the encounter with God as subject. Thus, as Lonergan observes, although 'a person cannot be an object if "object" is taken in a naïve realist, Kantian, or positivist sense . . . [still] if "object" means that towards which self-transcending heads, obviously persons are objects; we know them and we love them.'[133] Intersubjectivity is one thing and objectification another, but there is no contradiction between them for, as Lonergan remarks : 'Just as we pass from consciousness of the self as subject to an objectification of the self in conception and judging, so too we pass from intersubjectivity to the objectification of intersubjectivity.'[134]

Finally, in his most recent lectures on method in theology Lonergan has been stressing that God is not to be called an 'object' when he is viewed as the term of an orientation to transcendent mystery. Thus, for example, in mystical experience God is encountered in a 'cloud of unknowing'.[135] And in this experience which involves a withdrawal from all concepts and images and the worlds mediated by meaning, God is not properly met in the context of questions and answers, but as the *mysterium tremendum*.

With the mention of God as transcendent mystery it is appropriate to bring this dialectic as well as this work itself to a close. In concluding, it should be kept in mind that Lonergan does not pretend to have spoken the last word on the philosophy of God. In fact, seeing that recently he has dropped the terminology of faculty psychology and stresses the need to philosophise and theologise in the terms of intentionality analysis, we can confidently affirm that a richer natural theology remains to be worked out within systematic theology. The aim of this work, however, has not been to project the lines of a natural theology of tomorrow based on Lonerganian principles, but to outline systematically the basic features of Lonergan's philosophy of God as it exists today.

In a philosophy of God two extremes are to be avoided. One is to say less about God than can reasonably be said and the other is to say more about God than reason is capable of saying. Lonergan manages to achieve a happy middle position between these two extremes. On the one hand, he does maintain that it is possible for man to achieve natural knowledge of the existence of God and that, in fact, in *Insight* he has given evidence of just such an achievement. On the other hand, however, Lonergan clearly acknowledges the limits of natural reason in grappling with the problem of God. Thus, for example, he admits that although it is possible to show that there is no contradiction involved in affirming that God is infallible in his knowing, irresistible in his willing and yet that man is free, still it is not possible to explain the divine transcendence. In Lonergan's view, then, an authentic philosophy of God involves a basic testing or measuring of the *power* and *limitations* of the human mind in its ability to reflect on God. To overlook either of these aspects is to misunderstand both.

In the light of the preceding comment, Lonergan's insistence on the divine transcendence is a forceful reminder that one must steadfastly reject constantly recurring temptations to anthropomorphise God in terms of man's current image of himself. God is forever the transcendent one and is always much more dissimilar to man than he is similar to him. There comes a point where a man must, in his reflections upon God, choose either the silence of adoration or else the attempt to explain away mystery itself.

It is abundantly clear that the God Lonergan understands and affirms to exist is in no way a static, dull, inactive, uninvolved God. Rather, he is a God who is a rapturous, infinite act of understanding and love. He is liveliness itself and the fullness of actuality and life. He is benevolence and beneficence—Love Itself—and joyously, freely overflows in a self-transcending act of creation. Only when the attempts are made to imagine God's inner being in temporal terms are his pure actuality and possession of limitless life misunderstood, deteriorating into a caricature. In the final analysis it is God's eternity which explains our time and not the converse. Time is a creation of God and God's eternity transcends time in every respect. Time is as foreign to the inner being of God as is matter.

Finally, although the God of Lonergan's philosophy is intelligent and loving (and therefore personal), it is only in theology that the full meaning of the personal in God is revealed and God is seen to be Father, Son and Holy Spirit. Lonergan's philosophical conception of God, in other words, is open to further determinations from theology. Although in Lonergan's theological works the analogies of philosophy are constantly operative, yet, in the instance of the psychological analogy the analogy itself is implicit in Christian revelation. Lonergan is a Christian thinker in the grand tradition of Augustine and Aquinas. Lonergan's recent proposal that the philosophy of God be carried out as a distinct moment within theology tends to justify the title 'Christian Philosopher' most powerfully.

Epilogue

WITH these concluding words I would add a few further suggestions to aid the reader's private self-questioning. I use the word 'private' wittingly. A reader of such a work as Fr Tyrrell's, unless he or she has been framed into the stance of unlearning familiarising intake, comes questioning through with genuine self-interest, self full-specified perhaps as questioned : and privacy is called for. 'Our outer world is frequently isomorphic with our inner world, and the "external" problems we deal with "scientifically" are often also our own internal problems, and our solutions to these problems are also, in principle, self-therapies in the broadest sense.'[1] And the 'external' problem of the Interested All in its isomorphic core self-therapy is not for the public square—sometimes not even for a friend. What is called for is an axial transformation of evalued thinking about God and us; what is to be avoided is post-systematic conjugation of initial landmarks in an emergent zone. More patently, what is to be avoided is talk about an anthropological turn as if it were a curve in another universe and not a corner of the campus, a crux in the economy, an invitation to personal ex-sistence.

The point has been made already in the book, but perhaps I might give it a new twist by raising the question, Has the point been made 'too objectively'? Recall the citation, above, from Maslow, and note the following more recent comment of Lonergan : 'The trouble with chapter XIX in *Insight* was that it did not depart from the traditional line. It treated God's existence and attributes in a purely objective fashion. It made no effort to deal with the subject's religious horizon. It failed to acknowledge that the traditional viewpoint made sense only if one accepted first principles on the ground that they were intrinsically necessary and if one added the assumption that there is one right culture so that differences in subjectivity are irrelevant.'[2] Perhaps chapter XIX of *Insight* also is 'too objective'?

First of all I would note—and this is Fr Tyrrell's view after consideration of the St Michael's Institute lectures—that the thesis of the present book stands, and that this thesis includes the claim that the process through *Insight* to chapter XIX, inclusive, is valid. But, just as Fr Lonergan, in those lectures, emphasised continually the context of meaning necessary for grasping his comments, so Fr Tyrrell can require a like context for the understanding of precisely what he holds. Alas, in contrast to the Principle of the Empty Head, the Principle of the Personal Paradox in interpretation affirms the adequate interpreter to have necessarily more than arrived before he sets out.

Secondly, when I debate whether theorems and statements may be 'too objective', I am endeavouring to raise issues and foster dialogue beyond confusion regarding objectivity and subjectivity, beyond the rejection of shades of solipsism and confrontationism.

Thirdly, while that places the question in the rare zone of critical interiority, it none the less has an obvious aspect. So, for example, Fr Lonergan elsewhere in the St Michael's lecture remarks that 'philosophy of God must not attempt to prescind from the subject.' Is his expression an adequate going-forth of subject in meaning to contemporary reading subject? More generally, is the expression of chapter XIX of *Insight* adequate? Granted even its limitation to the intellectually-patterned subject, it would seem that the expression needs transformation to reader-interiority precisors.[3] To labour the obvious, it is all too easy for a reader to pass the print on the idea of being in chapter XIX without realistically plumbing the dimensions of personal desire, without ever keenly meeting the time- and soul-consuming challenge to root in his or her intentionality towards a conception 'greater than which I cannot think'.

Fourthly, there is the less obvious aspect to the question of 'adequate objectivity', and this withdrawal from obviousness corresponds to a withdrawal from concern with outer words to attention to explanatory mental words within the field of interiority. There is no discussion of the religious pattern of experience in chapter VI of *Insight* : what does this say regarding that chapter's validity and viability? Chapter XIX does not express a thematic of religion : is it then merely a chapter in the history of philosophy? In a sense the latter question twists us round full circle to the problematic of the present book. The question can neither be understood adequately, nor answered precisely, out of the context of fulfilled *de facto* and *de jure* conditions.

Fifthly, there is the responsibility of some judgment and some expression of it. From what I have gleaned of chapter XIX of *Insight* through several years of formally lecturing on it in a growing appreciation of its content, its context, its linguistic transformability, I would take a normative stand on its substantial survival within systematics. With Fr Tyrrell, too, I would hold for the need of another book, a book on Lonergan's Systematics of God, spelling out particularly the existential contemplative challenge of section 9 of chapter XIX of *Insight*.

Sixthly, not only do I see chapter XIX as thus surviving within systematics : I cannot see the survival of a serious significant Christian systematics without it. Fr Tyrrell mentions in chapter 5 certain parallels I drew between Aquinas's treatment of God in the *Summa* and the treatment in *Insight*. Let me bring the parallel a stage further. Section 9 of chapter XIX is an expression of a dense 26-point expansion of a hypothesis of unrestricted understanding. Aquinas's corresponding discussion runs to question 26, and in question 27 he launches into the hypothesis of intelligible emanations in God. Lonergan's systematics might well include in a 27th place the equivalent hypothesis, 'beginning where natural theology leaves off'.[4] Without such a serious Trinitarian systematics I can only see theologies of hope and such-like struggling to survive without a heart.[5] And, to touch briefly on the eighth functional specialty in the existential fashion of one just come from a Sunday parish liturgy darkened by a limp homily, when will our seminaries come to grips wholeheartedly with the hard fact that such systematic understanding has not a little to do with the contemporary preaching of the Word?

In existential continuity I conclude. Being a theologian in these closing decades of the twentieth century is no easy task. Functional specialisation is a lightening of that task, cognitional self-appropriation its core. Still, both *Method in Theology* and *Insight* teach new tricks, and even younger dogs at times have muscles moulded in old ways. Lonergan's systematics of God, it seems to me, is an elusive means which yet finds echo in each sapient man's grey gut. There are few of us who might not come to admit the faintness of its thematic echo in ourselves, come to admit 'rarissimos esse homines'.[6] There are few who might lay claim to incarnating the conditions of possibility spelt out by Fr Tyrrell. That fewness can breed a commonsense ecleticism. But it can also blossom out into a tonality of mystery which still fosters serious striving for some systematic, and most fruitful, darksome, glimpse of God. The challenge may be private, but its being recognised and met meshes into the dialectic of our communal way to God.

I would like, finally, to thank Fr Tyrrell for the privilege of assisting him in the recasting of his thesis for publication. Needless to say, I would also like to associate myself with the stand he takes, and most particularly with the esteem he expresses, in the conclusion to the Introduction and elsewhere, for Fr Lonergan. After fifteen years of serious searching for Lonergan's meaning I still find in all his speaking and writing an invitation to further transformations of personal perspective which are by no means mere accidental additions to an essential view.

Philip McShane

Notes

FOREWORD (pp. ix-x)

1. They first appeared in *Theological Studies*, 1941-42 and 1946-49. Later they were published in book form: *Verbum: Word and Idea in Aquinas*, ed. David Burrell, Notre Dame 1967 and London 1968; *Grace and Freedom*, ed. J. Patout Burns, New York and London 1971.

2. Papers presented at the congress have been edited by Philip McShane and published by Gill and Macmillan, Dublin, and by University of Notre Dame Press, Notre Dame, *Foundations of Theology*, 1971; *Language Truth and Meaning*, 1972.

INTRODUCTION (pp. xi-xiv)

1. For the location of Lonergan's method in further contexts see M. Lamb, 'Wilhelm Dilthey's critique of historical reasoning and Lonergan's meta-methodology', 115–66, and F. Lawrence, 'Self-knowledge in history in Gadamer and Lonergan', 167–217, *Language, Truth and Meaning*, vol. 2 of the Lonergan Congress Papers, ed. Philip McShane (Dublin: Gill and Macmillan, and Notre Dame, Indiana: University of Notre Dame Press, 1972).

2. Lonergan, 'Response', *Proceedings of the American Catholic Philosophical Association* XLI (Washington: Catholic University of America Press, 1967), 256.

3. *Ibid.*

4. Lonergan, in *Insight*, includes general transcendent knowledge within metaphysics: 'The metaphysics of proportionate being becomes a subordinate part of a more general metaphysics that envisages the transcendent idea of being', *Insight: A Study of Human Understanding* (London: Longman, Green and Co. 1957), 665.

5. *Ibid.*, 521; cf. also 484.   6. *Ibid.*, 484.   7. *Ibid.*, 522.

8. See 'Bernard Lonergan Responds', *Language Truth and Meaning*, ed. P. McShane, 307.

1. THE HISTORICAL DIMENSION (pp. 3-29)

1. Lonergan, 'Theology and Man's Future', *Cross Currents* XIX 4 (Fall, 1969), 460.

2. Lonergan, 'The Future of Thomism', an unpublished lecture delivered at Pittsburgh in 1967.

3. Cf. Lonergan, 'The Natural Theology of *Insight*', an unpublished lecture on the proof for the existence of God in *Insight* delivered at the Divinity School of the University of Chicago in 1967, 2.

4. *Insight*, 678.

5. Lonergan, 'The Absence of God in Modern Culture', *The Presence and Absence of God*, ed. Christopher F. Mooney, S.J. (New York: Fordham University Press, 1969), 165.

6. *Ibid.*, 165-6.

7. Lonergan, 'Theology in its New Context', *Theology of Renewal I*, ed. L. K. Shook, C.S.B. (New York: Herder and Herder 1968) 35.

8. See Lonergan, 'Dimensions of Meaning', *Collection* (Herder and Herder 1967), 259-60.

9. Lonergan, 'Theology in its New Context', *op. cit.*, 43.

10. In this discussion of classical Thomism, I am relying mainly on the unpublished lecture of Lonergan entitled 'The Future of Thomism'.

11. Lonergan, 'Belief Today', *Catholic Mind* LXVIII (May 1970), 17.

12. *Ibid.*, 16.

13. Lonergan, 'Theology and Man's Future', *op. cit.*, 456.

14. Lonergan, a book review of *Saint Augustin et le neoplatonisme* by M. F. Sciacca and of *Exist-t-il une Philosophie Chretienne?* by Maurice Nedoncelle, Gregorianum XL (1959), 182-3.

15. Lonergan, 'The Absence of God in Modern Culture', *op. cit.*, 173.

16. *Ibid.*

17. Lonergan, '*Existenz* and *Aggiornamento*', *Collection*, 247.

18. Lonergan, 'Belief Today', *op. cit.*, 13.

19. Lonergan, 'Dimensions of Meaning', *Collection*, 266.

20. See Lonergan's discussion of the controversies between Bréhier, Gilson and Blondel in 'The Origins of Christian Realism', an unpublished lecture delivered at Regis College in Toronto, Ontario, on 8 September 1961, 1-2.

21. Lonergan's studies on operative grace and the *verbum* have profound methodological implications, as David Tracy demonstrates in his 'The Development of the Notion of Theological Method in the works of Bernard Lonergan, S.J.' (unpublished doctoral dissertation, Gregorian University, Rome, 1969). In this context it is

important to note that when one speaks of Lonergan as philosophising in his *Grace and Freedom* and *Verbum*, this is to be understood in the sense that in these works Lonergan differentiates between the natural and the supernatural and is very clear about what is philosophical and what theological in his analyses. The study on operative grace, for example, is, in Lonergan's words, a 'history of theological speculation', *Grace and Freedom* (New York : Herder and Herder, 1971), 1. Yet, in Aquinas, as Lonergan indicates, *'the supernatural* is a scientific theorem : it has an exact philosophic definition; its implications are worked out and faced,' *ibid.*, 13. Lonergan then, in his studies on operative grace and the *verbum*, is performing a hermeneutical task and this task requires him to function both as a philosopher and as a theologian since Aquinas was a Christian thinker whose philosophising was a moment within his overall Christian reflectivity.

22. *Grace and Freedom*, 63.

23. For Lonergan's explanation of his plan of operations in the five articles on *verbum*, originally published in *Theological Studies*, see the book-form of these articles, *Verbum: Word and Idea in Aquinas*, ed. David Burrell, London : Darton, Longman and Todd, and Indiana : University of Notre Dame Press, 1967, 180.

24. *Ibid.*, vii.   25. *Ibid.*, x.   26. *Ibid.*

27. *Ibid.*, xi.   28. *Ibid.*   29. *Ibid.*

30. *Ibid.*   31. *Ibid.*, xii.

32. 'The Natural Desire to See God', *Collection*, 84.

33. *Ibid.*

34. Aristotle, *Metaphysics*, 1. 1. 980.

35. See *Verbum*, ix.

36. Bernard Lonergan, *De Deo Trino: I Pars Dogmatica* (Rome : Gregorian University, 1964), 154.

37. See 'The Origins of Christian Realism', *op. cit.*

38. *De Deo Trino: I*, 109.

39. 'The Natural Desire to See God', *Collection*, 88.

40. 'Openness and Religious Experience', *Collection*, 199.

41. *Ibid.*, 200.

42. See *De Deo Trino: II Pars Systematica*, 232-5.

43. 'Openness and Religious Experience', *Collection*, 200-1.

44. *Ibid.*, 201.   45. *De Deo Trino: I*, 108.   46. *Ibid.*

47. See, e.g., *Isaiah* 45 :18.   48. *Galations* 1 :8.

49. *De Deo Trino: I*, 110.   50. *Ibid.*, 36.   51. *Ibid.*, 39.

52. *Ibid.*, 40.   53. *Ibid.*, 98-9.   54. *Ibid.*, 93-4.

55. *Ibid.*, 48-50.   56. *Ibid.*, 94-5.   57. *Ibid.*, 93.

58. *Ibid.*   59. *Ibid.*, 103-4, 147-8.   60. *Ibid.*, 56.

61. *Ibid.*, 57. 62. *Ibid.* 63. *Ibid.*, 60-2.

64. Here it should be noted that in Lonergan's opinion it is incorrect to assert that the Nicene use of the term consubstantial—*homousios*—involved a corruption of pristine Christian revelation through the use of a profane Hellenic term. As Lonergan indicates in his review of Leslie Dewart's *Future of Belief, homousios* up to the Council was understood in one sense only, namely,' "of one stuff"; (and) as applied to the Divine Persons, it conveyed a metaphor drawn from material objects. The Fathers at Nicea, then, did not find ready to hand a sharply defined, immutable concept which they made into a vehicle for the Christian message; on the contrary, they found a word which they employed in a metaphorical sense.' *See* 'The Dehellenisation of Dogma', *Theological Studies* XXVIII 2 (June 1967), 344.

Lonergan proceeds to point out that what was Hellenic was not the concept but rather the technique employed to determine the meaning of the concept. This technique is what Lonergan refers to as the ability to operate on propositions, or the technique of second-level propositions. Thus, for example, Athanasius by reflecting on the true propositions of Scripture and tradition concluded that the Son was consubstantial with the Father and he explained exactly what he meant by this proposition by moving to an explanatory definition in which he affirmed that 'the Son is consubstantial with the Father, if and only if what is true of the Father also is true of the Son, except that only the Father is Father: *ibid.*, 345.

65. The Nicene Creed.

66. See *De Deo Trino: I*, 80. 67. *Ibid.* 68. *Ibid.*

69. It should naturally be borne in mind that in speaking of man's response to the revealed word in faith the term of man's believing response is not a proposition but rather the reality mediated through the true proposition, e.g., in the present context the Mystery which is the Trinitarian God himself.

70. *De Deo Trino: I*, 108-9. Lonergan expands on this view considerably in more recent essays.

71. *Ibid.*, 153-4. 72. *Ibid.*, 81-7.

73. 'Bernard Lonergan Responds', *Language Truth and Meaning*, ed. Philip McShane, 308-9.

2. THE EXISTENTIAL DIMENSION (pp. 30-68)

1. *Insight*, 248. 2. *Ibid.*, xix. 3. *Ibid.*, 743.

4. Lonergan, *De Constitutione Christi ontologica et psychologica* (Rome: Gregorian University, 1956), 14-19.

5. *Ibid.*, 14-15. 6. *Ibid.*, 17.

7. Lonergan, 'Theology in Its New Context', *Theology of Renewal I*, ed. L. K. Shook (New York : Herder and Herder, 1968), 45.

8. *Ibid.* 9. *Ibid.*

10. *De Constitutione Christi*, 17; *Insight*, xx.

11. *Insight*, 272. While the term 'conversion' does not occur in *Insight*, Lonergan used it in a philosophic context in his Montreal lectures on 'Intelligence and Reality', 1951, 14, 16. His notes—25 pages—are available in the Lonergan Centre, Regis College, Toronto.

12. Andrew J. Reck, 'Bernard Lonergan's Theory of Inquiry vis-à-vis American Thought', *Proceedings of the American Catholic Philosophical Association* XLI, 244.

13. Lonergan, 'Response', *Proceedings of the American Catholic Philosophical Association* XLI, 257.

14. *Ibid.*

15. *Insight*, xx-xxi; see also 412.

16. Plato, *Republic* VII, 518.

17. Lonergan's '*Insight* : Preface to a Discussion', *Collection*, 158, note 10.

18. Plato, *Republic* VII, 516.

19. Lonergan, *The Subject* (Milwaukee : Marquette University Press, 1968), 18; see also *Method in Theology* (London : Darton, Longman and Todd, and New York : Herder and Herder, 1972), 238-40.

20. *Insight*, xx.

21. Lonergan, 'Bernard Lonergan Responds', *Foundations of Theology*, vol. 1 of the Lonergan Congress Papers, ed. Philip McShane (Dublin : Gill and Macmillan, and Indiana : University of Notre Dame Press, 1971), 234.

22. *Insight*, 558. 23. *Ibid.* 24. *Ibid.*, 561.

25. Newman, *Grammar of Assent* (New York : Image paperback, 1955), 143.

26. *Ibid.*, 142-3. 27. *Insight*, 561. 28. *Ibid.*

29. '*Insight* : Preface to a Discussion', *Collection*, 158, note 10.

30. *The Subject*, 18.

31. *De Constitutione Christi*, 18.

32. *The Subject*, 19.

33. *De Constitutione Christi*, 15. The original Latin reads : '*quamdam sensitivae animae noctem.*'

34. *Ibid.*, 16.

35. Lonergan, 'Natural Knowledge of God', *Proceedings of the*

Twenty Third Annual Convention of the Catholic Theological Society of America XXIII (Washington, D.C., 1968), 64; see also *Method in Theology*, 240-3.

36. 'Natural Knowledge of God', *op. cit.*, 64.

37. *Ibid.* 38. *Insight*, 220. 39. *Ibid.*, 223. 40. *Ibid.*, 227.

41. *Ibid.*, 238-42; 663; 690. Cf. also, 'The Role of a Catholic University in a Modern World', *Collection*, 115.

42. *Insight*, 234. 43. *Ibid.*, 600.

44. 'Natural Knowledge of God', *op. cit.*, 54.

45. *Ibid.*, 68-9. 46. *The Subject*, 26.

47. *Ibid.*, 28. 48. *Insight*, 599-600. 49. *Ibid.*, 633. 50. *Ibid.*

51. *De Constitutione Christi*, 17. The translation is my own.

52. *Ibid.*, 18. The Latin reads : '. . . *fere cogat ad ex-istendum.*'

53. *Insight*, 739.

54. This phenomenological analysis of questioning is taken from a summary of a series of lectures on Existentialism which Lonergan delivered at Boston College in July 1957. The summary was reprinted by the Thomas More Institute of Montreal; see especially 19-20. The lectures are available on tape at Regis College, Toronto, Canada. See also *Method in Theology*, 235-7.

55. *Insight*, 627.

56. 'Metaphysics as Horizon', *Collection*, 213.

57. *Ibid.*, 214.

58. *De Methodo Theologiae* (notes for lectures presented at the Gregorian University in Rome in 1962; the notes were xeroxed at the North American College in Rome), 11. The translation is my own.

59. *Ibid.*, 3. 60. *Ibid.*, 11.

61. Lonergan, 'Metaphysics as Horizon', *Collection*, 213.

62. Lonergan, '*Existenz* and *Aggiornamento*', *Collection*, 240-51.

63. *Ibid.*, 243. 64. *The Subject*, 2. 65. *Ibid.*, 18.

66. 'Metaphysics as Horizon', *Collection*, 214.

67. *Ibid.* 68. *Ibid.*

69. *Method in Theology*, 131.

70. 'An Interview with Fr Bernard Lonergan, S.J.', edited by Philip McShane, *Clergy Review* LVI 6 (1971), 426.

71. Lonergan, 'Hermeneutics', an unpublished lecture delivered at Regis College, Toronto, Canada on 20 July, 1962, 3.

72. *Ibid.* On this topic see also *Method in Theology*, 157-8; chapters 7-9 of the same book, of course, provide a richer treatment.

73. *De Deo Trino: II*, 12. The translation is my own.

74. Lonergan, 'Hermeneutics', *op. cit.*, 7.

75. This citation is from a summary made by Lawrence K. Shook of certain comments of Bernard Lonergan on theology. The summary is published in a work entitled *Congress of the Theology of Renewal* (Toronto : Pontifical Institute of Medieval Studies, 1968), 7.

76. Dante, *The Comedy of Dante Aligheri: Hell*, E. tr. Dorothy L. Sayers (Harmondsworth : Penguin Books, 1964), Introduction by Dorothy Sayers, 49-50.

77. *Ibid.*, 11.   78. *Ibid.*   79. *Method in Theology*, 131.

80. Charles Curran, 'Christian Conversion in the Writings of Bernard Lonergan', *Foundations of Theology*, ed. Philip McShane, 41-59.

81. *Ibid.*, 59.

82. See Lonergan : 'Natural knowledge of God.' In this article Lonergan writes (p. 66) : 'Thirdly, it was urged that we have to drop the words, nature, natural, that we should be content to speak with Scripture and the Fathers of God's grace and man's sinfulness. Now I have no doubt that such words as nature and natural, no less than object and verification, can be abused. But I also have no doubt that if we are not only going to speak about God's grace and man's sinfulness but also we are going to say what precisely we mean by such speaking, then we are going to have to find some third term over and above grace and sin.'

83. Lonergan, 'Faith and Beliefs', an unpublished lecture delivered at Boston College in 1969, 14.

84. *Ibid.*   85. *Ibid.*   86. *Ibid.*, 11.

87. *Ibid.*, 14-15. Lonergan acknowledges Professor Wilfred Cantwell Smith as the one from whom he derives the notion of a 'universalist faith'.

88. *Ibid.*, 15-16.

89. Lonergan, 'Faith and Beliefs', *op. cit.*, 13.

90. *Ibid.*, 14.

91. Lonergan, 'The Future of Christianity', *Holy Cross Quarterly* 2 (1969), 10.

92. Lonergan, 'Faith and Beliefs', especially 14-21.

93. *Ibid.*, 21.   94. *Ibid.*

95. Lonergan, *'De Methodo Theologiae'*, *op. cit.*, 4.

96. Lonergan, *'Existenz* and *Aggiornamento'*, *Collection*, 246.

97. *Ibid.*   98. *Ibid.*

99. Lonergan, *De Constitutione Christi*, 17. The translation is mine.

100. *Insight*, 683-4.

3. CRITICAL SELF-AFFIRMATION AS BREAK-
THROUGH TO INTELLECTUAL CONVERSION
(pp. 71-94).

1. *Insight*, 635. 2. *Ibid.*, 636. 3. *Ibid.*, 3. 4. *Ibid.*, 4.
5. Lonergan, *The Subject*, 22.
6. The data for self-affirmation of oneself as a knower are immediately given in consciousness.
7. *Method in Theology*, 4.
8. *Insight*, 391. 9. *Ibid.*
10. See above, Introduction, x; also *Method in Theology*, 25.
11. Lonergan, 'Cognitional Structure', *Collection*, 226.
12. Lonergan, 'Christ as Subject: A Reply', *Collection*, 173.
13. *Ibid.*, 177. 14. *Ibid.*, 176.
15. 'Cognitional Structure', *Collection*, 226.
16. *Insight*, 321. 17. *Ibid.*
18. 'Christ as Subject: A Reply', *Collection*, 186.
19. *Ibid.*, 180, note 18. 20. *Ibid.*, 181, note 18.
21. *Insight*, xiii.
22. Aristotle, *De Anima*, III, 7, 431^b.
23. *De Verbo Incarnato* (Rome: *Gregorian University*, 1964),
333.
24. *Summa Theologica*, I, q.14, a.2 c.
25. *Verbum*, 72, note 115.
26. *De Verbo Incarnato*, 333.
27. *Verbum*, 73. 28. *Verbum*, 72.
29. *Summa Theologica*, I, q.84, a.7 c.
30. 'Christ as Subject: A Reply', *Collection*, 186; *Verbum*,
215-16.
31. '*Insight*: Preface to a Discussion', *Collection*, 162.
32. Etienne Gilson, *Réalisme thomiste et critique de la connaissance* (Paris: Librairie Philosophique J. Vrin, 1939).
33. Lonergan, 'Metaphysics as Horizon', *Collection*, 202-20.
34. It should be noted that this analysis and critique of Gilson
is limited to *Réalisme thomiste et critique de la connaissance*. The
question of possible later developments or changes in Gilson's thinking on this matter is a valid one but is not of concern here.
35. Gilson, *Réalisme thomiste*, 215.
36. *Ibid.*, 225-6.
37. Lonergan, *De Methodo Theologiae*, 33.
38. Gilson, *Réalisme thomiste*, 160.
39. *Ibid.*, 125 and 207.
40. '*Insight*: Preface to a Discussion', *Collection*, 152-63.
41. Lonergan, *The Subject*, 10-11.

42. *Insight*, x.   43. *Verbum*, 179.

44. *Insight*, 407, footnote.

45. In *Verbum*, 177-81, Lonergan speaks of objective, apprehensive and formal abstraction. It is not essential here to enter into the details of these scholastic distinctions, but it is helpful in the light of *Insight* to indicate briefly the meaning and implications of each since this is an aid to understanding in what way abstraction may be viewed not, as is often the case, as essentially impoverishing but rather as enriching.

Accordingly, objective abstraction basically constitutes the imagined object as something to be understood. It is enriching because it anticipates an intelligible unity or relationship to be added to data, cf. *Insight*, 88. Apprehensive abstraction is the very moment of insight itself and it is enriching because it actually adds to data the intelligibility sought in terms of objective abstraction, cf. *Insight*, 311. Finally, formative abstraction is the moment of meaning or defining what one has understood. Only at this point may the abstraction be viewed negatively since it involves 'the omission of the insignificant, the relevant, the negligible, the incidental, the merely empirical residue' : *Insight*, 89.

46. *Insight*, 274 : 'By questions for intelligence and reflection are not meant utterances or even conceptual formulations; by the question is meant the attitude of the enquiring mind that effects the transition from the first level to the second and, again, the attitude of the critical mind that effects the transition from the second level to the third.'

47. *De Methodo Theologiae*, 23.

48. *Ibid.*, 23.   49. *Insight*, 550.

50. *De Methodo Theologiae*, 23-5.

51. Lonergan, taped lectures on *Insight*, lecture 5 on judgment.

52. *Verbum*, 47.   53. *Ibid.*, 65-6.   54. *Insight*, 325.   55. *Ibid.*

4. CONFINEMENT IN OPENNESS : THE POSITION ON BEING (pp. 95-117).

1. *Insight*, 388.   2. *Ibid.*, especially 521-3.

3. Lonergan, 'Cognitional Structure', *Collection*, 221-39.

4. Lonergan, *De Notione Structurae*, a Latin address delivered on the feast of Thomas Aquinas, 1964, at the Aloisianum in Gallarate, Italy. The lecture, which is transcribed from the original tape, consists of eight single-spaced typed pages.

5. *Insight*, 522.   6. *Ibid.*, 388.   7. *Ibid.*, xxviii.   8. *Ibid.*

9. *Ibid.*   10. *Ibid.*, 523.   11. *Ibid.*, 392.

12. '*Insight* : Preface to a Discussion', *Collection*, 155-6.

13. *Insight*, 350.

14. Lonergan, *De Constitutione Christi*, 30. The translation is my own.

15. *Insight*, 350-74. See also *De Constitutione Christi*, 9-13; *Verbum*, Index under Being.

16. *Insight*, 369.

17. Jean Langlois, 'The Notion of Being According to Lonergan', *Spirit as Inquiry: Studies in Honour of Bernard Lonergan*, S.J., *Continuum*, 1964, 130.

18. Aquinas, *In Boethium De Trinitate*, q.5, a. 3.

19. Lonergan, *De Notione Structurae*, 3.

20. *Ibid*.

21. Lonergan, 'Isomorphism of Thomist and Scientific Thought', *Collection*, 14.

22. *Insight*, 399.

23. *The General Character of Mathematical Logic*, Section III, 2. (This and citation 24 are from a summary of a series of lectures on mathematical logic which Lonergan delivered at Boston College in July, 1957. The notes were reprinted by the Thomas More Institute of Montreal. The lectures are also available on tape at Regis College, Toronto, Canada.)

24. *Ibid*. 25. *Insight*, 399-400. 26. *Ibid.*, 523.

27. Lonergan, *De Notione Structurae, op. cit.*, 3.

28. Needless to say, it is not being asserted here that it is impossible to understand an essence without *eo ipso* affirming its existence. What is being stated, however, is that essence is of itself ordered to existence as possible being to its existential actualisation. Again, finite existence can only be affirmed of essence. It cannot stand alone in affirmation.

29. *De Notione Structurae, op. cit.*, 4.

30. In discussing Lonergan's view of science as involving the verification of hypotheses in instances, mention should be made of the fact that James Albertson, S.J., in a review of *Insight* in *Modern Schoolman* XXXV (March 1958), 236-44, and Edward MacKinnon in his three-part study of Lonergan's thought entitled 'Understanding According to Bernard Lonergan', in *The Thomist* XXVIII, Nos. 2, 3 and 4 (1964), 97-132, 338-72 and 475-522, object to what Albertson refers to as 'the characteristic' of *Insight*, namely, 'the absence of a distinction between those intelligibilities immanent in the objects and patterns of experience, and those intelligibilities projected by the knower into objects and patterns of experience' (p. 238). For Albertson and for MacKinnon, to the extent, as he says, that Albertson's criticism 'applies to Lonergan's explanation of science' (p. 488), the absence in Lonergan of the distinction between

immanent and projected intelligibilities is a basic inadequacy in his thought.

Now it is not possible here to enter into a discussion of the various arguments proffered to bolster the position that the distinction between immanent and projected intelligibilities is valid and must be upheld. The distinction which most fundamentally means that the mind discovers certain unities, relations, and necessities in data but in certain sophisticated scientific instances imposes or projects certain intelligible unities, relations or necessities into data is a counter-position of the most fundamental sort.

Here, perhaps, it would be most expeditious to cite verbatim with only a few incidental verbal modifications a taped reply which Lonergan made at the *Insight Seminar* held at St Mary's, Halifax, Nova Scotia, in 1958 to a question regarding the Albertson objection and hence implicitly that of MacKinnon as well:

> The point to the distinction between immanent and projected intelligibilities is, of course, a distinction that is necessarily made by an empiricist or a naïve realist. The immanent intelligibility is the one you know by taking a look at what really is there and the projected one is the one you think out in your mind, but do not see in the object.
>
> Now, since I disclaim both empiricism and naïve realism I consequently have no use for that distinction. For me the significant distinction is between intelligibilities that are affirmed in true judgments and intelligibilities that are not affirmable. If your criterion of reality is a look, you have to distinguish between the immanent and the projected intelligibility entirely or say that all intelligibilities are subjective.
>
> Man, however, does not know intelligibilities by taking a look. Man has insights but what he grasps by insight is not yet known to be true. There is required a further reflective act in which you affirm what you grasp by insight. There are conditions for the affirmation and the conditions have to be fulfilled before the affirmation can be rational. Accordingly, if one is going by the look, the logical position is to say that no intelligibility is objective. However, if you hold that the criterion of reality is truth, then you divide intelligibilities into those that enter into true judgments and those that do not.
>
> Finally, if you say that certain intelligibilities are not so or that something does not pertain to this intelligible law or however you conceive the intelligibility, then it does not pertain to the real. In conclusion, from one viewpoint of the nature of knowledge a distinction between immanent and projected

intelligibilities may be plausible but if one's criterion of the real is truth then the only relevant division of intelligibilities is between those truly affirmed and those not affirmed or able to be affirmed. (Lecture 8, Side 1, Discussion.)

31. *De Notione Structurae, op. cit.*, 4.   32. *Insight*, 498.

33. *Ibid.*, 399.   34. *Ibid.*, 623.   35. *Ibid.*, 512.

36. On these issues see P. McShane, *Randomness, Statistics and Emergence* (Dublin : Gill and Macmillan, and Indiana : University of Notre Dame Press, 1970).

37. Lonergan, 'Natural Knowledge of God', *op. cit.*, 59.

38. Lonergan, 'Cognitional Structure', *Collection*, 228.

39. *Insight*, 375-6.

40. *Ibid.*, 376.   41. *Ibid.*, 377.   42. *Ibid.*

43. Lonergan, 'Cognitional Structure', *Collection*, 230.

44. *De Notione Structurae, op. cit.*, 6.

45. *Ibid.*, 7.   46. *Insight*, 378.   47. *Ibid.*   48. *The Subject*, 14.

49. *Insight*, 388.   50. *The Subject*, 14.   51. *Insight*, 499.

52. *Ibid.*, 501.

5. THE AFFIRMATION OF GOD (pp. 118-79)

1. Lonergan presented a series of ten lectures on his *Method in Theology* in Dublin, Ireland in the period of 2-14 August 1971. The lectures and responses given by Lonergan during eight question periods are all available on tape at Milltown Park in Dublin, where the lectures were presented, and at the Lonergan Centre, Regis College, Toronto.

2. Karl Rahner, 'Theology and Anthropology', *The Word in History* ed. T. Patrick Burke (New York : Sheed and Ward, 1966), 9.

3. Lonergan, 'Theology and Man's Future', *Cross Currents* XIX/4 (Fall, 1969), 457.

4. Lonergan, *Method in Theology*, 129.

5. *Insight*, 672.   6. *Ibid.*, 675.   7. *Ibid.*, 689.

8. 'An Interview with Fr Bernard Lonergan, S.J.', edited by Philip McShane, *Clergy Review*, LVI/6 (1971), 423.

9. *Ibid.*, 426.

10. *Insight*, 640.   11. *Ibid.*, 684.   12. *Ibid.*, 640.

13. 'An Interview with Fr Bernard Lonergan, S.J.', *op. cit.*, 426. This comment should be understood as a *spontaneous* one occurring in an interview.

14. *Insight*, 638.   15. *Ibid.*

16. Lonergan, 'The Absence of God in Modern Culture', *The Presence and Absence of God*, ed. C. F. Mooney, S.J., cf. especially 169-78.

17. *Insight*, 683.   18. *Ibid.*, 692.

19. Lonergan, 'The Natural Desire to See God', *Collection*, 84-95. In this article the classical difficulties with the view that man naturally desires to see God are raised and succinctly answered.

20. *Collection*, 198-201. In this article Lonergan sketches a basic philosophy of religious experience.

21. *Insight*, 683.   22. *Ibid.*

23. Lonergan, *Grace and Freedom*, 105.

24. *Insight*, 640.   25. *Ibid.*, 682.   26. *Ibid.*, 634.

27. Lonergan, 'The Natural Theology of *Insight*', *op. cit.*, 1.

28. *Ibid.*, 2.   29. *Ibid.*

30. This question is from a letter from Lonergan to this writer dated 8 November 1970, posted from Regis College, Toronto, Ontario.

31. *Insight*, 653.

32. Cf. also for a very brief outline approach to Lonergan's argument Gary Schouberg's 'A Note on Lonergan's Argument for the Existence of God', *Modern Schoolman* XLV (March 1968), 243-8.

33. *Insight*, 678.   34. *Ibid.*, 672.

35. This extrapolation is both from the side of the subject and from that of the object. As Lonergan put it (*Insight*, p. 644) : 'We are led to the conclusion that, while man cannot enjoy an unrestricted act of understanding and so answer the question, What is being? still he can determine a number of features of the answer by proceeding on the side of the subject from restricted to unrestricted understanding and on the side of the object from the structure of proportionate being to the transcendent idea of being.'

36. *Ibid.*, 651.   37. *Ibid.*, 674-5.   38. *Ibid.*, 657-8.

39. Lonergan, 'Natural Knowledge of God', *op. cit.*, 63.

40. *Insight*, 672.

41. *Ibid.*, 673.   42. *Ibid.*, 676.   43. *Ibid.*, 643.

44. *Ibid.*, 644.   45. *Ibid.*, 642.   46. *Ibid.*, 642-3.

47. *Ibid.*, 643.   48. *Ibid.*   49. *Ibid.*, 645.

50. *Ibid.*, 518.   51. Lonergan, *Verbum*, 184.

52. *Ibid.*   53. *Insight*, 677.

54. *Verbum*, 188.   55. *Insight*, 516.

56. *Ibid.*, 647.   57. *Ibid.*, 648.   58. *Ibid.*, 647.

59. Lonergan, *De Deo Trino; II*, 108.   60. *Ibid.*

61. Lonergan, 'The Natural Theology of *Insight*', *op. cit.*, 2.

62. *Insight*, 652.   63. *Ibid.*

64. This is a direct quotation from the tape-recording of lecture 10 of Lonergan's seminar on *Insight* held at St Mary's, Halifax, in the summer of 1958.

65. *Insight*, 678-9. 66. *Ibid.*, 678. 67. *Ibid.*
68. *Ibid.*, 657. 69. *Ibid.*, 656. 70. *Ibid.*, 432.
71. Philip McShane brings out this point in an unpublished set of lecture notes on natural theology. I wish also to express here my indebtedness to Philip McShane for a number of the ideas stressed in this chapter.
72. Lonergan, 'The Natural Desire to See God', *Collection*, 85.
73. On analogous knowledge, see *Collection*, 85; 191, note 47.
74. See Philip McShane, 'Foundations of Mathematics', *Modern Schoolman*, XL (1963), 380.
75. *Insight*, 677. 76. *Ibid.*, 658-9. 77. *Ibid.*, 659. 78. *Ibid.*, 378.
79. Lonergan, *Grace and Freedom*, 104.
80. *Insight*, 695. 81. *Ibid.*, 660.
82. Lonergan, 'On God and Secondary Causes', *Collection*, 54-67.
83. Lonergan, *De Ente supernaturali: Supplementum schematicum* (published only in mimeographed form at L'Imaculée-Conception, the Jesuit theologate, Montreal, in 1946, 83 pages); also *Supplementum schematicium de praedestinatione: De scientia atque voluntate Dei* (published only in mimeographed form at Regis College, Toronto, Canada in 1950, 48 pages).
84. *Insight*, 663.
85. Lonergan, 'On God and Secondary Causes', *Collection*, 58.
86. Lonergan, *Grace and Freedom*, 88-9.
87. Lonergan, 'On God and Secondary Causes', *Collection*, 57.
88. *Ibid.*, 58. 89. *Insight*, 664.
90. Lonergan, '*Existenz* and *Aggiornamento*', *Collection*, 249.
91. *Ibid.*
92. F. E. Crowe, S.J., 'The Origin and Scope of Bernard Lonergan's *Insight*', *Sciences Ecclésiastiques* IX (1957), 290-1.
93. *Grace and Freedom*, 103-4.
94. This translation of the saying of Boethius is taken from *Basic Writings of St Thomas Aquinas I*, E. trs. Anton Pegis (New York: Random House, 1945), 74.
95. *Insight*, 662, the second corollary.
96. *Ibid.* 97. *Ibid.*, 666. 98. *Ibid.*, 666-7.
99. *Ibid.*, 667. 100. *Ibid.*, 667-8. 101. *Ibid.*, 672.
102. *Ibid.*, 670. 103. *Ibid.*, 674. 104. *Ibid.*, 675-6.
105. David Tracy, 'Lonergan's Foundational Theology: An Interpretation and a Critique', *Foundations of Theology*, ed. P. McShane, 218-19.
106. *Ibid.*, 218. 107. *Ibid.* 108. *Ibid.*, 219. 109. *Ibid.*
110. This and the following two citations are from a letter sent

to this writer by Bernard Lonergan in response to certain enquiries. The letter is dated 17 August 1968, posted from Regis College, Toronto, Canada.

111. *Ibid.* 112. *Ibid.*

113. Lonergan, 'Natural Knowledge of God', *op. cit.*, 63.

114. *Ibid.*, 66. 115. *Ibid.*, 63.

116. Edward MacKinnon, 'Understanding According to Bernard Lonergan', *The Thomist* XXVIII/4 (1964), 518.

117. *Ibid.*, 514. 118. *Ibid.*, 512.

119. David Burrell, 'How Complete Can Intelligibility be? A Commentary on Insight: Chapter XIX', *Proceedings of the American Catholic Philosophical Association* XLI (1967), 252.

120. Lonergan, 'Response', *Proceedings of the American Catholic Philosophical Association* XLI, 258.

121. *Ibid.*, 259. 122. *Ibid.* 123. *Ibid.*

124. David Burrell, 'How Complete Can Intelligibility Be?', *op. cit.*, 253. See also *Insight*, 650.

125. *Ibid.* 126. *Insight*, 658-9.

127. 'Lonergan and the Subjectivist Principle', *Language Truth and Meaning*, ed. Philip McShane, 218-35.

128. Schubert Ogden, *The Reality of God* (New York : Harper and Row, 1963).

129. *Ibid.*, 17.

130. Lonergan, *Supplementum schematicum de praedestinatione: De scientia atque voluntate Dei*, 41-3.

131. Ogden, *The Reality of God*, 17-18.

132. Lonergan, 'Natural Knowledge of God', *op. cit.*, 58.

133. *Ibid.*, 67. 134. *Ibid.*

135. Lonergan, *Doctrinal Pluralism* (Milwaukee : Marquette University Press, 1971), 18.

EPILOGUE (pp. 180-83)

1. A. Maslow, 'Are Our Publications and Conventions suitable for the Personal Psychologies?', Appendix A of *Towards a Psychology of Being* (New York : Van Nostrand, 1968), 217.

2. Quoted from one of three lectures on 'The Relationship between Philosophy of God and the Functional Specialty, Systematics' delivered at St Michael's Institute, Spokane, Washington, December, 1972.

3. The problem of 'expressing the subjective experience in words and as subjective' (*Method in Theology*, p. 88, note 34).

4. *Verbum*, 213.

5. For some suggestive thinking in this area, see F. E. Crowe, S.J., 'Pull of the Future and Link with the Past : on the Need for Theological Method', *Continuum* 7 (1969), 39-45.

6. *De Constitutione Christi*, in the section 'De ex-sistentia'.

Index

Anthropocentric turn, 4-5, 180
Anthropocentricism, 3
Aquinas, Thomas, 34, 80, 82, 102, 106, 137-8, 148, 182, 185 n.21; proof for God's existence, 4, 129
Aristotle, 14, 16, 19, 80, 106, 137-8
Arius, 24-5
Athanasius, 25
Augustine, 14-15, 19, 32, 35
Authenticity, 31-2

Bañez-Molina controversy, 13
Being, 96-101; components of, 138-40; concept of, 99, 100-101; definition, 109; idea of, 99, 101-2, 130, 136, 138; and intelligibility, 121, 136, 143, 168, 171; and intentionality, 133; notion of, 96, 99-100; pure notion of, 134-5; heuristic notion of, 134-5; proportionate, 105, 130, 134, 143-4; and the real, 37, 98, 116, 121, 132, 143; spheres of, 169-70; and understanding, 98, 130, 132, 134; as unrestricted act of understanding, 136-7, 138, 139, 140, 141, 142
Bias, 41, 43; antidote for, 41, 43; general, 42; group, 42; individual, 41, 42; and intellectual conversion, 47-48; and moral conversion, 43
Bréhier, Emile, 12, 185 n.20
Burrell, David, 128; criticism of Lonergan's proof, 171-3
Butterfield, Herbert, 6, 7

Causality, 8, 130, 132, 142-7; efficient, 154-5, 156, 174; exemplary, 153, 156; final, 156-7; Lonergan-ian, 142; and modern science, 8
Clement of Alexandria, 23-4, 28
Cognitional analysis, xi, 5, 93, 121
Cognitive operations, 71, 91, 176
Consciousness, 39, 76-80, 92; and

awareness, 77; and intellective activity, 78; moral, 44; and questioning, 79
Context, 3, 5, 9-10, 89; of Lonergan's work, 3, 118, 181; and philosophy, 55-7
Conversion, 28, 30, 31, 41, 116-17, 188 n.11; intellectual, 31, 32, 35-9, 121; intellectual defined, 37; intellectual and self-transcendence, 37-8, 40; and interpretation, 57, 58-9, 67; moral, 31, 32, 35, 39-49, 119, 164-6; moral defined, 39; moral and self-transcendence, 39-40, 60; and philosophy, 33, 34; qualities of, 32; religious, 32, 35, 49-68, 119, 164-6, 167; religious and being in love with God, 61, 67; religious as de facto condition of possibility for validating Lonergan's proof, 61, 65-6; religious defined, 49; religious and grace, 61; nature of religious, 59-61; religious and self-transcendence, 60
Cosmocentricism, 3
Cosmopolis, 43
Cultural shift, 5-11
Culture, 6; classical, 6, 7; defined, 5-6; and meaning, 6; modern, 6, 7, 10-11
Curran, Charles, 60

Data, xi; of sense, 76, 79, 82; of consciousness, 76, 79, 82
Divine Comedy, 58-9

Epistemology, xii, 5, 95-6, 99
Evil, 31, 160-61; basic sin, 160, 161; moral evil, 160; physical evil, 160-61
Exist, 30, 31, 49, 169
Existence, 30, 106, 107; contingent, 101
Existential, 30
Experience, 76-80

Openness, 18-20
Origen, 24, 28

Philosophy, 177-8; Christian, 9,
11-12; conditions of possibility for
Christian, 17-20; context of
Lonergan's, xi, 13, 118, 120;
process, 173-4; of God, 177-8,
181; conditions of possibility for
philosophy of God, 32, 35-7; 40,
46, 61
Plato, 34
Presence, 76-7
Principle of the Empty Head, 56,
57

Rahner, Karl, 116, 118
Real, the, and being, 132-3; intelligibility of, 116, 162-3
Realism, 20; Christian, 16, 17; conditions of possibility for Christian,
17-20; critical, 20, 21, 26, 27, 97;
defined, 21; dogmatic, 21-2, 23-6;
intuitive, 84; naive, 20-21, 23-4;
origins of Christian, 21-8
Revelation, 16-17

Science, 107, 124, 144; classical,
7-8; and hypothesis verification,
8, 107, 193 n.30; and metaphysics, 108; modern, 7-8; and problem of God, 9, 149
Self-affirmation, 37, 91-3, 95, 98,
105; as immanent law, 92-3; and
intellectual conversion, 37
Self-appropriation, 4, 16, 30, 44,
182; and intellectual conversion,
35; and moral conversion, 43
Self-transcendence: cognitive, 51,
73, 134; moral, 39-40, 60; religious, 60

Sin, 161; conditions of, 44
Structure, 102-4; of things known,
103, 106, 107
Subject, 3, 95

Tertullian, 23, 24
Theology, 116, 123; functional
specialties, 120; natural, 4, 5, 116,
120, 123; systematic, 116, 120,
128
Tracy, David, 71, 163, 185 n.21;
criticism of Lonergan's approach
to God problem, 163-8
Transcendence, 72, 130; divine, 178;
general, 72
Transcendental method, 75; and
cognitive process, 74; invariant
in, 8; radical, 74-5; thematic, 75

Understanding, 80-86; act of, 80;
and intelligibility, 138-9; reflective, 88-91; restricted, 134-5, 136,
171-2; unrestricted, 132, 134-6,
146-7, 151-2, 171-2

Value, 43, 119-20; and moral conversion, 43

Will 36; and, assent to truth, 36;
bad, 36, 45; and conversion, 36;
good, 36
Word of God, 26
World, 51-2; defined, 52; as good,
48; and horizon, 50-51; mediated
by meaning, 51; of immediacy,
51; of interiority, 52; of meaning,
52
World-view, 5